Computer Networking

This Book Includes:

Computer Networking First steps, Computer networking Course, Computer Networking Beginners Guide.

Author:

Tim Wired

Table of Contents

Computer Networking First Steps

Introduction 11
Chapter 1: Basics of a Network 13
    Definition of a Network and Why It Exists 13
    What Is a Client/Server Network? 16
    Server Access 19
Chapter 2: Network Topology 23
    Physical and Logical Topologies 23
    Wireless Technologies and Wired Technologies 24
Chapter 3: Types of Network Topology and Network
Administration 29
    Ring Topology 31
    Star Topology 33
    Mesh Topology 35
    Hybrid Topology 37
    Tree Topology 39
Chapter 4: Network Administration 41
    Principles of Network Administration 45
    Home Network Administration 47
    Building a Career in Network Administration 48
        Job Titles in Networking 48
        Gaining Experience With Networking 50
        Education and Experience 53
        Representation of the Skills and Abilities 53
Chapter 5: Network Infrastructure 57
    What Exactly Is Network Infrastructure? 57
    Challenges Surrounding Network Infrastructure 59
        Centralization of Traffic 59
        Data Duplication 60
        Relaying the Right Data to the Correct Tool 60
    Network Protocols and Standards 61
    How Do Network Protocols Work? 63
        Network Communication Protocols 64

Protocol Design Principles..70
Layering 71
Software Layering..74
Strict Layering...76
Protocol Development and the Need for These
Standards 76
Chapter 6: Network Protocols and Standards 79
Network Protocols..79
Communicating Systems 81
Basic Requirements for Network Protocols....................83
Data Formats for Exchange of Data 83
Address Formats for the Exchange of Data 84
Mapping of Addresses..84
Detection of Errors That Occur During Transmission .84
Routing...85
Acknowledging...85
Timeouts and Retries...85
The Direction in Which Information Flows..................86
Control of Sequences 86
Control of Flow 87
Design of Protocols 87
Protocol Layering 89
Software Layering..94
Strict layering..95
Development of Protocols 96
The Process of Standardization......................................98
Cable Infrastructure...105
LANs and Ethernet...108
Chapter 7: Servers and Virtualization..............................111
Components of a Server...111
Motherboard 111
Central Processing Unit 112
Random Access Memory..112
Network Connection...113
Hard Drive..113
Graphics Processing Unit (An Optional Component).113
What Is Server Virtualization? 113
Benefits of Server Virtualization 121
Limitations of Server Virtualization..............................125

Determining if Server Virtualization Is Necessary for Your Business 127

The Potential in Server Virtualization and the Trend It Is Likely to Take 130

Understanding Containers and Virtual Machines 131

Server less Computing and Virtual Machines 132

Chapter 8: Securing Computer Networks 135

The Basics of Network Security 137

Types of Network Security 137

Conclusion 149

Description 150

COMPUTER NETWORKING COURSE

Introduction..155

Chapter 1: Computer Networking.......................................157

Chapter 2: Storage Architecture..199

Chapter 3: Transmission control protocol (TCP) and

IMPLEMENTATION 221

Chapter 4: Planning a Network 235

Chapter 5: WIDE AREA NETWORK 257

Chapter 6: Configuration Windows servers......................269

Conclusion 285

Description...287

Computer Networking Beginners Guide

Introduction 293

Chapter 1: What is Computer Networking 297

Chapter 2: History of the Internet................................... 303

Chapter 3: Components of a Computer Network 325

Chapter 4: Firewall.. 345

Chapter 5: Network Components 351

Chapter 6: Wireless Technology 359

Chapter 7: OSI Reference Model 371

Chapter 8: Transmission Control Protocol and Internet

Protocol (TCP /IP)... 381

Chapter 9: IP Address.. 389

Chapter 11: Remote Access Protocols, Network Storage

Systems & File Transfer Protocols................................. 403

Chapter 12: SECURITY PROTOCOLS 415

Chapter 13: BASIC NETWORK UTILITIES...................... 425

Chapter 14: NETWORKING ISSUES.............................. 429

Conclusion... 435

Description 437

Computer Networking
First Steps

Introduction

Congratulations on downloading your copy of *Computer Networking First Step*. It is a source of delight to me that you chose his book as you set out on a journey to learning more about computer networking. Computer networking is an important part of our lives in the workplace, at school, and even at home, and that is why many seek to understand how computers connect with each other.

As you continue to read, you will discover that networking is versatile and that different people may understand it differently depending on the part of the network that they are handling. However, you will understand that networks are what connects computers at the basic LAN level and even further as the networks extends over larger geographical areas.

While you may have never thought of networking in detail, this book will introduce you to the basics of networking, the different types of networks available, the types of network topologies that you will encounter, the concept of server virtualization, and details of how to handle network breaches. The book also offers an explanation of network protocols, design, and infrastructure—information that will help you understand how computers interact with each other.

There are indeed a variety of books that have been written about computer networking, and it is a privilege that you should choose this book to help you advance in the field, even in the slightest. Thank you for choosing this title. As a token of appreciation, every effort was made to ensure that this book carries only the most up-to-date information that will be useful for you, whether you are a starter at networking or are already established in the field

Chapter 1: Basics of a Network

This chapter outlines the basics of networking. As a starter, you probably have no idea what the term network means, or you may just have a slight idea. Do not worry because that is the purpose of this book. In the next sections, you will understand the definition of a network and the different types of networks, depending on whether you are cabling, working on networking devices, or servers. You shall also understand in detail the servers, clients, big and small networks, topology, and network administration.

Definition of a Network and Why It Exists

There are networks almost everywhere in the world. Look at your body; for instance, there are various networks of tissues, organs, and cells that allow your body to work efficiently. Even in plants, it is easy to see a network of leaves and branches that lead to the stems and, finally, roots. The concept of networks, however, has defied the natural world and has permeated virtually into every aspect of our lives. There are human networks that enable us to connect with one another at home, at school, and even at work. In this chapter, we focus on computer networks and how the components of the network communicate with each other

When it comes to the concept of computer networks and networking, it is important to understand that different people understand it differently. Going forward, you may realize that you come to your own conclusions and understanding of this concept. This notion simply means that even as you begin to understand networks, you should not really judge the next person's perception of the same. Also, the fact that you will understand networking differently shows you that this is a technical field and there are many interconnections involved. Therefore, finding an efficient order in which to present the world of networking may be difficult. The approach in this book, however, is friendly and takes a path that you are likely to understand without a lot of stress. Dive in for some more.

A network, essentially, is an amalgamation of different components, including hardware, software, and cabling that allows communication between multiple computing devices.

The essentials that will be presented in this chapter are:

· LANs- Local area networks

· IP-Internet protocols

· TCP- Transport and connections protocol

The three essentials mentioned above are also known as layers. LANs are the link layer; the internet is the work layer, and TCP is the transport layer. There is another type of layer, the application layer, which constitutes the software that you use. Together, they form the four-layer model that is known in networking. In this context, you can view a layer as a library, and each layer communicates with the layers that directly border it. The application layer will, therefore, communicate a set of data to the transport and connections protocol library, which will, in turn, communicate with the internet protocol library, which will further communicate with the LAN to ensure the delivery of the message. As such, the application does not have direct interaction with the other parts of the network, such as the IP and LAN.

The LAN layer is the one responsible for the delivery of data pockets through LAN-layer supplied addresses. LAN is divided into the logical and physical component. The logical component comprises the abstract LAN layer that is digital, while the physical layer is often the optical or electrical signaling mechanism involved. The physical layer of the LAN concerns the designers of physical hardware. The five-layer model, as represented below, comes as a result of the LAN'S physical/logical division.

| Application |
| Transport |
| IP |
| Logical LAN |
| Physical LAN |

The explanation that follows will follow a logical model that will see the reader oscillating between concepts to fully understand how networks operate.

What Is a Client/Server Network?

This is a network in which a centralized and often more powerful machine or computer, also referred to as the server, works as a hub that supports less powerful workstations or computers, also referred to as clients. The clients are connected to the server and run programs and access data that are already existent or stored on the server. The server is, therefore, designed and dedicated to the running of services that serve the needs of other computers within the network. The server could be a database, file, print, home media, or web server, depending on the running service. The client, on the other hand, is not necessarily a computer but can be a computer software or hardware that accesses the services of the servers. Often, servers are located on separate physical computers, but sometimes, they can be connected within the same system. The client, typically, does not share its resources but requests the service function and content of a server. Therefore, clients will initiate communication with the server that will usually be waiting for incoming requests.

When looking at the roles of servers and clients, you will realize that servers are classified based on the role of the play and services provided. For instance, the file server serves computer files, while web server provides services for web pages. The resources shared may vary from data, processors, programs, and storage devices, and this sharing of server resources constitutes a service.

The image below shows a set-up of the network client relationship:

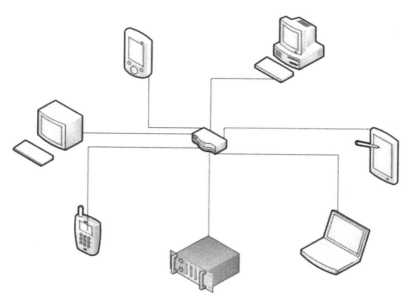

The communication between servers and clients

Services are generally involved with the abstraction of the resources of the computer. As such, clients are not really concerned with how the server works and performs to fulfill the request and deliver a response. What concerns the client is the response based on the application protocol.

A communications protocol defines the rules and language to be used, as explained above. The client-server protocols operate in what is called an application layer, which, in turn, defines the patters of the dialogue; further data exchange is formalized through the server's implementation of application programming interface. The API is a layer for accessing service and facilitates parsing by restricting communication to a specific format. Sometimes, a server may receive abundant requests in a short span. Normally, computers rely on scheduling systems to determine which requests from clients to accommodate first. Servers may provide limited availability by denying services to some clients. These types of attacks work by exploiting the server's process request obligations by overloading it with requests. An example of how client-server systems work is when an online banker accesses banking services through the web browser. The login credential of the customer is stored in the database, and the web server will act as an intermediary between the database server and client by accessing the database server. The application server responds to the data returned by applying the business logic of the bank and providing output to the web server, which will return the results to the web browser that is what the client sees. You notice that in each step of the sequence, there is a processing and requesting and returning data— the messaging pattern. When explaining clients and servers, a related concept is a host. A host connects with other computers. A host is, therefore, a reflection of the logical relationship between computers on a network. To bring this concept to life in your mind, imagine that you want to download from another computer on the computer that you are using. The other computer is hosting the image and is, hence, referred to as the host computer. When a computer downloads pictures, for example, from other computers, the one that is being downloaded from becomes the host. Routers have the ability to host each other, and computers can do the same thing, too. However, a host must have an internet protocol address. Other components, therefore, do not qualify as hosts.

Server Access

Servers are connected either outside or within a local area network. Accessing a server will depend on whether it is a private or public internet protocol address. If the IP address is public, then it is possible to access it from the web. If, however, it is private, it can only be accessed from within the local area network. An alternative for accessing a private address would be to setup port, forwarding that allows remote access.

The speed at which data is retrieved from the server depends largely on the bandwidth required for data transfer. If the server is within the local access network, then the router determines how fast the data is transferred to the client from the server. You, therefore, need a quality router with high speeds. The logic applied for LAN network follows if the server is on the internet. Once you visit a webpage, the speed of the page load will depend on:

· The size of the webpage

· Speed of the website's server packets

· The bandwidth allowed by the ISP

· The speed of the router in routing data packets

Latency and bandwidth determine the performance experienced between clients and servers.

From the explanations above, it is logical to wonder if there is a difference between a server and the host. There are indeed differences, as the technology works differently from technology for sharing files. Usually, servers:

· Can be software programs or physical devices

· Provide specific services

· Are installed on the host computer

· Are of service to clients

Hosts, on the other hand:

· Are always physical devices or computers

· Serves multiple devices and users

The set-up shown below shows the server and clients and how they operate:

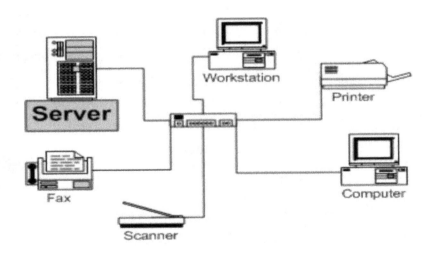

In this arrangement, you can see the server provides services to the rest of the machines on the network.

You have probably noticed that in the Windows workgroup environment, PCs within the network always have access to folders considered public on other computers within the environment.in the same light, it is not uncommon to find one computer hosting the media files of another because the former has a lot of space in the hard drive compared to the former. It is considered a host and not a server because, to be a server; the computer must serve only clients.

The advantage of using the workgroup in such a case is that it gives you easy access to media and any other files within the computers on your local area network. The disadvantage is that the files cannot be accessed beyond the LAN, and you can only access files if you have a server running on the host machine. Computers with static IP addresses can, however, function as servers with dual-purpose configuration.

Chapter 2: Network Topology

In simpler words, network topology involves the logical connection of computers within a network. It is the layout pattern of the computers and how they are interconnected within the network. It is the virtual structure or shape of the network. In topology, the devices found within the network are commonly referred to as nodes. Topology is, hence, depicted by showing the nodes and how they connect using cables. I will illustrate further below in what can be considered a logical explanation.

The network is crucial for the activities of an organization. Specific guidelines and models must be followed so that one device is connected to another. Below, we outline why network topologies are important:

· Topology plays an important role in network functioning.

· It plays a vital role in determining performance.

· It helps in creating an understanding of the concepts of networking.

· It helps in reducing the maintenance and operational costs, for instance, cabling costs.

· Network topologies make it easy to detect faults and errors within the network.

Physical and Logical Topologies

Logical and physical topologies are the basic categories in this kind of topology. The physical topology is the transmission layout that links devices. In fiber-optic mediums, physical topology involves cabling layout, node location, and the link between cabling and nodes. The topology of a network, in this case, is determined by the network access media and devices' capabilities, the level of fault or control tolerance desired and the cost of telecommunication circuits and cables. Logical topography, on the other hand, involves how signals act on network media. In simpler terms, logical topography is involved with how data passes from one device to the next in a network without regard to the physical interconnectedness of the device. The network's logical topography is not concerned with the physical, which means that they can be different within the same network.

Transmission media is also known as physical media. Transmission media is used to link devices that are within a network and includes:

- electrical cables
- radio waves
- optical fiber

Ethernet is a widely used physical media in the LAN network. Ethernet uses copper and fiber to transmit data. LAN standards use infrared signals.

Wireless Technologies and Wired Technologies

In the list below, the order of wired technologies is made from that with the fastest transmission speed to that with the lowest.

- **Optical fiber.** An optical fiber is a glass fiber that carries light pulses that represent data. There are advantages of optical fibers over metal wires that have low transmission and are always are not immune to electrical interference. This wired technology can carry multiple light wavelengths, which has a positive effect on the rate of data that can be sent. With optical fibers, you can send data at rates of up to trillions per second. This type of cable is needed for cables that carry high rates of data and are used to interconnect continents as undersea cables.

- **Twisted pair wires.** These are the most widely and commonly used medium for all telecommunication. They typically consist of a pair of copper wires twisted into one. They are used, for instance, in ordinary telephone wires. A normal telephone wire consists of a twisted pair, while Ethernet wires consist of copper cables that enable data and voice transmission. This improvisation of twisted wires is important because it helps reduce electromagnetic conduction and crosstalk. The transmission speed in twisted pairs can range between 2 million to 10 billion bits per second. They come in two forms: unshielded and shielded twisted pairs. Each of the forms comes suited and designed for used in different scenarios.

- **Ribbon cables.** The ribbon cable is popular as a cost-effective technology for serial protocols. They come in handy, especially over short distances and with lower data rates. They can be rolled within copper braids and within metallic enclosures.

- **Signal traces.** Signal traces are typical for board level serial communication and common in SPI.

- **Coaxial cable.** Coaxial cables are used for systems such as televisions. Usually, the cables are made of aluminum or copper that is insulated by a high dielectric constant material. This insulation is important for the minimization of distortion and interference. The transmission speeds for coaxial cables vary from 200 million bits per second to over 500 million bits per second.

Wireless technologies are quickly becoming common today. Below, we explain them.

- **Communications satellites**. These types of satellites communicate through microwave radio waves that do not get deflected on the atmosphere of the earth. Satellites are found in space, 22,236 miles above the equator in geostationary systems. These systems can relay and receive voice, TV, and data signals.

- **Terrestrial microwaves**. Terrestrial microwaves use special technologies that resemble dishes for outposts for communication. They are in the lower GHz assortment, which means all communications are limited to the lie of sight. The dispatch locations are placed about 30 miles apart.

- **PCS AND Cellular systems**. These systems utilize radio communication technologies. They divide a region that they cover into several geographic areas. Each geographic area then has a radio relay antenna device or lower power transmitter for relaying calls form an area to the next.

· **Free-space optical communication**. This type of technology uses both visible and invisible light for communication. They use the line of sight propagation to limit the physical position of the devices in communication.

· **Radio and spread spectrum technologies**. Wireless LANs make use of great occurrence hi-fi technology that is like low-frequency radio technology or digital cellular. This technology enables wireless LANs to enable communications between devices in a limited area. One of the common open-standards wireless radio-wave technologies is the Wi-Fi.

Chapter 3: Types of Network Topology and Network Administration

Physical and logical network topologies do not stop at that. Often, they can further be classified into five major models, as discussed below:

Bus Topology

To understand bus topology, consider the diagram below:

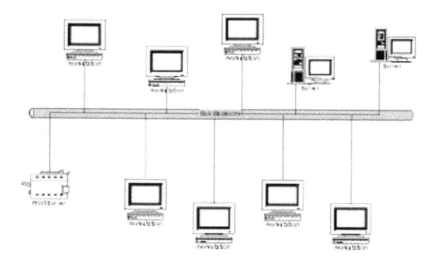

Bus topology is easily the most basic network setup for both logical and physical topologies. In this case, the devices and nodes are interconnected through the use of a single cable. In this type of topology, data is transmitted in one direction, and all devices are connected to a single cable. This simple setup is the reason that sometimes, this type of topology is referred to as backbone or line topology. A coaxial or RJ45 cable can be used to connect the devices in bus topology, depending on the devices and nodes. This main cable, therefore, acts as the network's backbone and one of the computers works as the server. The bus topology has advantages. First, it makes it relaxed to link a CPU or marginal device to the network. Also, it lowers the costs associated with cabling because the cable requirements are generally on the low compared to other topologies. Additionally, it is very easy to understand the bus topology due to its basic nature; it is an ideal type of topology for small networks, and it makes it easy to reduce or extend a network.

There are also disadvantages that come with the bus topology. While it can be ideal for small network setups, you may have to look elsewhere as the network becomes bigger. Also, if the primary cable fails, then the whole network will be affected, and it will fail as a result. Another disadvantage is the fact that the bus topology is unidirectional and that the speeds of transmission reduce greatly when the number of nodes increases. Also, compared to a ring topology, this kind of topology is slow.

Ring Topology

Ring topology can be understood from the next image:

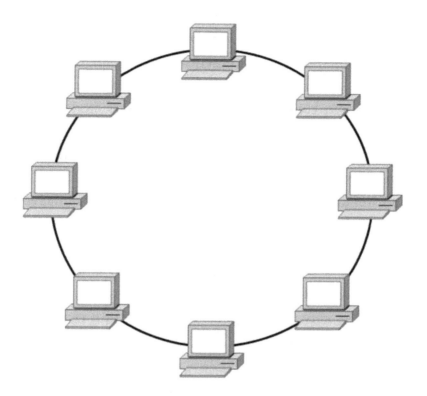

Ring topology is commonly called ring because the formation of a ring is evident as one computer connects to the next, and the last computer connects back to the first one. Each device has two neighbors, and the computers within the network form a circle as a result of their interconnection. Usually, one node within the network acts as a monitor that handles the configurations. Some of the features of ring topology include the use of repeaters for ring topology where a large number of nodes is involved.

For instance, if someone wants to send information to the last node in a series of 100 nodes, then it has to pass through 99 others to reach the last, which presents the possibility of data loss. Repeaters are put in place to prevent loss of data within the network. Also, just like bus topology, transmission here is unidirectional. However, there is a possibility of making the transmission bidirectional by ensuring two connections between network nodes. When this is done, it is referred to as dual ring topology. What happens when this type of topology is introduced is that there are two ring networks in play, and data flow is in opposite directions to each other. This is advantageous because if one ring fails, the other ring comes in handy, acting as a backup that keeps the network up. In a ring topology, the transfer of data is sequential which, in this sense, means bit by bit. Data, therefore, pass through every node in the network and goes that way until it reaches the designated destination.

Ring topology is not just interesting but has advantages too. For instance, ring topology has the ability to maintain its speeds without slowing down, thanks to the fact that the transmission is not affected by the addition of nodes or high traffic. This happens because only nodes with tokens take part in data transmission. Also, this kind of topology is relatively cheap to install and easy to expand, making it a rival to bus topology when it comes to cost reduction. For ring topology, it assures better performance than bus topology, especially when the loads are heavy. Also, the point to point connectivity among nodes makes it a tad easier to know where faults and misconfigurations occurred, and it offers an orderly flow in the network.

Every good thing must have a disadvantage. Such is the case of ring topology. Some of the disadvantages of ring topology are the fact that it can be difficult to troubleshoot when a problem happens in the ring topology network. Also, network activity suffers a major blow should you try to add or delete computers from the network. Imagine a network of 100 computers and a possible disruption that requires you to remove two from the network. Also, if just one computer fails within the ring topology, it is bound to disturb the rest within the network. Also, there has to be a shared bandwidth among the devices within the network, and delays in communication are proportional to the number of nodes within the ring network. The more the nodes, the worse the communication delays will be.

Star Topology

Below is a picture that describes star topology

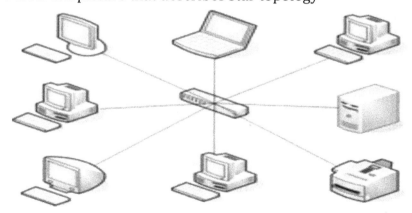

Just like the name suggests, star topology offers an arrangement where there is a central hub, which is a node or a computer which cares for the entire network and is surrounded by devices. They connect to the hub through a cable. In this arrangement, every node has a direct connection to the hub. Each of the devices within the network, therefore, has a direct connection with the central hub and the nodes have an indirect connection with the other nodes within the network through the central node. In star topology, data flows through the central hub before reaching the preferred destination. The central hub is, therefore, responsible for the control and management of data connectivity and transfer within the network. The central hub also has another role, the role of a repeater. A repeater, whose role is played by the central hub, ensures that there is minimal to no data loss when the transmission is taking place. To configure star topologies, coaxial or optical fiber wires are used.

There are advantages, as well as disadvantages associated with the use of the star topology. We begin with the advantages. One advantage of using star topology is that the failure of one node is inconsequential to the rest of the network as it is often not affected. Also, you can add remove, modify, and even possibly reconfigure devices without having to worry about disturbing the peace of the entire network. Another advantage that comes with this type of topology is the fact that you require minimum cabling for the configuration of the topology, and it is relatively easy to modify and even set up. When a problem occurs, it is equally easy to troubleshoot. On top of it all, there can still be fast performance even there is low network traffic, and there are a few nodes.

There are disadvantages, as well. For instance, there is the fact that the hub is the life of the entire network, and the network completely relies on it for survival. A failure in the hub means the failure of the entire network as the whole of it will be down. Also, unlike the topologies discussed so far, the star topology is expensive not only to install but to use as well. Most disadvantageous, however, is the fact that the network relies on the hub for configuration, efficiency, and even power.

Mesh Topology

Mesh topology is characterized by a point-to-point connection to other devices or nodes such that every node is connected to another within the network of computers (as shown below).

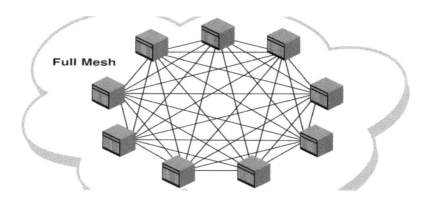

These node connections are not just direct but also non-hierarchical. Unlike the star topology, the network here is not dependent on one machine, and every node is active and playing a critical role in information relay. This type of topology is ideal ,especially in cases where there are workstations located in groups and when there is the use of a wide area network instead of the local area network. There are two vital techniques used to relay data in this type of topology.

· Routing

· Flooding

Routing involves making use of every node within the network such that every node in the network has a routing logic and data transfer is done through the routing logic. The routing logic is used as a tool to figure out the shortest route possible that can send information efficiently from the sender to the receiver. The trick is to use this logic to avoid broken data transmission lines.

Flooding involves transferring data to every node within the network. Here, there is no requirement for a routing logic as is required during routing. However, there are similar advantages here as no data is likely to be lost. In this case, this efficiency can be achieved because every node carries the same data within it. The network is, therefore, not only fault-tolerant but robust as well. Also, there is an increased load on the network as a result.

Just like the other topologies described above, the advantages and disadvantages of the mesh topology shall be discussed here. One interesting fact that also doubles as an advantage, in this case, is the fact that that the mesh topology is in actuality an extension of the star and bus topologies as addressed above. Also, another advantage is the fact that it is easy and very possible to expand nodes, while at the same time, the topology is easy to manage and maintain. It is also relatively easy to detect an error within the network with this type of topology. There is also a high level of security and privacy associated with this type of topology, and the network is robust.

One disadvantage here includes the fact that the initial costs of installation and implementation can be high. It does not end there; the cost of cabling is high as well. For the untrained eye, mesh topologies can be difficult to understand. Another problem or disadvantage posed by this type of network is that installing and reconfiguring in a network that utilizes the mesh arrangement can be a big task. Also, with the presence of a central hub, the entire network is at risk should the hub fail.

Hybrid Topology

A hybrid topology typically consists of a mixture of two or more topologies. For example, one department within the office may utilize bus topology, another utilizes mesh topology, and the last utilizes ring topology. When these topologies are connected, they result in what is commonly known as a hybrid topology. Interestingly, with such a combination of topologies, it is certain that the hybrid kind of topologies inherits the advantages and disadvantages of the individual topologies that make it up. Usually, what determines the components of the hybrid topology is the fact that they are configured according to the requirements of the company. Therefore, the hybrid of one organization or company could easily differ from the next. With proper configuration, there is a likelihood that hybrid topologies provide an office with the best of all the topologies involved. The hybrid topology is illustrated below:

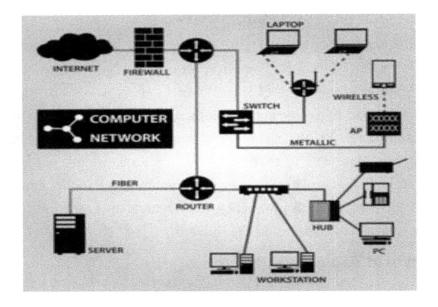

The advantages of hybrid topologies include the fact that they are reliable as it will be easy to troubleshoot and detect errors within the network. Also, as highlighted above, with proper connection, it is easy to get an effective network. The scalability of this type of topologies also gives it a competitive advantage compared to other types of topologies. Also, with different types of topologies in one, this topology is relatively flexible.

The disadvantages of hybrid topologies are few, including the fact that it is overly complex in design and can be costly during installation and even maintenance.

Tree Topology

The tree topology is considered a type of network topology by itself and yet, it qualifies as an exemplar of the hybrid topology. This is because it is a combination of the bus and star topologies. Typically, star topologies connect to each other within the network through the use of line topologies. There is a hierarchical type of connection between the nodes as they connect with each other, earning this type of topology its second name, which is hierarchal topology.

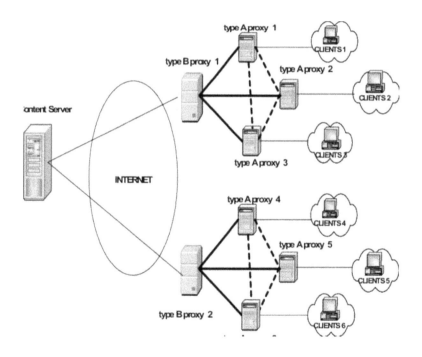

One of the major advantages that make this type of topology a favorite among many is the fact that it is highly flexible. In addition to flexibility, it is a scalable topology type as you can easily add or remove nodes according to your requirements and expectations of the network. Also, if you have a large network and have not quite figured out the right topology for you or your organization, then this may be it. With tree topology also comes the advantage in the ease of management.

There are a few disadvantages associated with a tree topology. For instance, the topology is definitely costly to install as a result of the robust cable work that will need to be done. Also, getting the right design to use after figuring out that the organization may need tree topology can be difficult. Maintenance costs that come with this type of topology can make it excruciatingly costly to maintain.

From the detailed explanation of the different topologies above, you will come to realize that choosing the right network may not be an easy job, but, it is possible when the right factors are put into consideration. These factors include the geographical distance between a node and the next, the number of nodes likely to be involved in the network, finances, and the flexibility in operation, maintenance, and many others that you may come across as you begin to figure out what may be the right fit for you. By now, you understand that, no one type of topology is fully superior to the next and that each has advantages and disadvantages that may come in handy when you are in the process of choosing. There is, therefore, no straight and correct answer or solution when you want to build and configure the right networking model for your organization or company, for instance. For any person thinking of adopting a topology, it may be wise to gather information and understand your needs and requirements before resting on a final decision for which topography will be best for you.

Chapter 4: Network Administration

By now, you must have understood that businesses, libraries, school, small, and even large corporations rely heavily on computer networks for the running of their day-to-day activities. It makes sense, in a world that is quickly becoming a global village to aspire for efficiency. This is where network administration comes in. In the midst of all these operations, there must be someone or even a group of people who are held account for the administration of these networks. The perfect word that can be used for this is network administrators. These very important people are the brains responsible for keeping the technology behind networks updated and ensuring that the networks run smoothly. This type of job is well-suited, especially with individuals who are technically inclined. However, it is important to realize that network administrators are, more often than not, critically skilled, and possess a combination of interpersonal skills, problem-solving skills, and technical skills. As a network administrator, you will not only interact with these machines but also with people, and, therefore, you need to have an understanding of the machines through technical and analytical skills and must be armed with interpersonal skills to maintain the human touch. It is a delicate play, but a lot of people have the right skills to help them get fully involved in network administration even as a career.

At this point, you may be wondering what the duties of network administrators are. We outline them below:

- Installation of hardware, including network printers, wireless access points, and video conferencing systems in an organization

- Deployment of upgrades and also enterprise applications

- Monitoring the network traffic of an organization to establish any suspicious activities and performance bottlenecks. Suspicious activities in such a case could include inappropriate network usage among employees and security breaches.

- Organizing, planning, and management of other administrators, especially as an administrator begins to climb higher up the career ladder

- Training the employees of an organization on the basics of networking and how they can handle user support calls

- Management of servers, mobile, and desktop equipment within the organization.

- In some instances, network administrators may work hand in hand with network architects in the designing and analysis of network models

- Supervision of computer support specialists

From the duties outlined above, it is clear to see why there is a need for the combination of technical and interpersonal skills when undertaking network administration duties. They require a deep knowledge of the technical world, and they should be able to quickly learn the details of server software and new networking packages. The role of network administrators is not always clear-cut, especially in small companies. In such settings, it is possible to find that the duties of the network administrator are pegged to those of network engineers. Also, sometimes, the terms system administrator and network administrator are used interchangeably as a result of related job roles in the two positions.

The responsibilities of network administrators fall within the four areas outlined below:

· **Designing the network.** Typically, this is the first phase of the life cycle of the network. While this is the initial phase of network administration, it is usually not carried out by new network administrators, as it can be a daunting task. This task will often involve making decisions on a variety of issues, for example, which network type best suits a given organization. In many large organizations, there is usually a senior network architect, basically a highly experienced network administrator that is familiar with the software and hardware of a network that will make decisions during the design phase of network administration. There are many factors involved in network design.

· **Setting up the network.** This is the step that comes after the initial design phase of network administration. This phase involves not just setting up but configuration of the network as well. If you are a network administrator, this is where you install any hardware that makes up the network's physical parts and configures databases, routers, hosts, and the servers for network configuration. This is a part played quite well by network administrators as the tasks within this phase are major responsibilities associated with the role of network administration. As such, as a network administrator in an organization, you should expect to perform these tasks unless the organization you work with is sufficiently large and with a system already in place.

· **Maintenance of the network.** After design and installation are done, the network must be maintained. There are many tasks that are involved in maintenance, including addition of new host machines to the network in question, administration of network services, such as name services and electronic mail and network security. Also, another duty is the troubleshooting problems within the network. These responsibilities constitute the bulk of duties performed by a network administrator in an organization.

· **Expansion of the network.** Sometimes, there is a need to expand existing networks. Interestingly, the more a network stays in place and functions efficiently, the higher the probability than an organization will need to expand its network's services and features. At the early stages, it is possible to expand the network by expanding network services and adding new hosts. However, over time, a network expands so much that further expansion will yield inefficient results. This is when the fourth phase of network administration comes into play. There are many different options available for this type of expansion, including the possibility of setting up a new network, then connecting it to the already existing network via a router, hence creating an internetwork. Also, it can involve configuring the machines in the office or even homes to remote networks thus enabling machines to connect to the network over social lines. Also, it may involve connecting the network to the internet so that those within it can retrieve information from the other systems, even when they are in different parts of the world. Lastly, a configuration can be done by configuring UUCP communications such that users can exchange files and emails through remote machines.

Principles of Network Administration

Administration of a network is done to ensure that it is under control in terms of resources and how they are utilized within the network. To maintain a network, there are principles that have to be followed and practiced. Below is an analysis of these principles:

- Firewall rules. A firewall ensures protection of an individual against threats within the computer network because it monitors all the traffic that comes in and goes out of the network, making a decision whether to permit or refuse it based on some set safety procedures. Firewalls have been the most popular and widely used line of defense in networking. They work by creating a barrier between untrusted outside sources, for example, the internet and internal networks that are trustworthy. Firewalls come as software, hardware, or both. There are various types of firewalls, including proxy, stateful inspection, unified threat management, next-generation, and threat-focused next-generation firewalls, all of which will be discussed in the later chapters of the book.

- VLAN management. The logical interface of a VLAN is known as the switched virtual interface. This interface is crucial in helping share resources and communication between layer three switches so that there can be inter-VLAN communication. To create an SVI, you will initially have to create Layer 2 VLAN on a switch, after which you will assign an IP address on the Layer 3 VLAN interface. This Layer 3 will have an IP address just like physical routers. The difference, in this case, is that the third layer, in this case, is virtual. So, clients connected to the VLAN use the SVI interface as their gateway.

- Secure route configuration. To ensure a proper configuration of the router, there are several steps taken. For instance, there must be a change in the default username in the website of the router to ensure that the account information cannot be hacked. The SSID has to be changed and the MAC or physical address activated and the SSID broadcast feature disabled. Also, static IP addresses must be assigned, and the option for auto-connecting to Wi-Fi networks automatically must be disabled. Statistic IP addresses are then assigned to all devices in the network. Firewalls are also enabled to ensure security.

- Access control lists. Access control lists are typically catalogs of access control entries. Each access control entry identifies a specific trustee and specifies what rights are allowed and even denied for that specific trustee. There are basically two types of trustees, DACL and SACL. DACL is a discretionary access control list that identifies every trustee that is allowed or denied access to an object. When a procedure, therefore, attempts to gain admittance to a securable entity, the DACL comes into play, and the systems will scan the ACE to determine whether it should be granted permission or not. SACL is also known as the system access control list. It works by authorizing administrators who log on to try and reach a securable object. The log attempts of different administrators are itemized by every ACE, and therefore, a record in the security event log is generated.

Home Network Administration

Home network administration is just the same as professional network administration. As such, the duties of a network administrator in the workplace reflect what can be done in the home setting; the only difference is that it is done on a smaller scale. Some of the activities taken by home network administrators include:

· setting up broadband features with advanced features, such as QoS and wireless security keys

· troubleshooting performance issues and any outages that come within the network

· training family members on the technical details of network usage and network devices

· building a network backup system for the home

It is vital to realize that home networking cannot act as a substitute when it comes to network administration.

47

However, when doing network administration in the home, you get a snippet of what network administration is all about. This educational value increases when you use your home networking expertise to help neighbors and friends with their network connection. For other people, network administration is a hobby that they love to undertake.

Building a Career in Network Administration

Computer networking is an attractive career that many have set their eyes on. It became a field of interest in the early 2000s and has not gone down the ladder of popularity since. The reason why computer networking continues to be popular is that there is a shortage of professionals that can take up jobs in the field, and yet, it can be an easy way for a person in the field to land a relatively lucrative position and scale-up in a fast-growing company. Whatever side of the debate you lie on, there are some things you should know about beginning a career in networking, expanding. Also, we outline some of the things you will need to be keen on when hunting for a job in this field. Luckily, these tips apply for other jobs in technical careers as well.

Job Titles in Networking

There are several positions when it comes to professional computer networking, and each of them comes with a variation in salaries and a high potential for long-term careers. The only disadvantage with this field is that job titles in networking can always be a source of confusion and not just for beginners but experienced people as well. There may be bombastic or bland titles that may fail to capture the essence of the actual work a professional may need to carry out in the field. There are some job titles that should be clearly spelled out as is done below:

✓ **Network administrator.** It is only fair, to begin with, that a large chunk of the discussion in the above sections has been focused on network administration. Basically, the job of a network administrator entails managing and configuring WANs and LANs.

✓ **Network engineer.** A network engineer is also called a systems engineer. The job role primarily focuses on system upgrades and evaluation of vendor products. Also, a systems engineer is always responsible for security testing.

✓ **Network technician**. Sometimes, network technicians are referred to as service technicians. The job, in this case, tends to give more focus on setting up, troubleshooting, and repairing both software and hardware products. It is not uncommon to find network technicians traveling to remote locations so they can upgrade fields and offer support as needed.

✓ **Network analyst**. A network analyst is also known as a network programmer. Their duties revolve around writing software scripts and programs that are useful in network analysis. Network analysis, in this case, involves monitoring of utilities and diagnostics. They also must evaluate third party products and integrate these products and software technologies into the already existing network environment. Conversely, they can easily build new network environments as well.

✓ **Network systems manager**. A network systems manager can also be called an information systems manager. Their main duties revolve around supervision of the work of network administrators, technicians, engineers, and programmers. They have a special focus on longer-range planning and make strategy considerations.

It is vital to realize that there are no uniform salaries in networking; in fact, salaries may vary, depending on different factors. These factors include which organization is in question, the market conditions within the locality, and the skill level and experience of the person being hired. This is why it is important to get into networking with a straight face and realistic expectations. Rarely will you find it a smooth walk in the park, but when you have the passion and determination for the job, you will find that your movement upward is a simple task. Advancement up the career ladder will often carry with it more lucrative opportunities when it comes to networking. Read on for more about gaining experience in networking.

Gaining Experience With Networking

Well, getting a job in networking can be quite an arduous task. This is because most employers are always seeking employees with experience, but where are you supposed to gain experience when you are fresh out of college? It is not uncommon to hear job seekers lamenting about this reality, and many people complain that the best and only way to gain experience is through getting hired. These sentiments may be true, despite the many promises of a lucrative job in the IT industry. The conditions are increasingly becoming harder and landing an entry-level position in networking can be difficult. However, you can still gain experience in other ways, as will be discussed in the next paragraphs. With these tips, you can have better chances of getting a good job and faster.

One great tip for gaining experience in networking is to pursue a help desk or programming internship full time in the summer months. Alternatively, you can take up a work-study job in these fields as they will work equally well. Internships are not assuring of the best pay, but the work could turn out to be more interesting or uninteresting for some. If the job is not interesting, there is a likelihood that an individual will not finish a substantial project during the limited time they have there. However, there is a clear advantage for you should you manage to complete your work-study or internship. Besides, you will gain hands-on experience, and you will be adequately trained, so you are ready for the market. With you being able to obtain and work well in these jobs, you demonstrate to your future and potential employers that you have an interest in the networking role you are applying for, and that is exactly what they like to see when hiring.

Another useful tip that can help you to gain experience is to self-study. Being handy can pay, albeit in different ways. One thing for sure, however, is that being hands-on can work in your favor as the skills you have can be useful and powerful when you demonstrate something to a potential employer. For instance, you may have just completed a class project recently. Do not stop there, extend the project in some way that will show that you can think out of the box, and show your abilities. You can also create a personal project that you have not been tasked to and complete it. A good way to start would be, for example, to experiment with network administration tools.

Also, earlier on, I mentioned something about home computer networking. This can be quite a useful way to gain experience. You can start with setting up the networks of friends and family and acting as an administrator for the same, for free. While this may not be the best idea for earning income, it will provide you with a basic understanding of how networks run. Should you find a job in business, however, remember that business computer networking is more complex. Therefore, you should expect that there is a different level of complexity and that you will use different technologies than you did in the home environment.

Also, the field of networking is vast and can be overwhelming for many people who may just be starting out. Instead of trying to eat more than you can chew by mastering every language and trying to keep up with every trend, make your life easier. Simply focus on the basic technologies that will be most important as you enter into the market. Over time, you will realize that you keep learning and keeping up if indeed, your interest is in the computer networking industry. Some core technologies that you can build expertise in include TCP/IP, as this will form a foundation for you to learn other specialized new ones in later life.

Education and Experience

As a person that is interested in venturing into networking, you may wonder the value that education holds when placed against the value of experience. As you may have noticed by now, a lot of employers seek out employees who have completed a four-year degree in university. This may not make sense in some instances, but it is important because they use this as a gauge for your commitment in the industry and field at large. The technology utilized in networking is not constant, and it keeps changing every other day. This is why employers find it important to know that you possess current information when it comes to networking and that you are willing to learn and adapt in the future as technology continues to change. Certifications in networking help prove that you have the basic knowledge base, but college degrees are the real thing; they demonstrate your general ability to learn.

Experience is also important because it demonstrates that you have skills that are needed for the workplace. The more experience you have in the field, the better because it tends to put you in a better position to get a job. However, nothing beats the combination of experience and education when it comes to getting into networking as a career. This is because when you have both experience and education, it sets you apart from individuals who have one of each.

Representation of the Skills and Abilities

I discussed in the earlier sections that to get into network administration, a person should have a great combination of technical and interpersonal skills. I need to emphasize that interpersonal skills are important, and yet often, they are underrated. Also, you need to understand how to explain and exchange information pertaining to the technical aspects of networking. You will most likely be working in a team and not alone and having the ability to explain yourself verbally and in writing, both email and formal, you have the advantage of getting the chance to enjoy communicating with other networking professionals throughout your life as you seek to build your career.

Before even going further about the importance of communication skills at the networking workplace, let us start with the initial stages. You will definitely need good communication skills during an interview. Your ability to articulate yourself in the work environment is important, and the interviewers will be looking for possible clues into how well you can be understood within the networking environment as you work in a team. Therefore, understand the jargon used in such places and learn to relax when making conversation about such technical subjects. This is not something that will simply come to you in one day, but over time and with practice, you can learn so much that you can answer impromptu questions when asked. You can learn to articulate yourself through many tactics. For instance, you can visit local job fairs and discuss professional subjects with the people you will find there and with your friends. You will find that you gain indispensable knowledge on these subjects.

There are some tips that have been outlined above that may not work for people who are already in the field of networking. However, they can be used by those who aspire to venture into fields related to networking. Furthermore, there are tips that can be used no matter where you are in your career, for instance, visiting job fairs to help polish your skills. I hope that the information given can be of help to you, even in the slightest of ways.

Chapter 5: Network Infrastructure

Network infrastructure is part of IT infrastructure found within companies in enterprise IT organizations. Network infrastructure is interconnected and is usable for both internal and external communication. The network infrastructure in organizations is important because, in the digital age, the productivity and agility of a company are pegged on excellent equipment, as much as smart employees are also involved. For smooth running of operations, you require secure network infrastructure that will not let you down. Without the right infrastructure, you may find yourself suffering from security issues and poor user experience, which can impact the productivity of employees and customer experience and cost your brand its reputation.

It is, therefore, important that you and your organization understand how important network infrastructure is and be aware of the opportunities and possible challenges that come with network infrastructure. When you have the right knowledge of network infrastructure, you will be better placed to have maximum production and helping your organization reach optimum performance. Below, we dive deeper into the topic.

What Exactly Is Network Infrastructure?

The network infrastructure consists of resources needed to make the network work. These resources make network or internet connectivity, business operation, management, and communication within the organization possible. It consists of both software and hardware components, and it is what enables communication between services, uses, application, and processes and allows computing.

There is a common and interrelated term to network infrastructure. The term is IT infrastructure. In the simplest way, it is the same as network infrastructure. Interestingly, the terms are even used interchangeably and yet; there are ways in which they can differ subtly. IT infrastructure is used to define the large collection of elements of information technology that form the foundation for IT service. It encompasses the physical elements; in essence, the hardware and software components needed to form a healthy IT network. The network infrastructure, on the other hand, is seen as a smaller category compared to IT infrastructure. It is, therefore, as described before, a component of larger IT infrastructure. To have sustained success and cohesive solutions, a company should put in place both network and IT infrastructure. Below, the diagram expresses some of the components within a network infrastructure:

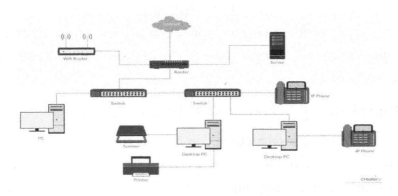

Why is network infrastructure important?

Network infrastructure is important because it can make or break a company and its reputation. It is, hence, important not only to have reliable IT infrastructure but also qualified personnel. These three components will work hand-in-hand to ensure a good and reputable company. The network is important mostly because it allows communication and connection. If there is no network infrastructure, other IT components such as software and hardware hardly make any sense and are not of much use. If, however, your network infrastructure is rich, clean, and secure, you are on your way to organizational excellence.

Challenges Surrounding Network Infrastructure

There are also challenges that surround network infrastructure that can prevent optimal functioning. Some of these challenges include:

· Centralization of traffic

· Duplication of data and how to deal with it

· Relaying the right data to the correct tool

Centralization of Traffic

An organization usually has several different locations or sites and subnets. If there is no centralized hub, it can be difficult to monitor and manage the network, and network visibility may also be an issue. Some companies have found a way around this, and typically, they use network infrastructure solutions to better understand what their network is and to centralize the heavy traffic. Infrastructure solutions also help companies to monitor and understand any data that traverses their networks. Using network infrastructure solutions, therefore, helps improve the security of a network and helps network operations teams address their issues with performance.

Data Duplication

Data duplication is also a major issue when it comes to network infrastructure. In Extreme instances, duplication can occur for up to 50 % to 66 % of network traffic. Duplicate data may present problems, especially with regards to network security solutions. If network security solutions encounter a lot of duplicate data, there are new risks involved. First, the duplicate data makes the solutions slow down, and eventually, they are not able to detect threats within the network infrastructure. Removing duplicate data is, therefore, not just important but critical for the well-being of the organization as well.

Relaying the Right Data to the Correct Tool

Different organizations use a variety of different cybersecurity providers and tools. These security providers charge organizations based on the amount of data they need to process. It is, therefore, important that the data sent is relayed to the right tool. If data is sent from various sources to one and the same tool, it may end up not only being ineffective but also costly, especially in a case where one tool suits a different type of data than another one.

There are solution providers that help organizations and companies to keep an efficient, clean network, as this work is not a small task. It may, therefore, be helpful to have a team with deep security and networking expertise in your organization. Unlike in the past, where network infrastructure was clear cut, today, the network infrastructure field is dynamic and complex, with a mixture of cloud and on-premise management. Even when on-premises networking happens, it is possible for a company to have a mix of vendors and networks. When companies merge, and when there is organic growth, there tends to be further mix up in the network infrastructure, which eventually, ends up having a negative impact on network infrastructure. When such eventualities come about, sometimes companies end up with up to five tools for monitoring and managing what is now a hybrid network. If you want to have your company and network safe and performing at its peak, this may not be the best or ideal environment. You may need to establish a central hub where you can view all your network traffic and get the tools to direct the right traffic to the right tools.

Network visibility remains important mainly because the good performance of a company relies mainly on the infrastructure and its ability to monitor performance and detect threats. If a company is able to deal with network blind spots, then they are able to uncover the blind spots, identify threats from the sources uncovered, and remediated solutions quickly. With these solutions in place, it is possible for the organization to remove duplicate data and allow for efficiency in the network and security tools.

Network Protocols and Standards

The definition of terms is important in networking. From the above sections, we have had a step-by-step development of concepts that have so far given an idea of how networks function. Now, the reader is going to be introduced to network protocols, what standards are, and what role they play in networking.

Network protocols are the policies and standards, including formats, rules, and procedures that define how two or more devices communicate over a network. These protocols govern end-to-end processes and ensure that data and network communication is secure and also timely. Protocols include all the requirements, processes, and restraints involved in initiating and accomplishing communication when it comes to servers, computers, and other devices within the network. Protocols have to be affirmed and installed by both receivers and senders so that data and network communication is possible and to ensure the application of software and hardware nodes that do the communication over a network.

There are types of network protocols:

· Network communication protocols, such as HTTP and TCP/IP

· Network security protocols, such as HTTPS, SFTP, and SSL

· Network management protocols, including SNMP and ICMP

It is important for anyone who is seeking to understand networking to understand network protocols. This information is usually key to understanding communication and troubleshooting communication problems within networks. Also, these network protocols give the network devices a common language through which they can communicate. Without protocols, therefore, computers cannot achieve communication with each other. Network end users heavily rely on these network protocols to connect.

How Do Network Protocols Work?

You may be wondering how network protocols work. In the simplest terms, these protocols work by breaking down what are seemingly large processes into narrowly definite, more discrete tasks across each level within the network. In a standard model, the Open Systems Interconnection model, there are network protocols that govern the activities in each layer in the exchange.

A protocol suite is a set of network protocols that work together. The TCP/IP suite is a type of suite that includes a number of protocols across layers. These work together to enable internet connectivity. The network protocols involved include:

·   **User Datagram Protocol.** This protocol is simply referred to as UDP and takes the responsibility of acting as an alternative protocol of communication to the transmission control protocol. UDP is used in establishing loss-tolerating and low-latency connections between the internet and various applications.

·   **Transmission control protocol**. Also known as TCP, this control protocol uses rules that have already been set to ensure communication exchange between internet points in information packets.

- **Internet protocol**. Also known as IP, this protocol uses rules that have been set to receive and send messages based on the internet address level.

- **Other network protocols, including hypertext transfer protocol and FTP**. These protocols have defined a set of rules that help in the exchange and display of information.

All packets that are transmitted and received within a network have binary data. Usually, a packet will have a header at the beginning of a packet. This header stores information regarding the sender and the intended destination of the data. Some packets also have footers at their end, and they contain additional information about the sender and destination. The network protocols involved then process the headers and footers and sieve messages of each kind as they move among devices. There are groups that set up these industry standards and publish them.

Network Communication Protocols

Communication protocols include formal descriptions of rules and digital message formats that are required during the exchange of information between and in computing systems and devices and in telecommunications at large. Communication protocols cover a wide range of processes, including error detection, authentication, and signaling and error correction. These protocols also describe the synchronization of digital and analog aspects of communication, semantics, and syntax. These protocols are implemented in both hardware and software, and it is not surprising that there is an abundance of communication protocols used in both digital and analog communications. In short, computer networks cannot be existent without communication protocols. The properties of transmission that a protocol is able to define include transmission size, packet speeds, techniques of synchronization and handshaking, types of correction errors, sequence control of packets, address formatting, routing and address mapping. Some well-known communication protocols are Hypertext Transfer Protocol (HTTP), Simple Mail Transfer Protocol (SMTP), User Datagram Protocol (UDP), File Transfer Protocol (FTP), and Internet Message Access Protocol (IMAP).

Where digital computing systems are involved, the rules of the communication protocols are expressed by data structures and algorithms. Protocols, therefore, serve the same purpose to communication as algorithms and programming do to communications. Operating systems contain processes that cooperate and manipulate data that is shared so that they connect with each other. The connection is usually guided by protocols that can be entrenched within the very course. There is no shared memory, and so, the systems that are communicating have to do so using s common transmission medium. Transmission is such a case is not fully reliable, and there may be the use of different operating systems and even hardware.

For the successful implementation of a networking protocol, the software models have to be interfaced with the machine's operating system's framework that has already been implemented. The framework is responsible for the implementation of networking as a functionality in the operating system. Protocol algorithms are articulated in what is a transferable language in programming, and the protocol software becomes independent of the operating system. Some of the well-known frameworks are the OSI model and the TCP/IP models.

When the internet was developed, the successful design approach for both operating systems and compiler was abstraction layering. A remarkable resemblance between programming languages and communication protocols exists, which is the reason that the original monolithic schmoosing plans were disintegrated into liaising protocols. Eventually, this contributed to the upsurge of the layered protocol perception, which, today, is the center of protocol design. Typically, systems cannot utilize a solitary protocol for broadcast. As an alternative, systems utilize collaborating protocols, which has been described above as a protocol suite. Protocols are arranged according to their functionality in clusters, for example, a cluster of the transport protocol. In this case, functionalities are plotted into layers, and each layer solves a specific type of issue. For transmission of a message, protocols are selected from every layer. The next protocol is accomplished through the extension of the message with the next layer's protocol selector.

There are other basic requirements needed in this process, and getting files transverse the network is only a small fragment of the protocol. When files are acknowledged, it is evaluated so that the context of progress within the conversation is established. The protocol, then, contains guidelines that describe the context as well. The syntax of communication is expressed through the rules of context. There are other rules that express the semantics of communication. To begin communication, the communication systems facilitate the sending and receiving of messages. Thus, protocols govern the rules of transmission, while the following must be adhered to:

✓ Data formats that will enable records interchange

Bit-strings of digital messages are exchanged and divided into fields such that a field will carry only material pertinent to the protocol. The bit-string is usually separated into the payload and header. The payload carries the message while the header has information pertaining to the protocol operation. If a bit-string is longer than the SMTU, then it is divided into pieces that are of the right size.

✓ Address mapping

In some instances, protocols are required to map addresses of a particular scheme on those of another. For instance, for an Ethernet MAC address application to translate a specified logical IP address, it has to map addresses.

✓ Address formats for data exchange

Addresses exist solely for the purpose of identifying senders and recipients. Bit-strings contain headers that carry addresses, allowing for the receivers to resolve if the bit-strings are appropriate, thus must be processed or if they must be ignored. The connection between the receiver and sender is identified using what is known as an address pair. Address values, sometimes, consist of special meanings. For instance, if an address is comprised of all -1s, then it can be supposed that it is addressing every station of the network and the message shall be broadcast so that the entire local network receives it. The rules that are used are referred to as addressing schemes, which determine the meanings corresponding to the address values.

✓ Routing

Routing typically happens when systems do not have a direct connection with each other. Intermediary systems are, therefore, needed to send messages in place of the source along the route, which are called "routers." The way the routers connect through routers on the internet is known as internetworking.

✓ Detecting transmission errors

If there is a possibility of data corruption anywhere within a network, then it is necessary that errors are detected and eliminated as soon as possible. Usually, the CRCs of any data are attached to the packet's end, and this makes it possible for whoever is receiving the data to detect corruption in it because they can see the differences. In such a case, the receiver rejects the packet-based in these CRC differences and makes arrangements for fresh transmission.

✓ Time outs and retries causing loss of information

Sometimes, packets may be delayed in transit, or they may be lost on the network. To deal with such issues, some senders who are operating under protocols can expect that the receiver acknowledges that they received the correct information within a relatively short time. When, therefore, there is a timeout, the receiver may need to inform the sender who retransmits the information. In the case where links are permanently broken, there is really no need for retransmission, so the number of retransmissions is usually limited. If the limits for retrying are limited, then what occurs is an error.

✓ Flow control

The importance of flow control resides on the sender's task of transmitting data fast—faster than what the receiver's network equipment can actually process. It is, however, possible to control flow by messaging to the sender.

✓ The direction of the flow of information

If transmissions can only occur in one direction at a time, as transmission happens on half-duplex links, then there is a need to address transmission direction. Arrangements are made to accommodate contention, like in a situation when two parties concurrently need to transfer data.

✓ Control of sequence

> As we explained above, bit-strings may sometimes be divided into pieces. When this happens, the pieces of bit-string sent on the network may get delayed or get lost completely. Sometimes, they may end up taking different routes to their destination and what results is that the bit-strings arrive out of sequence. Resubmission, on the other hand, can result in pieces that are duplicate. However, it is still possible to mark pieces with sequence information such that the receiver is able to determine what was duplicated or lost and ask for retransmission where information was lost. It also becomes possible to reassemble what could have been the original message.

Protocol Design Principles

Network protocol design principles have been based on systems engineering principles. Therefore, to design complex protocols, decomposition into smaller cooperating protocols is necessary. Operating systems operate synchronously. The synchronization of software is a primary aspect of concurrency in programming. This receives and sends communication in the right sequence. This type of programming, when it comes to operating systems theory, has always been a topic among programmers. If carefully studied, you will realize that there are several analogies between programming and communication. In such a case, the CPU is likened to a transfer mechanism of a protocol. Below, I introduce the rules that allow programmers to design protocols that are independent of each other but can cooperate.

Layering

Protocols are layered in modern protocol design so that they can form a protocol stack. Layering comprises a design principle that splits the protocol into smaller phases that complete specific parts while interrelating with the protocol's other areas in minor but well-defined means. The layers have a role of testing and designing independently the protocol's various parts, thereby eradicating the chances of combinatorial explosion while keeping the designs simplistic.

The internet's communication protocols are supposed to function in, not only complex but also, diverse settings and are designed for modularity and simplicity, and they fit into the hierarchy of layers as defined by the internet protocol suite. TCP and IP, the first two protocols that cooperate come as a result of decomposing the original TCP into a layered suite of communication.

Another protocol is the seven-layered model or the "OSI model." This was developed for general communication as a reference model. The difference is that this layer has a more rigorous concept of functionality and stricter rules of protocol interaction. Application software is always built on a strong transport layer the routing mechanism, and datagram delivery underlies the transport layer. The routing mechanism is connectionless when it comes to the internet. Network link technologies are the layer on which packets relay upon networks. Network link technologies include

Ethernet which is physical layer technologies. Layering allows the exchange of technologies when necessary; for instance, to accommodate the connection of networks that are not similar, protocols can be stacked in a tunneling arrangement.

Protocol layering is, hence, the basis for protocol design. Protocol layering allows the decomposition of complex protocols into simplistic ones that can cooperate. Also, since every protocol goes into a protocol layer, this can be seen as functional decomposition. Each distinct protocol layer has distinct problems related to communication. The IP suite consists of internet-network and application-transport functions. Together, they make up a layering model or layering scheme.

Network architecture and protocol layering design are interrelated, so they have to be designed alongside each other. The features of these two in relation to each other are as described in the next paragraphs:

The internet is a source of universal connection. Any two computers that connect to the internet can, therefore, communicate. All computers on the internet are identified by an internet address and reach the user as one huge network composed of interrelated physical networks. This is what we know as the internet, which is a system of interconnection that is also known as "internetwork."

Internet addresses consist of the host-id and net-id. The host is identified by the hosted, while the network is identified by the net-id. The term host can mislead, as often, a computer may have multiple work interfaces, and each will have its own unique address. The internet address, on the other hand, does not identify a connection to one computer but rather to the network. This is the id that is used by routers to determine where a packet should be sent.

Routers ensure the interconnection of physical networks. They forward packets that appear between the interconnected networks and make it possible for one host to reach another when on a physical network. There is a flow of communications between two systems that communicate through routers, and datagrams are delivered from router to router until one that can deliver the datagram to the attached network is reached. A routing table is consulted in the case where a decision has to be made, whether a datagram needs to be sent to a router closer to the destination or it can be delivered directly to the network. The routing table typically consists of paths and networkids that need to be followed to reach a network. The path prescribed is, therefore, either direct (there's a sign that the datagram can be brought straight to it) or not (there is an alternative route that is closer to the destination).

All networks, be it WAN, LAN, or point-to-point links, are treated as the same network.

The internet offers a packet-switched system that adapts well to a range of hardware, including Ethernet. Connectionless delivery involves streams and messages being allocated into pieces and are multiplexed on high-speed interconnected machines that allow simultaneous use of connections. The divided pieces each carry information that helps identify what the destination is. The delivery is, however, unreliable, as sometimes, packets get lost, delayed, delivered despite defect, or duplicated without warning to either the source or receiver. This unreliability comes as a result of a shortcoming in which the underlying networks fail, or resources are exhausted. The internet protocol defines an unreliable connectionless system. Also, the routing function is specified by the IP protocol. Virtual circuits between senders and receivers are built up through connection-oriented systems. Once virtual circuits are built up, datagrams are sent like any other data through virtual circuits. This data is forwarded to IP protocol modules.

The transmission control protocol defines a reliable stream transport service. These services are layered; on top are the application programs, also called "application services," which can utilize the transmission control protocol. Should the program interrelate with the packet delivery system, the process takes place through the user datagram protocol.

Software Layering

Software layering/design is done after the protocols, and protocol layering has been established. Software is layered in an organization and has a relationship with protocol layering. To send messages on a system, the modules have to interact such that the top one interacts directly with the one below it. It then hands over the message for encapsulation. The module establishes a reaction, which is encapsulating the data presented within its data area and filling the header with the data according to the protocols. To interrelate with the module right beneath it, it passes over the newly compiled information where it is appropriate. The module at the bottom directly interacts with the module at the bottom of the next receiving system such that the message gets sent across. The reverse happens on the receiving system such that the message is eventually delivered to the destination in its original form if, by good luck, it does not experience any protocol violations or transmission errors.

When it comes to protocol errors, the delivering module discards any received pieces and hands to the source of the piece on the same layer, the report of an error condition. It does this by dispensing an error message below or delivering it across, in the case where there is a bottom module. The layer that introduced division and reassembly handles the stream of data and division of the messages into pieces, and their final reassembly is done at the final destination. The translation of programs is divided into the following:

· Loader

· Compiler

· Link editor

· Assembler

This signifies the layering of the translation or software, which allows them to be designed independently. The complexity of program translation could be conquered in some ways, and these ways could be applied to protocols; the brains behind the TCP/IP protocol suite ensured that they imposed the same layering when it came to software frameworks.

Strict Layering

Strict layering involves adherence to a layered model. However, this cannot be considered an ideal method of networking since strict layering typically can cause severe effects on the performance of a system. There must, therefore, be a trade-off between performance and the simplicity offered by layering. Researchers criticize the rather widespread use of protocol layering for the primary reason of having a probability of duplication between a higher layer and a lower layer's functionality.

Protocol Development and the Need for These Standards

Protocols have the selected standards for communication to happen ultimately. Rules are expressed through data structures and algorithms. The operating system and hardware are independent, and this is enhanced by the expression of the algorithms into what is a portable programming language. The standards of protocol are achieved by obtaining the support and, ultimately, approval of a standards organization. The standards organization is responsible for protocol development. An agreement is created for the organization's members to adhere voluntarily to the result of the work. Often, these members control the larger market shares relevant to protocols, and the standards are reset by the government because they also serve an important public interest. Sometimes, they do not gain enough acceptance, and the government or law has to come in disclosing the source code and enforcing it for the sake of the public.

To further enhance an understanding of the importance of these standards, you can take the example of IBM's bi-sync protocol. This early link-level protocol was for use in correcting two nodes that were separate. When it was used in a multimode network, some deficiencies were realized. Manufacturers and organizations can enhance the protocol as they see fit in the absence of standardization, and this has led to the creation of versions that are even incompatible on networks. Today, there exists over 50 variants of the BSC, something that could have been stopped by the presence of standardization.

Sometimes, protocols fail to go through the standardization process and yet still gain dominance in the market. The protocols, in this case, are called de-facto standards. De-facto standards tend to be a common trend in monopolized markets, niche markets. Sometimes, they are used to scare away competition, and this can have a negative impact on the market. Standardization is, therefore, a way to counter-act de-facto standards and their ill results. However, de-facto standards are not always negative. In some instances, such as the case of GNU/Linux, there is no undesirable control on the market. The reason for this is that the sources are published and maintained openly, which invites the existence of competition. The solution for open systems interconnection, therefore, does not have to be standardized.

Chapter 6: Network Protocols and Standards

Network Protocols

Network protocols in the simplest sense are the policies and standards, including but not limited to, the formats, procedures, and rules that define how devices, two or more, communicate within a network. These policies and standards govern the end-to-end processes involved in communication and ensure timely, secure delivery of data, and network communication. Protocols in a network incorporate the processes, constraints, and even requirements of accomplishing communication between servers, routers, computers, and other devices that may be network-enabled. Normally, these network protocols are installed and confirmed by the receivers and senders so that network and data communication is done, and they apply to both the hardware and software nodes that communicate with each other on a network.

As such, a protocol can be likened to the language through which communication happens on the internet. This is because there is a set of mutually accepted rules that are also implemented as both ends of what is perceived to be the communication channel to ensure proper communication exchange. Two devices can exchange information only if they adopt the rules. We, therefore, cannot even dare communicate over the internet without the use of protocols. Every protocol is defined using unique terms, and each has a different name. Typically, messages travel from the sender to the receiver through a medium just like normal communication does. In this case, the medium refers to the physical path over which the information will travel once it is sent and expected by the receiver. It uses a protocol.

These formats are used among communicating systems to exchange messages, where each has a precise meaning and is intended for a particular recipient. This recipient then produces a singular response from a pool of all probable responses predetermined for the specific situation being examined. This characteristic is typically autonomous of its intended implementation communication protocols agreed to by the parties involved, and to do this, protocols are developed according to technical standards. This kind of arrangement is also the same for a programming language, and it can, therefore, be said that protocols act to communication as programming languages do to computations. Different protocols describe different aspects of communication. A group of protocols that have been designed to work in collaboration is known as protocol suites. When protocol suites are implemented in software, they are known as protocol stacks. The Internet Engineering Task Force publishes internet communication protocols, and hence, it handles both wired and wireless networking that has become a prominent part of present-day networking. The International Organization for Standardization, also known as ISO, on the other hand, handles other types of networking. Yet another organization, the ITU-T, handles protocols for telecommunications and public switched telephone network

(PSTN) formats. This and internet coverage are uniting over time. As such, the standards are doing the same and are moving towards convergence as well.

Communicating Systems

Between other media and the devices in a network, communication is exchanged in every instance. This type of exchange is administered by predetermined agreements set out in communication protocol specifications. These specifications work to define the state-dependent behaviors, actual data that is exchanged, and the nature of communication. Digitally, in computing systems, the rules are expressed as data structures and algorithms, while in communication, they are expressed as protocols. Operating systems, which we will discuss later in the book, usually contain cooperating processes that work to manipulate the data that has been shared within devices to know what was being communicated. The protocols that govern this communication and protocols are also embedded in the process code. Communicating systems do not have shared memory, and therefore, they have to use a shared transmission medium for communication with each other. Transmission as the way to achieve the ultimate goal of communication may not be reliable. As such, individual systems sometimes end up using different operating systems and different hardware. When implementing a network protocol, software modules for protocols and frameworks within the operating systems of machines interface. The framework is responsible for implementing the operating system's networking functionality. Protocols are usually expressed in portable programming language, and when this happens, protocol software and the operating system are made independent of each other. The TCP/IP and OSI models are the most popular frameworks.

A design approach that has been deemed successful is abstraction layering from the days as early as when internet development was taking place. Abstraction layering was a useful design approach for both the operating system and compiler design. There are similarities between communication protocols and programming languages, and this meant that the monolithic networking programs could be broke down into protocols that could work together, giving rise to the concept of layered protocols. As a result of such developments, today, layered protocols are the basis of protocol design. One protocol is generally not enough for systems when transmitting information. Instead, there are sets of protocols that cooperate to ensure transmission, and they are known as protocol suites. Protocols are arranged based on the way they function in groups. To illustrate, take a group of transport protocols, for example. Here, the groups of layers pertain to certain functionalities, where each of the layers solves a particular class of problems that relate to different aspects, such as internet, application, transport, and network functions. For a message to get transmitted, each layer gives a chosen protocol. The subsequent protocol's selection is attained when the message is drawn-out by a protocol selector in each of the layers.

Basic Requirements for Network Protocols

For data to get across, an entire network is just a small part of the equation when it comes to transmission. Once the data is received, more things happen. For instance, data has to be evaluated so that it can be understood how far the conversation has reached. Protocols, therefore, must be inclusive of rules of engagement that will describe the context. The rules in question express communication syntax. There are other rules as well, and these ones determine the usefulness of the data that has been transmitted according to the context of the exchange. They are the rules that express the semantics of communication. Communication, in this case, involves semantics and syntax.

There is the sending and receiving of data on communication systems, and protocols define and specify the rules that are responsible for the government of transmission. The aspects described below are, therefore, to be addressed

Data Formats for Exchange of Data

In this sense, there is an exchange of information bit-strings. There is a division of the bit-strings into fields, and every one of these fields carries information that is relevant to the protocol in question. There is a division in the bit-string, so it consists of two parts: the payload and header. The payload is responsible for carrying the actual message, and the header, on the other hand, is responsible for fields that are relevant to the protocol's operation. There is a maximum transmission unit for bit-strings, and sometimes, some bit-strings are longer than this specified minimum. In such cases, the bit-strings end up being divided into smaller appropriate-sized pieces.

Address Formats for the Exchange of Data

Addresses in networking are just like addresses for humans in real life. They identify who the sender of information is and who the intended receiver is. The header area in the bit-string described above contains this information, and this allows the recipients of the message to determine if the bit-strings will be of use to them or not so that they can process or ignore the message therein. There may be a connection between the receiver and the sender, and this is identified using what is known as an address pair. Address pair come with values that have meanings for the receiver and sender. Sometimes, the addresses come with special values that have meaning. This is what results in a broadcast message in a local network. An address scheme is the set of rules that describes the meanings of the address values in the address pair.

Mapping of Addresses

This happens when protocols need to address one scheme to another. For example, when there is a need to translate an application specified logical IP address to an Ethernet Mac address, address mapping must happen so that the address of the first scheme is understood to the second scheme.

Detection of Errors That Occur During Transmission

Data detection is a necessary and important part of the process of data transmission in networks. It is especially necessary in cases where data corruption has occurred. The most common approach to this issue is the attachment of CRCs to the end of packets. When the CRCs are added, then it is possible for the receiver of data to establish that there are some differences that have occurred as a result of corruption. This gives the receiver a basis for rejecting the packet, and therefore, arrangements are made for retransmission.

Routing

Sometimes, you may find that systems do not connect to each other directly. In such cases, there is the employment of intermediary systems that work to connect the intended receiver with the message. These routers forward the message on behalf of the sender and make it possible for the receiver to get the intended message. "Router" is a term that is used when these connections happen on the internet, and the resulting interconnection of networks is referred to as internetworking, as mentioned earlier.

Acknowledging

When there is the expectation of communication, then acknowledgment that the correct data was received is necessary. The receiver usually sends the acknowledgment to the original sender of the message.

Timeouts and Retries

Interestingly, despite taking all the necessary precautions, packets tend to be lost in networks sometimes. At other times, there may be a simple delay in the delivery of the packets. This is where acknowledgment plays a role because the sender expects that the receiver sends an acknowledgment so that they are sure that the message was received. The acknowledgment is expected in a set amount of time, and this gave rise to the concept of timeout. When the time lapses and the sender has not received an acknowledgment, it becomes a cue that there is a need to retransmit the information. In other cases, links may permanently be broken. In such cases, retransmission usually loses its effect, resulting in a restricted number of retries. When number of retries exceeds that of the limit, then an error follows.

The Direction in Which Information Flows

Sometimes, transmissions occur in one direction as would be on the case of information that flows from one sender at a time or half-duplex. If this happens, then there is a problem that will need to be addressed. This is the root of the concept of media access control as arrangements are made so that the case of contention and collisions are involved. Collisions happen when two senders want to simultaneously send out information, and contention happens when the two senders both wish to transmit data.

Control of Sequences

As we had discussed above, sometimes, bit-strings may need to be transmitted after division into smaller pieces. However, problems may arise as most times, when these bit-strings are sent individually on the network, they may get delayed and sometimes, lost as they may take different routes to reach their destination. In such cases, these pieces of bit-string end up reaching the destination out of sequence. Retransmissions, on the other hand, will result in duplicate pieces, which does not solve the problem. As such, the pieces are marked with sequence information when they are still with the sender. If, therefore, they reach the receiver when out of sequence, the receiver has the right tool to determine what is duplicated and can know what was lost and either reassemble or ask for retransmission as is best seen.

Control of Flow

The flow needs to be controlled when the sender is transmitting packets of data faster than can be received and processed by the intermediate network or receiver. As we have mentioned earlier, the best way to establish flow control is by messaging the sender and receiver.

Design of Protocols

To generate a group of common principles governing protocol design for networks, the system engineering principles have been put into use. Therefore, to design complex protocols, it is necessary to decompose simpler protocols that can cooperate within the conceptual framework. There is a concurrent type of operation in communicating systems. Synchronizing the software that receives and transmits messages in proper sequences is an essential part of this type of programming. Traditionally, concurrent programming has been discussed in theory when it comes to operating systems. Formal verification is important because concurrent programs usually contain a big number of hidden bugs. Communicating sequential processes is the mathematical approach that studies communication and concurrency. Alternatively, concurrency can be modeled using machines that are finite, and such machines include Mealy and Moore, which is utilized in digital electronic systems as design tools and are encountered in the telecommunication and electronic hardware used in devices.

There are a lot of analogies between programming and computer communication. A protocol's transfer mechanism, in this case, is comparable to the central processing unit. Among the programmers, there are rules governing the design of protocols that can cooperate even when independent of each other.

We have mentioned layering before in the book, and now, we delve deeper into it. Usually, protocols are layered to form what is known as a protocol stack. As a protocol design principle, layering involves breaking protocols into smaller pieces, each of which will work to accomplish a specific task while interrelating, in trivial and undefined ways, with the other aspects of the protocol. The idea behind layering is that it allows individual aspects of the protocol to undergo testing and design without having to face combined explosion cases, and yet, the design can be kept relatively simple.

Internet communication protocols are made for complex yet diverse settings. Their design, however, is simple and modular and fit into the coarse hierarchy of function as defined within the internet protocol suite. The first cooperating protocol, the TCP/IP protocol, was a result of the decomposition of the Transmission Control Program, and what resulted was a layered communication tool. Another model is the OSI model, which consists of seven layers, as we have mentioned earlier. This one was modeled as something that would eventually guide general communication and has strict guidelines of protocol interaction, as well as rigorous notions of layering as a functionality concept.

Application software is constructed on a layer of data transport, and under the data transport layer, there is delivery of datagram and a typically connectionless routing mechanism on the internet. The relaying of packets happens in a layer that involves network link technologies such as Ethernet. Layering, hence, provides the opportunity for exchanging of technologies whenever there is a need. As such, sometimes, protocols are stacked in different arrangements, such as tunneling, that allows the connection of networks that are not similar. The asynchronous transfer mode has the internet protocol tunneled across it.

Protocol Layering

Protocol layering forms the basis for protocol design. Apart from allowing decomposition of single and complex protocols, a functional decomposition additionally exists. Each protocol goes into a protocol layer, which is essentially a functional class. The suite of internet protocol contains the network interfaces that serve as functions, including the application-transport-internet. The diagram below expresses protocol layering:

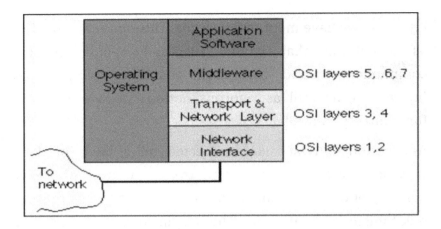

In networking, computations and algorithms go together while communication and data involve messages and protocols. A data flow diagram, therefore, consists of messages flowing. In a message flow diagram, the system has a vertical flow in protocols and a horizontal flow between systems. This flow is governed by data formats and rules as specified by protocols. Vertical protocols are, however, unlayered mainly because they are not obedient to layering principles that stipulate that protocols must be layered to enable the layer at the destination that accepts the same object handed by the source layer. Horizontal protocols, on the other hand, are layered and obey the layering principles as they are from a protocol suite. The designer of the protocol is permitted by the protocol layer to focus on a certain layer at a time or an instance, while it does have to worry about the performance of other layers.

The vertical protocols do not need to be identical in the two systems. There is a need, despite this, to satisfy even the small assumptions that the principles of protocol layering are obeyed particularly for layered protocols. How? Mostly by encapsulation. A message will be divided into small pieces, and these pieces can be called either message, packets, streams, network frames, or IP datagrams. The names will largely depend on the layer in which they are. The header area data contain information that classifies the source, as well as the packet's final destination on the network or packet. For vertical protocols, the rule is that transmission pieces are meant to be encapsulated in the lower protocols' data areas. The data is encapsulated as described on the side of the source, and the opposite takes place on the side of the destination. The rule of encapsulation, therefore, ensures that the rules of principles of layering persist in every transmission line except the lowest layer. For the purpose of ensuring that both sides are governed by a similar set of protocols, the messages carry information that identifies the protocol in their header.

The network's and protocol layering's design architecture are interrelated, and one cannot function without the next. To fully understand the features that define the relationship between network services and internet architecture, read below.

· The internet is a source of universal interconnection. All networks that interconnect physically appear as part of a single large network or the internet or internetwork, a concept we have discussed earlier.

· The internet addresses defined above consist of two main components: the net-id and hosted, which have been introduced earlier. The net-id gives an identification of the network, and host-id identifies who the host is. The internet address is an identification of the address to the network and not the individual computer. The net-id is useful for routers, as they decide where a packet should be sent.

- Independence in the network technology is achieved using the ARP, A low-level address resolution protocol. The ARP allows the mapping of internet addresses to physical addresses in a process called address resolution. The physical addresses, in this case, are, therefore, used by the network interface layer's protocols. The TCP/IP protocols, for instance, makes use of any underlying technology.

- Physical networks are connected through routers that function by forwarding packets between these interconnected networks. Routers, therefore, make it possible for one host to reach another on the physical network. The message will flow between two systems that are in communication and datagrams are passed from a router to another until the message reaches the intended recipient or destination on a network that is physically attached. To make the decision to deliver a datagram directly or whether it is to be sent to a router that is nearby, an IP routing table comes into the picture. An IP table typically consists of pairs of networkids and all paths that can be taken so that a destination is reached. These paths can either be those of direct delivery or it can be an indication that the address of another router can reach the destination quicker. There can be a special entry that specifies the default path that is used when there are not any other known paths.

- All networks are treated equally in this case, and, therefore, a point-to-point link, a LAN and WAN network are all considered as one network with no special privilege allotted to one or the other.

- Packet-switched system and service is an offering via the internet. This is preferred because it adopts well with different hardware, including the Ethernet. As a result, connectionless delivery implies that messages or streams can be divided into pieces that are separately multiplexed on the high speed interconnected machines that allow the concurrent use of connections. Every information piece, therefore, identifies the destination. Data packet delivery is sometimes unreliable, as mentioned earlier. Aside from the losses and delays, there can be duplication and delivery data packets that are out of order. This irregularity may be a result of a failure of the underlying networks. This unreliable connectionless system of delivery is defined by the IP. The IP is also responsible for the specification of the routing function as it chooses the path over which a set of data will be sent. TCP/IP protocols can also be used on connection-oriented systems. These systems build up exclusive use virtual circuits between receivers and senders. Once these virtual circuits are set up, IP datagrams are sent over the circuits as if they were data and are forwarded to IP protocol modules in a technique called tunneling. Tunneling is used on ATM networks and X.25 networks.

- The TCP defines the reliable stream transport service using connectionless packet delivery systems. The services and the application programs within the layer above are layered, and they are called application services that make use of the TCP. If a program wishes to have direct interaction with the packet delivery system, it does so using the user datagram protocol.

Software Layering

After the establishment of protocols and protocol layering, software design can follow. The software design is also layered in organization and has a relationship with protocol layering. To send a message on a system, the top module has to interact with the modules that are directly below it and hand over the message meant for encapsulation. The module will, therefore, encapsulate the message in the data area and fill the header with information regarding the protocol it implements. What follows is an interaction with the module below it, and it carries out the interaction by handing over the new information to the place deemed most appropriate. The module at the bottom interacts directly with the bottom module of the next system, so the message is sent across to the other system. The reverse happens on the receiving system so that the message that was sent on one system gets delivered ultimately in its original source to the module on top of the receiving system.

Sometimes, there are protocol errors. When this happens, the receiver will usually discard the received piece and send a message back to the original source about the condition. This is done by sending the message across and or sending it across the network if it happens at the bottom layer. The message is divided and reassembled at the point that introduced the reassembly or division.

The translation of programs us divided into subproblems:

- Compiler
- Assembler
- Link editor
- Loader

Translation software is also layered, and this allows independent designing of software layers. There is an analogy between programming languages and protocols, and the designers of the TCP/IP protocol were keen enough on this fact to ease the complexity that comes with translating programs when layering. Take the example of translating a pascal program that is compiled into an assembled into a program. The assembler program is assembled to the object code which links together with a library object code by a link editor. The product is an executable code that is loaded into physical memory. The modules that fall below the application layer are considered to be part of the operating system, and the data that passes within the modules are less expensive if compared to passing data between the transport layer and an application program. The operating system boundary is that which exists between the transport and application layers

Strict layering

Strict layering involves adhering strictly to a layered model. However, this practice is not usually the best when it comes to approaching networking as it can usually have an impact on performance. There somewhat has to be a trade-off between performance and simplicity within the network.

Using protocol is already universal today when it comes to computer networking. However, this does not mean that it is free from criticism as it has faced the same among researchers because abstracting protocol stacks may cause higher layers to copy the lower layers' functionality.

Development of Protocols

The selection of protocols precedes communication. The rules that govern the selection can be expressed by data structures and algorithms. Expressing algorithms in a portable software language enhances operating system and hardware independence. The protocol specification is wide, and even source codes can be considered as such. However, it is only source independence of the specification that provides wider interoperability.

The standards for protocols are created by obtaining the support of a standards organization, and obtaining this support also initiates the process of standardization. This process is what is commonly referred to as protocol development. Voluntarily, the members of the standards organization agree to adhere to the work that results. Members, in this case, are often in control of large market shares that are relevant to the protocol and the standards are enforced by the government and in some cases, the law. This implementation of standards by law is important because standards are of importance in regards to the public interest. Unfortunately, in other cases, protocol standards may not be sufficient for widespread acceptance and hence, the source code may need to be disclosed and even enforced by the law.

There is a need for protocol standards, but to understand fully, the point is going to be demonstrated by what happened to IBM's bi-sync protocol (BSC). BSC is a link-level protocol that is used in the connection of two separate nodes. Originally, the design was meant for use with the multimode network, but his use only revealed the dearth of the protocol. There was no standardization, so what happened was that organizations and manufacturers alike felt the need to create other versions that were incompatible on their networks. They did this with many motives, including to discourage others from using any equipment designed by other manufacturers. Today, there are over 50 variants of the same BSC protocol. Having a standard would have prevented the eventualities.

On the inverse, some protocols can indeed gain market dominance without standardization. Such protocols are often referred to as de facto standards, and they are most common in developing niches and emerging markets. Also, they can be common in monopolized markets. These kinds of protocols usually hold the market in a generally negative grip, especially when the intention is to scare away competition. Historically, standardization can be viewed as a measure against the de facto standards. There are, however, positive exceptions to the ills brought about by de facto standards. For instance, if you take the case operating systems, such as the GNU/Linux, you find that there is no negative grasp of the market in any way. The sources are published for this operating system and are maintained in this way, and hence, they invite competition. There may be other solutions for open systems interconnection apart from standardization.

The Process of Standardization

The process of standardization is not really complex but involves a series of steps. First, it starts off with ISO commissioning of a sub-committee workgroup. The workgroup then does the work of issuing the working drafts and discussions that surround the protocol to interested parties, which may include other bodies involved in standardization. With such intense discussions, there is bound to be debate, a lot of questions and even disagreement on what the provisions of the standard should be and the needs that it can satisfy. All these conflicting views are always taken into consideration, and what they strive to achieve is a balance. After a compromise is reached, a draft proposal of what comprises the working group is made.

This draft proposal is then taken for discussion with the standard bodies for the member countries. Further, a discussion is also done within each country. There are more comments and suggestions that are collated, and eventually, national views come together and are formulated before being taken to the members of ISO who will vote for the proposal. If by any chance, a proposal is rejected, the draft has to consider every counter-proposal and objections and use the information to draft a new proposal that will be taken for the vote. Before the end of this process, there is usually a lot of feedback, compromise, and modification. The final draft that is considered reaches a status called draft international standard, and once it is standardized, it is considered an international standard.

The process that a draft proposal takes to reach international standard status can often take years for completion. The original draft created by the designer will differ significantly from the copy that makes it the standard and will have some of the features outlined below:

· Various modes of operation that will allow for different aspects of performance, for instance, the set-up of different packet sizes at the time of startup. This is usually advisable when parties are unable to reach a consensus on what should be the optimum packet size.

· Undefined parameters or some that are allowed to take values that are set at the discretion of the implementer. This, just like the various modes of operation described above, usually is a reflection of how much the views of the members conflicted.

· Parameters that are reserved for use in the future. This usually reflects that the members of the standardization board reached a consensus that the facility had to be provided. However, in such a case, they could not agree on how the facility should have been provided within the time they had available.

· There will be ambiguities and inconsistencies found as the standards continue to be implemented.

· OSI standardization

Before the internet, there was ARPANET. For the ARPANET, protocols were standardized. However, we had described above how sometimes standardization may not be enough. The reasons stated in the case of de facto standards are different from the case here. Here, what makes standardization insufficient is the fact that the protocol also needed a framework to enable operation. There is, hence, a need to develop a future-proof, framework that is also for general purposes that is suitable for protocols that are structured. Such developments are important because they would not only allow clearly definitions of the protocol responsibilities at different levels but also, they would be instrumental for prevention of overlapping functionalities. These needs resulted in the development of the OSI Open Systems Interconnection model for reference. The OSI Open Systems Interconnection reference model is a vital framework used for designing standard services and protocols that conform to the different layer specifications.

With this OSI model, the systems in communication are presumed connected through an underlying medium that provides a primary mechanism for transmission. The above layers are numbered from one through to 7, and each layer provides service to the layer above it using the services of the below layers. The interface through which the layers communicate with each other are called service access points, and the corresponding layers at the systems are known as peer entities. For communication to happen, the peer entities in a layer use a protocol that is implemented by a number layer below. If systems do not have a direct connection, relays-intermediate peer entities are used.

There are addresses that identify service access points, and the domains that provide these naming services are not necessarily restricted to one layer. This makes it possible to use the same naming domain in all layers. Each layer has two protocols: the service standards protocol and the protocol standards. Service standards define how a layer communicates with the one above it while the protocol layer defines communication between peer entities at each level.

Below, there is an explanation of the layers and functionalities of the original RM/OSI model. The order is from the lowest to the highest.

1. **The physical layer.** This layer describes all the physical connections, such as electrical characteristics and the transmission techniques used. It also includes the setup, clearing, and even maintenance of the physical connections.

2. **The data link layer.** The data link layer is responsible for setting up, maintaining, and releasing data link connections. Any errors that occur in the physical layer can be detected here and, subsequently, corrected. These errors are reported to the next layer, the network layer. This layer also defines the exchange of data link units.

3. **The network layer.** The network layer is responsible for setting up, maintaining, and releasing network paths to be used between transport peer entities. The layer also provides relay and routing functions as needed, and with

the transport layer, it negotiates the quality of service at the set-up of the connection. The layer also takes responsibility for controlling network congestion.

4. **The transport layer.** The transport layer provides the basis for transparent yet reliable transfer of data in a way that is cost-effective as described by the quality of service selected. This layer supports the multiplexing of many transport connections on a network. Also, it may support the split of a transport connection into many others.

5. **The session layer.** The session layer provides a variety of services to the presentation layer, including establishing and releasing session connections and quarantine services for sending presentation entities to instruct the entity receiving the session so that the latter is instructed not to release data to the presentation entity without any permission. It also establishes and releases normal and expedited exchange of data and performs interaction management so that presentation entities are able to determine whose turn it is to perform some control, resynchronize a session connection, and to report unrecoverable exceptions to the entity of presentation.

6. **Presentation layer.** The presentation layer provides services to the application layer,

including the request to establish a session and to the transferring of data. Also, it allows the negotiation of which syntax is supposed to be used between the layers of application. It also performs special-purpose transformations, for instance, data encryption and data compression.

7. **Application layer.** The application layer provides services to application processes, including identifying the intended partners of communication and establishing the necessary authority to allow communication. Also, it plays a role in determining the availability and authentication of partners and agrees on the privacy mechanisms necessary for communication and agrees on the responsibility for recovery and how to ensure data integrity and allows synchronization between application processes that cooperate. Also, it identifies any constraints, including data ad character constraints on syntax. Lastly, it also provides services dealing with cost determinations and acceptable service quality and selects dialogue discipline, such as what logon and logoff procedures are to be followed.

The table below represents the seven layers.

OSI Layer	Name	Common Protocols
7	Application	HTTP | FTP | SMTP | DNS | Telnet
6	Presentation	
5	Session	
4	Transport	TCP | SPX
3	Network	IP | IPX
2	Data Link	Ethernet
1	Physical	Ethernet

The RM/OSI layering scheme defers from the TCP/IP layering scheme because it does not assume a connectionless network. The RM/OSI has a connection-oriented network, and this type is more suited for local area networks. The use of connections for communication implies that there are virtual and circuit sessions are used hence the session layer and lack of one in the TCP/IP model of layering. ISO constituent members were concerned mainly with wide area networks, and the development on the RM/OSI reflects this as it concentrates on networks with connections. Connectionless networks were mentioned as an addition to the RM/OSI. Today, however, the RM/OSI model includes connectionless services, and this has caused the TCP and IP models to develop into international standards.

Cable Infrastructure

Structured cabling is typically a type of open network structure that is usable by data, access control, telephony, and building automation systems, among others. It is a source of economical operation and flexibility

· Concepts of data rate, bandwidth, and throughput

All network connections have what is known as data rates. A data rate is a rate at which bits are transmitted. In some networks, for instance, LANs, data varies with time. Throughput is a related concept that essentially refers to the effective rate of transmission when taking into account factors such as protocol inefficiencies, transmission overheads and competing traffic. Usually, throughput is measured at higher network layers compared to data rates. Bandwidth refers to either throughputs or data rates but is mostly used in relation to the data rate. Commonly also, the term is used in relation to radios, where bandwidth refers to the width of frequency band available and use proportional or equal to the data rate achievable.

When referring to TCP, an alternative term, 'good put,' is used to refer to the throughput of the application layer. When good put is calculated, retransmitted data can only be counted once. The measurement of data rates is done in kilobits or megabits per second (bps). When calculating data rates, remember that a kilobit is 10^3 while a megabit is 10^6.

· Concept of packets

The concept of packets is the brainchild of Paul Baran. In 1962, Baran wondered how networks would survive in the event of node failure. This kind of failure existed mainly because there were centrally switched protocols. Donald Davies in 1964 developed the same concept, giving it the name which it still uses today: packets and packet switching

Simply put, packets are modest-sized data buffers that get transmitted through shared links as a unit. Usually, packets come prefixed with a header that contains information for delivery. Just imagine how every envelope comes with a name to ensure delivery to the right place. Headers in datagram forwarding, for instance, contain a destination address while headers in networks have an identifier for the virtual circuit; most networking today is based on the use of packets. Packets are called frames when they are in the LAN layer and segments when in the transport layer. LANs have an intrinsic maximum packet size that they can support and usually, this comes to around 1500 bytes of data for

Ethernet. TCP originally held 512 bytes. You may wonder how packets are transferred from large data pockets to smaller ones, but this shall be addressed later on in the book.

Every layer adds its header: typically, IP headers-20 bytes, Ethernet headers-14 bytes, and TCP headers-20 bytes, and IP headers-20 bytes. Datagram forwarding networks have headers that contain the delivery information, including destination address. Internal network nodes are called switches/routers, and these will ensure that the packet is delivered to the specified address.

· Concept of datagram forwarding

When a packet has to be delivered, there is a data packet that contains a destination address. The switches and routers on the way must observe the address and deliver the packet to the destination. The packet can only be delivered to the right destination by the provision of each router with a forwarding table of pairs. This is typically the destination, next, hop pair. What happens is that a packet arrives then the switch/router will look up the next destination address in the forwarding table. When this information is looked up, then it is easy to find the next_hop information. The next_hop information is the immediate next address in the loop that the packet should be forwarded to so that it is one more step closer to its destination. Every router or switch is responsible for only one step in the path that is meant to deliver the packet to its destination. When all is well within the layer, a packet is delivered to its destination, one hop at a time without interference.

The destination entries are in a forwarding table. However, they do not necessarily usually correspond with the destination addresses except in the forwarding of Ethernet datagrams. What happens with IP routing is that the destination entries in the table will often correspond to the prefixes of the IP address. This is a strategy that is meant for saving space. The requirement here is that switches can perform lookup operations using the destination address and forwarding table in the packet that has just arrived to determine what the next hop should be.

LANs and Ethernet

Below is a simple diagram that captures the components of a local area network.

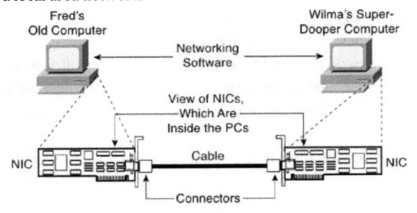

As earlier defined, LAN stands for local area networks. A LAN consists of physical links (serial lines), interfacing software that is common and connecting the hosts to the links and protocols that link everything together.

Ethernet is a physical/data link layer. As a physical layer of the network, Ethernet focuses on hardware elements, for instance, cables, network interface cards, and repeaters. Ethernet is the most used protocol in the physical layer. For instance, the Ethernet network specifies the type of cables that can be used, the topology and the length of cables.

The data link layer addresses how data packets are sent from node to node, and Ethernet makes use of the CSMA/CD access. SCMA/CD stands for carrier sense multiple access/collision detection. The SCMA/CD is a system in which a computer must put an ear out for the cable before sending information through the network. If there is a clear way, then the computer will continue with the transmission. If there is another node that is already doing the transmission, then the computer will have to wait before trying to transmit again once the line is clear. In other instances, two computers may want to transmit at the same time, and this causes what is known as a collision. In such a case, the computers will both take a step back and try to transmit again after random amounts of time before trying to retransmit. It is common for collisions to happen with this type of access method. This type of delay is, however, not big and usually small and does not affect transmission speeds on the network.

Originally, Ethernet was developed in 1983 and had speeds of 10Mbps. While this may not look like much now, it was good speed in the early days. Ethernet used a coaxial cable. The Ethernet protocol allows bus, star, and tree topologies, and these may depend on the type of cables used. The original Ethernet cabling was heavy and expensive to purchase and even install. Maintenance was an issue, and there was no easy way to retrofit the coaxial cable into existing facilities. The current Ethernet cables are now modified and use a twisted pair wire. They can transmit at speeds of 10, 00 and 1000 megabits per second.

The fast Ethernet protocol transmits at speeds of up to 100 Mbps and requires the use of not only different but also expensive network hubs and interface cards. Also, they make use of 5 twisted pair of optic fiber. There is also Gigabit Ethernet that has transmission speeds of 1Gbps, which is the same as 1000 Mbps. It is used along copper and fiber optic cabling. A summary of an Ethernet protocol is shown below:

Protocol	Cable	Speed
Ethernet	Twisted Pair, Coaxial, Fiber	10 Mbps
Fast Ethernet	Twisted Pair, Fiber	100 Mbps
Gigabit Ethernet	Twisted Pair, Fiber	1000 Mbps

Chapter 7: Servers and Virtualization

Imagine a typical data enterprise center with many servers. The majority of these servers sit idle as the workload of the enterprise is distributed among a small number of servers. This results in what can be considered a waste of resources, as these systems are not at work and yet will use power, require maintenance, and even cooling. This is a problem in many work environments today, and this is the exact kind of situation that server virtualization intends to solve. In this chapter, an exploration of server virtualization is done. The concept is explained, and so is the benefit of the approach.

Components of a Server

A server, basically, is also a type of computer. However, depending on the type of server in question, they are always set up differently from the average personal computer used by the average consumer. All the different kinds of hosting all involve the use of dedicated servers. However, the difference between shared, cloud, and VPS hosting are that the servers are organized and structured differently. The key components of a server are outlined below.

There are different components in servers; some are basic, while others are optional. They include the following.

Motherboard

The most basic explanation of a motherboard is that it is a circuit board that ensures the connection of all server components. This is where the heartbeat of the server is, and most consumers know little to nothing about it. The most important point to note when it comes to the motherboard is that it dictates the type of CPU, number of hard drives, and the amount of RAM that is needed for connection to the server.

Central Processing Unit

This component is also known as the processor, and it works like the brain of the server. It regulates performance but is not the only component that matters when it comes to performance. However, the importance of the CPU is trivialized. It is important for even the average consumer to understand the importance of processors and what makes a good CPU. You need to get enough information so that you know if you are getting a good deal on a central processing unit. Different hosts may offer outdated models or consumer-grade processors instead of the current gen-server grade processors.

Random Access Memory

Servers cannot be complete without memory, especially if the hosting of websites is involved. In the server, memory refers to the RAM and not the hard drive. RAM is similar to the human brain's short-term and is critical for the server's performance and the amount of memory that will need to be scaled up to meet the needs of the host. Apart from quantities, quality should also be considered when talking about RAM. There are four RAM generations currently, and the newer versions run faster than the older ones. To ensure that you have the best, look for the latest RAM technology as this will result in the highest value for your money and the best performance.

Network Connection

The network connection is yet another important component of servers. Servers are often connected to ports whose speeds are set by the host and can vary. Most of them start at 10Gbps, and others can go as high as Gigabit connections.

Hard Drive

The hard drive is yet another component of a server. The ultimate hard drive today is the SATA drive as they offer reliability and stellar performance. However, as is the case with many technological inventions, there are already better inventions threatening to take the place of SATA drives, for instance, Solid State Drives. All servers are beginning to embrace SSDs because they offer superior speeds for reading and writing, and they are highly reliable. Getting an SSD means a move towards increased server performance.

Graphics Processing Unit (An Optional Component)

Traditionally, GPUs were used only for gaming and graphic interfaces. Over time, however, these components have found their way in servers. They are accessed through a command line or terminal. There are other high-end GPUs that today are used in place of CPUs. Most servers, however, do not consist of GPUs. The ones that will be putting them in place are those that deal with artificial intelligence and machine learning especially

What Is Server Virtualization?

Server virtualization is a process through which software on a physical server is aided to create a number of virtual instances that can run independently. On a dedicated server, the machine has one operating system. However, with a virtual server, one machine can be able to run multiple instances, all of which will have independent operating systems. In this process, a physical server is taken, and the virtualization software helps to partition it and divide it so that it created what was referred to above as virtual instances. The entire system is dedicated to one thing, and thus, the server can be used in many different ways. So, unlike in the past before virtualization was mainstream, an operating system does not require a physical platform to host an operating system. A hypervisor is used to share the hardware of the host with the individual virtual machines. This technique, therefore, allows the sharing of resources, which enables organizations to reduce the cost of running a lot of physical software and reduce their datacenter hardware footprints.

Another way through which the concept of server virtualization can be understood is through the host/guest paradigm. Every gust will run on a virtual imitation of what would be considered the hardware layer. The guest OS runs without modifications and also allows the administrator to play the role of creating guests that use a different OS. The guest, in this case, does not usually know anything about the operating system of the host

The concept of data virtualization only hit the waves recently, and yet it has been in the oven for well over 50 years. IBM was the pioneer organization when it came to virtualization of system memory. This would eventually act as the precursor to virtualization hardware. IBM created the

VM/370, a propriety operating system. This operating system level of virtualization does not have much significance beyond mainframe computing, but even through its simplicity, it developed to the z/VM, which was the first virtual platform for severs that was used for commercial purposes in the market.

Today, server virtualization has become a norm, and the concept became dominant in the IT industry. Several companies are moving towards full virtualization and cloud-managed information technology ecosystems. This trend of virtualization's popularity came to life in the 90s with the release of the VMware workstation by VMware. The VMWare workstation was a savior that enabled the virtualization of x86/x64 machines and architecture and popularized virtualization. It became possible to run Windows, MacOS, and Linux on one host hardware, and, therefore, over the past two decades, virtualization of servers has served an important role in shaping the IT infrastructure market.

For virtualized server platforms, it is necessary to have a vendor or host hardware available. The hardware, in most cases, is usually a server that requires software as described above. The software is called hypervisor. The role of the hypervisor is to present the generic virtualized hardware to the operating systems that are installed onto it. The hardware included all the components needed to start the operating system, including the CPU, network drivers, hard disks, SCSI drivers, and memory allocations. The hypervisor, therefore, manages the resources of the host and allocates the same resources to every virtual machine that depends on it.

Virtualization can happen in either Windows, Linux, and Aix operating systems. Even more interesting is the fact that manufacturers are now offering virtual appliances of hardware devices. For example, Network Load balancers were traditionally physical devices in a rack. Today, however, things have changed, and they are many times virtualized. There is more power in host hardware, so offering virtualized dedicated appliances is quickly becoming commonplace.

There are several types of hypervisors. Below, we discuss information about hypervisors in detail.

As you may have already gathered, the hypervisor is the primary software that is meant to enable virtualization in servers. There are mainly two types of hypervisors:

· Baremetal. This is what is commonly referred to as the Type 1 hypervisor and is often installed directly on the host hardware. Directly, this hypervisor manages all the resources of server hardware that are installed in the bare-metal tin. Every hardware resource in this hardware is then allocated to virtual machines through the Hypervisor Operating system.

· The Type 2 Hypervisor. This hypervisor runs directly on top of the conventional operating system. It does so as an application or process. It virtualizes the hardware resources found in the conventional operating system. Interestingly, this type of hypervisor is common in non-production environments, and an example is the VMWare Workstation and Virtual Box.

Today, the VMware company has managed to keep every other manufacturer busy such that it has dominated the virtualization industry. So the software has ended up in use in many of the world's data centers. A giant in IT, Microsoft, produced its own version of the hypervisor-Hyper-V back in 2008. This hypervisor comes up with almost all Microsoft server operating systems, but recently, there has been a newer addition as the package comes bundled with Windows 10 Professional. The open-source community has its own hypervisor, known as Xen. Xen is a creation of the Cambridge University during the 1990s. However, it has continued to play a vital role in the world of virtualization today. It is, for instance, Amazon's virtual platform for cloud-based Amazon Web Services. Since Amazon is winning in the cloud ecosystem, other companies use Xen as a commercial product.

Server virtualization is not just a thing for software manufacturers. In fact, today, IBM, a company that manufactures its own hardware is a major manufacturer of hypervisors. The platforms of IBM, including System I, System Z, and System P, use the para-virtual hypervisor. The guest virtual machines have prior knowledge of each other and the resource requirements allotted to them through their host. The hardware resources of the host are divided and allocated to the virtual machine. Through this sharing, every partition knows of the partition requirements of the other, and every server has the least minimum hardware designed.

There is also operating system virtualization. At this level, virtualization works differently. There is no basis on the host/guest paradigm. Instead, the host runs an operating system kernel as the core and distributes the functionalities of the operating system to the guests. Guests then use the same operating system as the host, but it is allowed to use different distributions of the same system. Distributing architecture like this eliminates the system calls between layers, thus reducing the overhead of CPU usage. Each partition also remains isolated strictly from a neighbor so that security breaches and failure in a partition does not affect other partitions. Common libraries and binaries are shared on the same physical machine, which allows the operating system level virtual server to host an infinite number of guests all at once.

Server virtualization is part of an overall trend toward virtualization in IT involving enterprises. It works alongside network virtualization, storage virtualization, and management of workloads. Server virtualization is a component in autonomic computing development, which aims to enable the server to manage itself based on the perceived activity.

Types of server virtualization

There is more than one way through which virtualization can be achieved, apart from para virtualization that has been discussed. The ones that will be discussed below are:

· OS level virtualization

· Para virtualization

· Full virtualization

These share a few common traits, for example, they all have a physical server that is referred to as the host, and the virtual servers are called guests. The virtual servers exhibit behavior similar to physical machines, and every system uses a different approach for the allocation of physical server resources for virtual server needs.

Full virtualization. Full virtualization makes use of the hypervisor software. This hypervisor directly interacts with the CPU's and disk space's physical servers. The hypervisor serves as a platform that can be used by the operating systems of the virtual servers. The hypervisor does the work of keeping every virtual server independent and even unaware of the other virtual servers that are running on the same machine. Every guest server runs an operating system, and they do not have to be the same. One could be utilizing a Windows operating system, while the other operates a Linux operating system. The hypervisor also monitors the resources of the physical server. The hypervisor relays resources to the appropriate virtual server from the physical machine. The virtual servers, at this time, are running application. The hypervisor, as an application, has its own processing needs, and as such, the physical server reserves some processing resources and power that ensure the running of the hypervisor. If there are no reserve resources, then the overall performance of the system can be affected, and the speeds become slower.

Para virtualization. As a concept, para virtualization is a different approach from the full version. In para virtualization, the guest servers are aware of the existence of each other. The hypervisor in this type of virtualization does not do the kind of processing power needed to operate a guest operating system like in the full virtualization model. This is because there are interaction and recognition of the operating systems that are within the server without discrimination of one of them. There is a cohesive way of working here where the system is involved.

Operating system virtualization. This type of virtualization does not use a hypervisor in any way. The capability to virtualize is already part of the operating system. The operating system, in this case, performs the functions of a virtualized hypervisor. There is, however, a limitation to this approach. Every virtual server in this setup remains independent of the guest servers within the network, and there is no way that is operating among different operating systems. The environments in which the guest OS operates should be similar. As such, this type of environment is called a homogenous environment.

There is really no type of virtualization that is better over another. The choice to use usually depends largely on the needs of the network administrator. If the physical servers of the administrator run on the same operating system, then the operating system type of virtualization may be appropriate as these systems will be efficient and faster compared to further approaches. If alternatively, the administrator runs different servers on a variety of OS, then the network administrator may resort to the use of para virtualization. However, there is one disadvantage that may come with using para-virtualization, which is lack of support. Compared to the other types, this is a relatively new type of technique, and, therefore, only some organizations offer materials for para virtualization. Many organizations mainly back the use of para virtualization. However, para virtualization is quickly taking over and may eventually replace full virtualization.

Benefits of Server Virtualization

There are benefits to using server virtualization, and it is no wonder that many organizations invest in it. There are reasons that address technicalities, while others are purely based on financial motivations. Below, we outline the benefits of using server virtualization

- Through the method of consolidation virtualization helps in conserving space. Each server is dedicated to one solicitation. However, should many applications only make use of a minor quantity of electricity for processing, it is possible for the administrator of the system to combine many computers into one server that can run in different virtual environments. This can especially be helpful and beneficial for companies that have multiple servers, as it will significantly reduce or eliminate the need for servers.

- This technique provides a loophole through which companies can tend to like termination, all minus buying more components. Redundancy is when only one app is run on different servers. Often, it is practiced as a way to ensure safety such that if one server does not work well for whatever cases, then the other that is running this place can conveniently be a replacement. Through redundancy, there is a reduction in the service. It is not sensible to construct two servers (virtual) that perform the same presentation on a real server. In such a case, a crash in the server would mean that two virtual servers also fail. For many cases, people working within the system have the tendency to make redundant virtual servers on real technologies.

- Virtual servers give structures that are not only independent but also isolated so that programmers are able to test new operating systems and applications. Instead of buying physical machines, a virtual server can simply be created on the existing machine by the network administrator. Virtual servers are usually independent of the other servers, which give the programmer an opportunity to run the software as they need without worrying about the effect it will have on other applications.

- Server hardware eventually ends up obsolete. This creates further problems because, usually, switching across two differing systems proves to be not easy. Systems such as these can be referred to as legacy systems and offering services provided by these. These outdated systems could be the answer needed for proper functionality. In such cases, the obvious and most practical thing the system administrator can do is to create a virtual account of the hardware on a server that fits today's context. When looking at this approach like it is from the application, everything remains the same at the very core. The tasks will work the same way they would if they were still on the preliminary hardware.

The company can, therefore, buy time for transitioning to new processes without having to worry about the server breaking down. This can especially be beneficial in cases where the corporation that fashioned the original hardware ceased to be, and so, it may be impossible to fix broken equipment.

- Also, migration is a trend that has come with virtualization and is, by extension, the advantage or benefit of using virtualization. If you have the right software and hardware, then it can be possible to physically remove the network of a physical machine from one to the additional. Formerly, this stood probable but merely if the two bodily technologies run on the same computer technologies that are needed, in this case, to ensure proper functionality. Today, it is possible to rove virtual servers across many different machines, even when the machines are processed rather differently due to differences in hardware. The only condition that remains is that the processors must come from the same manufacturers.

- These servers help in cost minimization within enterprises. This reduction happens because virtualization helps to increase the utilization of already existing resources, and it is an efficient solution for small to medium-scale applications. As a technology, virtualization is used as a cost-effective way of providing web hosting services. Companies will acquire much less hardware for new infrastructure, and older hardware can simply be migrated to new and more efficient hardware. This equally benefits the data centers, as there will be less power and cooling requirements and reduces the datacenter footprint, thus reducing the overall costs associated with managed service provision.

- Yet another benefit associated with virtualization is functionality. The key functions include the ability to roll back changes, which eliminates the need for the many requirements that were associated with rebuilding a network from scratch. Management features such as Cloning, vMotion, and Fault Tolerance changed how administrators could increase infrastructure uptime while offering the best service level agreement to customers. As a result, network administrators can deploy new virtual machines almost instantly through the use of templates. Server provisioning has equally improved. Now, it is possible to build new virtual infrastructure from scripts. With tools such as Terraform, you can build virtual networks and use other toolsets for configuration such as Ansible to configure new infrastructure in exact and uniform ways as per the requirements.

- Lastly, virtualization has played a vital role in improving disaster recovery. You do not need to restore lost data from a tap to re-provisioned hardware as would have been the case in the past. Instead, you can replicate the entire virtual network infrastructure between sites using different tools that are required for virtualization. These tools may include VMware Site Recovery Manager, which can be automated. Other products, for example, CloudEndure can replicate servers to the cloud, and the entire system is replicated in a staging area that can be activated when a disaster recovery scenario is invoked.

Limitations of Server Virtualization

Above, we have explored the different benefits of server virtualization. But just like every other thing, server virtualization also has its limitations. It is vital for a network administrator to investigate the changing of servers and their architecture so that they can engineer the right solution.

One of the limitations is that if you have servers that are dedicated to applications that have high demands on power for processing, then this may not be the most viable choice. Virtualization works by dividing the processing power of the server among the virtual ones. When the processing power of the server is unable to meet the demand of the application, then the entire system will slow down. Even tasks that typically take a short time for completion begin to take hours. There is also a possibility of the system crashing if the server cannot meet the demands of all the virtual servers within the system. As such, it is vital that the network administrator takes a close look at the use of the CPU before the physical server is divided into several virtual machines.

Additionally, there is a limitation in migration. It is possible to carry out a migration of a virtual server from a physical device to the next if, together, the equipment makes use of a unified constructor's design. When a system customs a single server, that, for instance, goes on an AMD workstation, and an added one customs an Intel processor, it will be intolerable to carry out porting in a virtual server from a physical machine to the next. You may wonder why an administrator would require the migration of a virtual server from a physical machine. The physical server may require maintenance and porting the simulated ones to supplementary equipment can help in reducing the downtime of the app. Relocation is, hence, important because when migration ceases to be a preference, the requests that run on the computer-generated server will be unavailable until maintenance is done.

The downsides of virtualization are not as many as the benefits, and with the right considerations in place, a network administrator can identify the type that will work efficiently for the enterprise. The benefits are the reason that many companies are still investing in the virtualization of servers. Technology keeps advancing, and as this happens, the need for big data centers continues to decrease as well. The power consumption of servers may also be on the way, and this makes the concept of virtualization not only attractive financially but also a green alternative that can help in the reduction of the carbon blueprint of many companies. As networks use servers, there will be the development of more efficient yet larger computer networks. In fact, virtual servers can top an upheaval in the computing trade over time.

Determining if Server Virtualization Is Necessary for Your Business

If you are wondering if server virtualization is what may be best for your company and you need a few pointers to help you start, then the following section may be useful to you.

Server virtualization brings together multiple operating systems on one server. You can consider it if you need any of the things described below:

· If you need to use more operating systems and applications without necessarily breaking the budget for electricity, space, and hardware, then virtualization may be the best option for you. This is because the approach can be instrumental in reducing all these while not affecting the enterprise's budget in the long-term.

· Also, if you wish to reduce the work hours for your IT staff so that they do not have to spend a lot of time on patching, installation, administration and supporting application servers, then this may be the right time for you as it is an approach that consolidates many of these aspects, making work easier.

· If you wish or need to simplify backup and reduce the downtimes of applications, by adding storage space, then virtualization is the best option for you and should ultimately be considered.

· Sometimes, you may need to expand your technical skills in the field of networking. Server virtualization may help you to learn the ins and outs of converging network operations and systems. In such cases, virtualization would be the right step to take.

- Virtualization may also be the best option for you if you feel that you need to master cloud challenges. With experience in handling cloud challenges, you will be better placed when your business will be migrating to virtualization. This is especially critical when you will eventually have to migrate services that are critical to your business to the cloud.

Just like with other technologies, virtualization involves more than just the purchase and installation of a product. There are four important steps that can be considered part of the virtualization process:

1. Evaluation of the network's and system's current capacity and performance and the requirements it may need in the future

When you consider the above, you may find that you are long overdue for a refresh at your enterprise. You know that it is time for a haul in your systems when you experience server sprawl, and you struggle to achieve stellar performance with old hardware. When looking at the systems, consider the capacity and speeds of the central processing unit, a disk I/O, and processors. You can also have a look at emails, servers, setup of the hard disk, database applications, and file servers when evaluating where virtualization could lead to improvement. At network levels, you should assess the performance of routing, switching, and even WAN links.

Acceleration of the wide-area network, for example, can make such a big difference in performance.

2. Calculation of the expected payoff if the system or network is virtualized

Look at your enterprise or business and try to establish what you will gain from embracing virtualization. Consider the enterprise's short and long-term goals and establish how they fit in with the possibility of virtualization. Consider when you should do it and make further evaluations so that you do not find yourself on the losing end when it comes to virtualization. Look at what you can use in your new endeavor and establish if indeed, it is the right choice for you.

3. Creation of a strong infrastructure

You can choose a virtualization technology at this point, but you have to ensure that this will be a technology that will work to improve performance while simultaneously reducing costs and complexity at the moment and in the future, too. You could look for a management interface that provides a single interface for the management of the infrastructure and ensures performance and reduction in costs. Consider what switches you will use, hypervisors, storage, and servers.

4. Map your timeline for virtualization

By the time you will be reaching this stage, you will have all the software and hardware that will be needed for virtualization. The timeline for migration can range from anywhere in a time frame of as little as two weeks, and sometimes, it can go for as long as three months. The time frame will depend on the number of servers and sites and the staff.

From the start, align the network staff and the servers of the company so that you do not end up with high operating costs. The person who deals with the systems will need expertise and skills in managing operating systems, applications, switching, traffic, and VLAN. The network person should understand how to do things such as pushing the quality of service in servers. This is really important because the performance of your network may depend on these people. If it is impossible to have people who can manage these tasks, then you will have to bring in expertise from the outside. With the right tools and virtualization expertise, you can plan and take the virtualization journey that will best fit your organization.

The Potential in Server Virtualization and the Trend It Is Likely to Take

After all is said and done, you may be wondering why it is important to learn about server virtualization. Below, I explain why it is important to learn about server virtualization if you have even the slightest interest in networking.

Virtualization of servers is a simple concept that has had a profound and even almost profound impact on data centers in many enterprises. It had its roots in the early 60s and was popularized by VMware. The virtualization software was later introduced in the early 2000s for the x86 servers. Since the inception of these servers, many other vendors have begun to develop their own platforms for server-virtualization, and there have been advancements in management, automation, and orchestration. These tools make it easy to deploy, move, and manage virtual machine networks with ease. Before virtualization, many enterprises had to deal with server sprawl, high energy bills, and underutilized computer power, all to be dealt using manual processes and with inefficiency and inflexibility in the data centers. Today, this has changed, and instead, it has become difficult to find enterprises that do not run their workloads in virtual machine environments.

However, every good thing usually meets yet another good thing that will knock it off its pedestal. The next big thing when it comes to virtualization is going small. The next way that this will transform is that developers will slice applications into microservices that are not only small but also run in containers. There shall also be experimentation with function as a service, otherwise known as server less computing.

Understanding Containers and Virtual Machines

Docker is a popular tool used for spinning containers. Kubernetes is an innovation of Google. These two are the major enablers for containerization as they help in the management of multiple containers. Containers can be thought of as execution environments that share the host operating system's kernel. They are self-contained, streamlined and even more lightweight compared to virtual machines as they bypass any startup overhead and redundant guest operating systems. Developers are, therefore, able to run as many as approximately 6 to 8 more times of containers as virtual machines on one hardware.

So far, containers seem to be a good thing. However, they also have a downside. The use of containers is a relatively new approach, and therefore, there is not a wealth of management tools that are associated with older technologies. There is, therefore, still a lot of work-related to set-up and maintenance that is yet to be done. Additionally, as a new technology, there are also concerns about the security of the containers.

Where virtual machines are concerned, it is relatively easy to move workloads from one host to another. However, bare-metal machines complicate such a movement because they make it hard to move or upgrade. This difficulty comes about because rolling back a machine on a machine state with bare metal servers can be challenging.

Server less Computing and Virtual Machines

In the traditional cloud movement, there is the provisioning of virtual machines, databases, storage, and every other associated management and security tools. After this, applications are loaded on to the virtual machine.

Server less computing, on the other hand, is different. In this case, the developers will write the code, and the other aspects are handled by cloud service providers. Developers do not have to contemplate operating systems, servers, managing, and provisioning. Even the physical server that runs the code is the responsibility of the cloud service provider. The code is broken down into specific functions instead of having a monolithic application. When an event occurs and triggers a function, the server less service runs the function. Customers are charged by function as specified by server less providers. With the container and microservices, server less computing usually bypasses virtual machine layers, and the functions run on bare metal. Server less computing is currently immature, and the cases where they are used are limited.

The use of containers is increasing, and server less computing as a concept is also growing. Server virtualization is a solid technology that will continue to power many applications in the enterprise environment. The saturation of virtual machines in the enterprise world is estimated to be as high as 90 %.

It is currently hard to think that enterprises can move their critical applications that run smoothly to either server less platforms or containers. More likely is the probability of having heterogeneous environments in which the use of virtual machines will still be common. Containers still need to run on the same operating system and cannot be mixed between Windows and Linux.

There are new applications that rebuilt with the latest agile methodologies and DevOps because developers now have an easier time with all the options available. They will be able to make case-by-case decisions whether they should run a new workload in either a container, virtual machine, or server less environment.

Chapter 8: Securing Computer Networks

As discussed in the earlier chapters, network security is a term that refers to the extensive policies, as well as procedures that an administrator implements in order to evade and keep track of various unauthorized access, modification, denial, and exploitation of the existing network and its resources. This implies that a properly implemented network security system is capable of blocking hackers and viruses from gaining access to secure information or altering it therein. There are different layers of network security systems. The first one is usually enforced by using a username mechanism that allows specifically authorized persons who have a tailored privilege. When the user is authenticated, accessibility becomes easier. But, even in this case, firewalls won't always be in a position to easily detect, as well as stop viruses from penetrating the network security platform. In that case, the malware can contribute to the loss of crucial information. Therefore, antivirus software and intrusion prevention system will be implemented in order to help prevent harmful malware from penetrating the network. In different instances, network security has been confused with the use of information security systems. This has a different unique scope that intensely interrelates to the integrity of data of various forms, including print, as well as electronic.

With that said, network security systems combine a broad range of several layers aimed at creating a defense mechanism on the network. Every network layer works by implementing various policies and controls. Therefore, users are authorized to gain access to various resources of networks. Malicious actors will be blocked from accessing the said network or rather threatening the network system and security. When used properly, network security systems help the user, in most cases, organizations to prevent thieves from penetrating into their systems. This is also a move towards securing vital information embedded in the network security systems. With that said, it becomes vital to use network security systems in protecting proprietary information. In the current era, computers, as well as security breaches, are in the news every other day. They also cost many organizations millions of dollars appended to creating a security system that can help in protecting their systems. In a report by the IBM department, about 10 % of organizations in the US were subjected to computer network breach in 2018. Most companies lost sensitive information in the process. The healthcare sector has also registered vulnerable experiences and lost up to $ 300 in seeking to recover patient personal data. These facts surrounding the cybersecurity system are downright scary. With that said, it's vital to protect your system from such situations. While it can be challenging to actually find the viable means of protecting information from theft, there are a few measures that can assist you in achieving this in the long run.

The Basics of Network Security

There are different phases of implementation when it comes to network security. Network security consists of the elements outlined below:

- Protection. This involves the configuration of networks and systems as correctly as possible.

- Detection. This involves the identification of when there has been a change in the configuration or when there is a problem in the network traffic.

- Reaction. This happens after the identification of the problem. The response or reaction must be swift so that the network or system is returned to the original state as soon as possible.

Network security experts do not depend on one line of defense, as this can prove to be dangerous. A single line of defense can easily be attacked and overcome by an adversary, and yet, the network is more than just a line of defense and more of a territory. Hence, even when a part of the network has been invaded, there is a probability that they can be expelled if the network or system's defense is well-organized.

Types of Network Security

- **Control of access**. This involves preventing just any user from having access to the network. Therefore, every user and device in the network must be recognized. There are security policies imposed at this point, and they may include giving limited access or blocking noncompliant endpoint devices.

- **Antimalware and antivirus software use**. Malware includes, but is not limited, to worms, viruses, spyware, ransomware, and Trojans. Interestingly, malware can penetrate the systems of a network and remain dormant for weeks on end before attacking. It is, hence, important that a network uses anti-malware programs that will scan for malware before it enters the system and continuously track files so that it can detect and eliminate any anomalies.

- **Application security**. Applying application security means that you will protect all the software that runs your business. Some applications will have vulnerabilities and cracks through which attackers can infiltrate the network. Securing your applications will, therefore, mean protecting the hardware, software, and even processes in ways that will close all the holes available that can be exploited by hackers.

- **Behavioral analytics**. Behavioral analytics involves checking the behaviors of the network for any behavior outside the norm. For you to understand what abnormal behavior is, you must understand what normal behavior is within the network. In an enterprise or organization, the security team will usually play a critical role in helping the network identify what seems to be out of place behaviorally. They also know how to look at all the factors necessary to determine if there are indicators of the network being compromised. After identifying that, indeed, there is a threat, they can offer remedies that will help return the network back to normal.

- **Prevention of data loss**. It is beyond vital that an organization takes the right measures to ensure that their staff members do not end up sending what may be considered sensitive information outside the network as this could lead to a significant loss of data. To help with this concern, data loss prevention technologies can be put in place. These technologies will work by stopping members of staff from forwarding, uploading, or printing any information that may be considered critical for the company and if there is a general suspicion that it is being downloaded in a manner that is unsafe.

- **Email security.** In many organizations, emails are the first avenue that is used for a data breach. Social engineering tactics and personal information are common avenues through which hackers build complex phishing campaigns that are meant to cheat unsuspecting individuals and send them to sites that serve malware to their systems. Email security applications may help to enhance the security of networks in such a case by blocking any incoming attacks and controlling outbound messages that may cause a loss in the data.

- **Firewalls.** This is, perhaps, the most well-known way of enhancing security in a computer network. This happens when you put a barrier between your network, which usually is trusted and other networks such as the internet. There are both software and hardware-software, and some are a hybrid.

- **Intrusion prevention systems.** These types of networks scan network traffic so that any active attacks are blocked. Most do this by correlating the world's global threat intelligence to block malicious activities and prevent further progression of any files that they may find suspicious. This helps prevent any further malware from infiltrating the system and also prevents the spread of malware outbreaks and reinfection with the same.

Here are top strategies to use in protecting your network security system.

✓ Install a Firewall and Protective Barrier for Security

A firewall refers to a network security device that can be used in monitoring incoming, as well as outgoing traffic within the network system. It also permits or blocks any form of information such as data packets founded on a set of various security alerts and rules. In the long run, the purpose of this network security system is to create a significant barrier between the internal network and the incoming traffic that comes from external sources, including the internet. The main purpose of this interface is to block any form of intrusion from different sources. Firewalls also carefully analyze the incoming traffic. This is highly based on the pre-established rules that govern the filtering of traffic generated from different suspicious sources in order to prevent attacks. At every point of your network security, firewalls will guard traffic via the entry point known as the port. This is where the entire information is exchanged with the existing external devices. For instance, if you have an IP address in the house and a port number in the room, then you'll need to have different filters for various data provisions and dockets. The owner of the room will be allowed to gain access to specific rooms, but this is highly reliant on the authority they have in the organization. Also, children will be allowed to gain access to certain entry points within the ports.

✓ Use Virus Protection Software to Secure Your Network

Antivirus software for protection is successfully used in setting a broad spectrum of programs created to safeguard a system from malicious programs, such as malware and Trojans. Therefore, the virus protection is carefully installed into the computer system in order to protect personal property while removing any form of glitches, as well as software viruses that could be bogging down the operating system and network. With that said, there are various forms of viruses that could be bringing down your network. That is why there are multiple types of antivirus software in the industry. As such, free antivirus software offers simple scans on the computer using signature-founded detection to locate the identified malware. Other than that, pain antivirus software includes different heuristics that can be used in catching any form of imminent threats within the computer system. That implies that the antivirus can be used in creating generic signatures that can easily be used in identifying malicious intent on the internet. Virus protection software can also ensure that there's the protection of a computer's identity and data, as well as classified identification and information. In the long run, you will be allowed to optimize the company's performance, as well as security details using antivirus protection. Most individuals are pretty familiar with an element known as Trojan. However, they are not aware that it refers to a precarious element that can harm the computer system. By applying genetic systems, virus protection helps in ensuring that company performance is successfully enhanced. In other words, Trojans can easily be identified in the presence of an antivirus security system. You shall also learn more about its ability to spread via social engineering since it may be challenging to detect because it resembles the actual software that's used in computer protection. With that in mind, it's evident that clicking on a certain link or email attachment from a trusted source that could be assumed in one way or another could lead to the penetration of strange Trojan devices within the computer devices.

✓ Use a Customized VPN

While you can have a new device, apps, coupled with games, you also need to understand how to make good use of them. With professional help from a reliable service provider who understands the value of protecting your network, you can learn more about the applications of different operating systems, such as Windows, Chrome, and macOS. You will also grasp lessons based on the vital applications of simple instructions regarding how you can install security measures into your gadget. Other than that, you will understand why it's vital to have a VPN installed on your system to enhance security. With that said, the strategy was implemented in the tech sector by some of the world's most trusted tech gurus in order to help in enhancing privacy and security. Today, most business professionals can rely on the applications of a VPN in enhancing a viable platform of security in many ways. As such, these individuals have learned the basics of incorporating a VPS into their service portfolio where the device, in this case, a gadget that has password security measures, can be used in the application of top-notch security in a certain computer system. With a VPN, you'll be able to control who can gain access into your computer by analyzing the benefits of using a VPN. As such, it has been discussed that by using this device, you will be adding another layer of security into your system. For vital instructions on how to have it installed into your gadget, you can read the manual provided by the manufacturer and take advantage of the possible hidden features presented. Also, it's vital to understand that, with a VPN, you shall be in a position to secure your WI-FI network, especially when you want to evade the invasion of prying eyes. It can also work for you if you are probably worried about your privacy in general.

With the VPN, you can easily gain a lot of benefits in the long run. Other than that, in a nutshell, the application of a VPS highly plays a concrete role in ensuring that your web browser is more secure. In essence, you shall also be learning more about how to take advantage of its applications when you are attempting to gain access to sensitive information from your systems. As such, a VPN will come in handy not only when it comes to securing such privacy but ensuring that even the closest person to your office or home cannot gain access to the same data.

✓ Update Your Passwords Often

As of now, you should be aware that it's vital to have unique employee passwords, unlike the common 123s that is appended to their dates of birth. Besides using the passwords that have features such as letters and numbers, in addition to uppercase letters, employees can be advised to often change their passwords and use business passwords in case there is a system that provides that option. In that case, you can work closely with the team to help in creating new passwords. But, that's not enough since you shall be required to incorporate the application of new passwords and change them every two months. Even with that in place, you shall still be required to create additional passwords that can be used by new entrants into the organization. For added security in the firm, you should consider training your workers to secure their passwords and network security with VPN and firewall. In fact, these are some of the most important details that you should share with your team in the office. Your business should also have its own computers in order to upgrade and enhance your security system and needs.

✓ Keep All Patches Updated

Because cyber-criminals are known for exploiting vulnerable operating systems, web browsers, as well as software applications, you need to secure your operating system and general networking system by using certain security measures. To be specific, you should be able to verify that your office computers are generally running their current versions using these programs:

· Adobe Acrobat, as well as Readers

· Oracle Java

· Microsoft Office Suite

· Internet Explorer

With that in mind, you need to keep a viable inventory in order to make sure that your devices are updated often. This should include mobile devices and network hardware. You should also make sure that Apple, as well as Windows laptops, have some automatic updating enabled in their systems. The inappropriate privileges granted to users also pose some threat to security measures imposed on various computer systems. With that in mind, it becomes important for employees to gain access to vital data regularly. This should be, by no means, overlooked. Over 4,000 firms have recently undergone some survey by the HP and the Ponemon Institute. The team leaders admitted that workers luckily had access to confidential information provided outside the main scope of job requirements. In a report finding by the same professionals, it was deduced that general business data, including documents and spreadsheets of the unstructured data, was mostly at risk when it comes to snooping. Customer data was also considered to be in a risky docket, given that it could be hacked by different people. The IT departments of these organizations were highly considered to be secure in different ways. As such, when a worker's job changes, it becomes crucial for the department to be notified of their departure so that the privileges to gain access to vital information can be modified in the long run.

✓ Using network security software

> It is important that you are able to cover all the bases when it comes to network security. This is why it is important to have with you a wide variety of hardware and software tools. The firewall, for instance, is a vulnerable layer of protection, as you will need to fight the threats, both in front and behind the firewall. You will need to deploy some relevant tools to help you keep track of what is happening within the network including corporate products from some of the largest vendors, and some may be in the form of free, open-source securities that have been used by system administrators over the years. To have an efficient system, you must

understand how easy or difficult it would be to penetrate the system. You may, therefore, have to engage in some form of ethical hacking to help you determine how efficient you are as a network.

The benefits of insisting on network security cannot be underestimated. As an enterprise existing in the digital world, it is important to deliver only the best to clients. Each company challenges itself to be the best, and this can only happen when the network is well-protected. Network security is a big part of the services offered by a company, as data breaches can usually lead to brand names becoming unpopular and businesses losing clients. It is, hence, important that network security shields the network from external threats, such as potential data breaches.

Conclusion

Thank you for reading the book *Computer Networking First Steps* to the very end. I am indeed glad that you made it far, and I hope against all hope that the book was informative and that it provided you with a platform on which you could learn the details of computer networking. With this information, I hope you can start on the journey toward the realization of your dreams, whatever they may be. I urge you to read extensively even after making it to the last page of this book because there is still so much that you can learn from other sources when expanding your horizon.

After reading this book, it is only logical that you will be better prepared to venture into networking at any capacity since the book offers you a boost in the knowledge you possess in this field. If you find that you still need help understanding some concepts, then it would be important that you continue reading and, possibly, consult with peers or professionals in the field.

The book is a source of a wealth of knowledge that is needed in navigating the everyday networks we come across or much more complex networks that you may need to interact with.

Once you have finished reading this book and understood the essentials of networking, you may find that you are better placed but still need refinement from other sources. You will, however, most certainly be prepared to approach networking at all levels.

If you found this book useful and resourceful, then please leave a review on Amazon; your efforts will be greatly appreciated.

COMPUTER NETWORKING COURSE

Learn the basic tools of the computer networking from the bottom up in 20 minutes a day. Planning the networks and configuring the windows servers

Introduction

In this book Computer networking course, you will learn the basic tools of computer networking from the bottom up. You will learn about planning the networks and configuring the windows servers.

The chapters will cover a wide range of subtopics that will leave you enlightened and knowledgeable about basic computer networking skills. Chapter one of the book gives you an insight into networking. Here, you will learn on the types of systems, and also get to understand more on the wireless networks. Further, this chapter takes you into details of the Internet. Here, the book dives into the history of the internet, and also the pros and cons of the internet. You will also get to learn about Addresses and numbers.

Chapter two of the book covers the storage architecture. Here, you will learn the various storage mechanisms in networking. You may be using the storage systems but do not know how the systems work. Well, you will learn it here in the simplest form possible. This includes the network-attached storage, storage area network, tape and tape libraries. Structuring the capacity framework is also discussed into details as well as virtualization architecture. The third chapter discusses transmission control protocol and implementation the book will strategically explain to you what this means. You will learn the layers of TCP as well as the benefits and downfalls. The book will introduce and give you the details of Round trip time.

The fourth chapter of the book discusses the planning of a network. The author dives into the organization set up, strategy and culture and also options analysis. Through this chapter, you will further learn the implementation of TCP. The fifth chapter discusses in depth on Wide Area Network. As much as this term may be familiar, probably you do not know what it widely entails. Get a copy of this book and get to learn more on point to point services, bundle switched services, fiber optic connectivity and much more on WAN.

Finally, the last chapter of the book will take you through configuration windows servers. The author discusses relocation scenarios, the essential steps of configuring a new server and much more.

We are in the internet age, and therefore, ignorance is not an option. This book enlightens you on the basis that you should know on computer networking. Thank you for choosing this book. Please remember to leave a review on Amazon!

Chapter 1: Computer Networking

Systems interface things together. Through the USA, the gathering of streets involves putting down a system where cars can meet at one point. The reason for a system of streets is to allow individuals to effectively move to start with one spot then onto the next. PC systems comprise of interconnected PC frameworks. The motivation behind systems administration these parts together are to share data and processing assets. The internet is an obvious case of a PC network where many people get internet and computer assets throughout the world. A huge number of people who use these assets do not know how they are made as well as how they are made accessible to them. While everything is considered, that is the work of a computer jockey or the system overseer. Framework and system executives possess the assignment of guaranteeing that PC assets stay accessible. While the undertakings of these two particular jobs regularly cover, it is the activity of the system head to guarantee that PCs and other devoted system gadgets, for example, repeaters, extensions, switches, and application servers, stay interconnected. To achieve this errand, the net-work executive should be comfortable with the product and equipment utilized to successfully interface the different segments. In this nature, the idea of the system types and models.

Types of System

In computer networks, there are various terminologies that we have encountered. These involve the Local Area Network

(LAN), Wide Area Network (WAN), Campus Area Network (CAN), and Metropolitan Area Network (MAN).

Local Area Network (LAN)

LANs include many connected hubs which are in a similar structure. A hub is any gadget which can be arranged, similar to a PC (frequently alluded as the framework), a copier, a machine, as well as a discovery gadget. It ought to be noticed that with the appearance of layer 2 steerings. The thought that the hubs inside a LAN must be topographically close winds up false.

Advantages of LAN

Benefits of sharing devices: Devices such as printers, flash disks, modems, and hard disks are inserted to assist in productivity. With these, there are minimal costs that you can incur in buying pieces of equipment.

Program sharing-With LAN, you can share the same programming on a system. One does not need to buy different programs for every system. This makes it affordable.

Easy straightforward and affordable messaging: Information can be sent over different computers. This makes it fast and affordable.

Integrated information: The data of all the clients in the system can be stored within the hard disk. Therefore, a client can still use any workstation and still get their information. Through the networks, every person can access information no matter which computer they are using as long as it is interconnected.

Data safety: Data is stored centrally on the server computer. Therefore, the information is secure since it is not difficult to oversee the information.

Network Sharing: Local Area Network offers the workplace the ability to share alone web relationship with all the LAN customers. In a cyber cafe, a single web affiliation sharing structure enables the sustainability of more affordable web costs.

Drawbacks of LAN

High installation costs: Although the LAN will do without the expense due to shared assets, on the other hand, the cost of installing LAN is high.

Security infringement: There is an option for the LAN manager to check information records for each LAN client. Also, there can be a review of the web and computer use history of the client.

Security risk: Customers who are not authorized can access important information when the server is not verified well. The LAN head needs to make sure that there is proper verification.

LAN repairs: A LAN administrator should do repairs on the issues that come up regarding programming or PC.

Spreads a small area: A Local Area Network does not cover a huge area. It is limited to one office or one structure. A small area in an organization.

Wide Area Network (WAN)

The Wide Area Network (WAN) is a get together of organized and geologically divergent centers. As often as possible, the genuine difference between a Local Area Network and a Wide Area Network is the usage of some sort of quick media to bring together the center points. Such media joins microwave, satellite, and the broadcast. WAN is an extraordinarily wide term that is routinely associated with aggregations of LANs and various WANs similarly as gatherings of center points. One model is the Internet, which is constantly depicted as a WAN; the Internet joins the two LANs and WANs.

Strengths of WAN

It extends into a wide region as long as the business can interface on one system.

It has programming and reserves with partner operating stations.

Information can be passed very fast to some other person on the framework. This information can have images and associations. Excessive things, such as printers to the internet can be shared among all the computers on the system without getting an optional periphery for each of the computers.

Comparable data can be used by everyone on the system. It keeps up a vital good ways from issues where a couple of customers may have more prepared information than others.

Weaknesses of Wide Area Network

It needs a firewall to constrain uncontrollable from coming in and disquieting the framework.

Building a framework can be exorbitant, sluggish and bewildered. For a valuable framework, it becomes more expensive.

At the point when set up, keeping up a framework is a throughout the day work which requires sort out boss and specialists to be used.

Security is a primary issue when a wide scope of people can use information from various PCs. Protection from software engineers and contaminations incorporates more noteworthy multifaceted nature and cost.

Campus Area Network (CAN)

CAN is an interconnection of LANs and WANs. It involves the accumulation of interconnected hubs having a place with a solitary organization or college/school however whose bury association reaches out crosswise over numerous structures.

Metropolitan Area Network (MAN)

It is usually connected within the accumulation of hubs inside the territory of a metropolitan which are based under the equivalent corporate control, for example, in broadcast communications organization or free specialist organization (ISP). If you think that the LAN, WAN, MAN and CAN are posh names. You are right because they are.

Moreover, almost certainly, they will get fuzzier over the long haul and innovation develops. As a result of the fluffiness of the words, we characterize the term nearby system to mean the gathering of all hubs associated through a similar medium and having a similar system number. As it were, hubs that offer a similar system number can speak with one another without requiring the administrations of a switch.

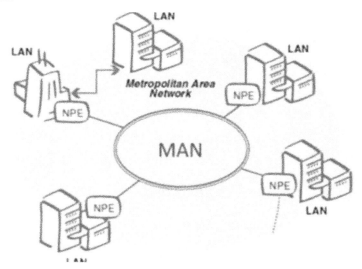

Pros of MAN

Incredibly productive and give quick correspondence using rapid transporters, for example, fiber optic links.

It gives a decent spine to the enormous system and gives more noteworthy admission to WANs.

The double transport utilized in Metropolitan Area Network assists in the transfer of information in the two headings all the while.

A MAN normally includes a few squares of a city or a whole city.

Cons of MAN

Progressively link required for a MAN association starting with one spot then onto the next.

Sometimes it is difficult to enhance security in the framework to from programmers and spying graphical districts.

Wireless Networks

Computerized remote correspondence is not another thought. Prior, Morse code was utilized to execute remote systems. Present-day advanced remote frameworks have better execution, yet the essential thought is the equivalent.

Remote can be divided into three;

Framework interconnection

Wireless Local Area Networks

Wireless Wide Area Networks

Framework Interconnection

Framework link is tied in with interlinking the segments of a PC utilizing short go radio. A few organizations got together to structure a short go remote system called Bluetooth to interface different parts, for example, screen, console, mouse, and printer, to the primary unit, without wires. Bluetooth likewise permits advanced cameras, headsets, scanners, and different gadgets to associate with a PC by just being brought inside the range.

In the most straightforward structure, framework interconnection systems utilize the ace slave idea. The framework unit is typically the ace, conversing with the mouse, console, and so forth as slaves.

Remote LANs

In this framework, there is a radio modem and reception apparatus in each Pc where it can serve at different frameworks. Remote LANs are usually winding up progressively regular in little workplaces and homes, where introducing Ethernet is viewed as an excessive amount of inconvenience. IEEE 802.11 is the standard for remote LANs, which most frameworks actualize and are also winding up across the board.

The radio system utilized for cell phones is a case of a low-transmission capacity remote WAN. This framework has effectively experienced three ages.

The original was simple and for voice, as it were.

The subsequent age was computerized and for voice, as it were.

The third era is computerized and is for both voice and information.

System Models

A system model is a reflection of an arrangement to achieve a connection between the frameworks. Also, system models are said to be system stacks. TCP/IP and Internet Package Exchange (IPX) are included in the system models. There are layers in a system model. Every layer has its full importance. There are conventions in each layer that are shown to implement assignments. A layer is a gathering of connections and comes with a certain value. There are many types of system models. They are all recognized with a specific task, for example, the TCP/IP system model. Other

OSI-RM

This is the World Wide firm for certification (ISO) which advances models. ISO started to take a blast at building up a standard for multivendor PC interconnectivity in the 1970s. The results that were spread during the 80s was the Open System Interconnection (OSI) model. The OSI model consolidates conventions which are utilized to execute a system stack. The conventions aren't utilized widely to a great extent because of the fame of the TCP/IP convention suite. Therefore, the model of OSI involves seven layers which are used mainly as a source of the perspective model, hence OSI-RM. System models are laid out in the way of OSI-RM. This is illustrated from layer 1 to layer 7.

Layer 7: Every effort of systems administration started in the submission layer. Folder move, informing, network perusing, and different applications are within the layer. Every submission will properly conjure handling information for broadcast using fine characterized layer interface under this one

Layer 6: This layer is the presentation layer. It is in charge of information organizing. It is responsible for requesting a bit and byte as well as representing a drifting point. Some of the examples include external data representation (XDR) and Abstract Syntax Notation (ASN).

Layer 5: This layer is responsible for information trading of information throughout exchange discussion conventions. This layer is to a great extent planned for the update and terminal correspondences. There is no pertinence with deference to TCP/IP networking.

Layer 4: This is the transport layer which is responsible for a solid exchange of information among frameworks. It is concerned with correspondence moment which involves; stream control, asking of data, mistake discovery and retrieving of information.

Layer 3: This is the Network layer. Its work is to convey information between various frameworks in the combined frameworks.

LAYER 2: This is the information link layer which gives guidelines for propelling as well as accepting information among two associated hubs along a specific material means.

LAYER 1: This is the physical layer that characterizes the needed equipment. This includes interfaces and cables for a specific vehicle of correspondence, for example, light-based and radiofrequency.

Along these lines, techniques for transmitting and receiving bit floods of data are characterized

Epitome and De-multiplexing

When information is transmitted from the top layer to the bottom layer, there is a specific

measure of data control that is usually connected in the information. The data in control is known as the header and it is largely included at the front of the data. A trailer is the control data attached to the information.

Not many trailers have conventions but every convention has headers. Exemplification is the procedure that involves adding headers and trailers to the information. Further, the payload is the information between the trailer and the header. Therefore, while connected, the trailer, header, and payload make up a data unit.

There involves show giving names to convention information components

Within the TCP/IP convention group: In TCP they have named sections, while in UDP and IP, they are named datagrams, further in the information connect layer, they are named outlines. Nonexclusive name parcel is usually utilized when the convention information piece does not submit to a particular convention/layer. The exemplification procedure is as follows; The procedure information element at one layer sums up the payload at the bottom layer. Every layer includes a header, Ethernet and also includes a trailer. Along these lines, there is an increase in the transparency of transmitting information from one layer to the another.

Headers as well as trailers which come from a certain layer prepared uniquely using substances at a similar layer. The header of a conveyed TCP portion is prepared distinctly using TCP convention at the host which obtains the TCP section. Every convention header information element is organized into several protocol explicit fields. The determination of a protocol is the organization of the header. The Header fields involve a foundation and a goal address, grouping numbers, payload length, and checksum for error control.

Just in case there is no fixed size in the header, then it has to be included as a header field. On the side of the beneficiary, every layer spreads from the header on that layer and goes through the payload into a convention at the top layer. Every layer has to select on to which top layer convention with which to transmit the payload. An example, Ethernet gadget host has to dole out the payload of a structure to IP or ARP. The payload of an IP datagram has to be appointed by the IP address to UDP or TCP or another convention. In this procedure of allotting of the payload to a top layer, the convention is known as demultiplexing.

Background of the internet

The beginning of the internet goes back to the late 1960s as an examination system financed by the United States Department of finance with an end goal to manufacture a correspondence system-dependent within the standards of the packet exchanges. The Advanced Research Projects Agency (ARPANET) was the system at first. By the mid -the 1970s, the rise of a few businesses and those, not businesses parcel exchanging systems, and the advancement of different networking technologies, for example, bundle radio and neighborhood, made a need to interconnect("internetwork") various kinds of systems through a typical convention design. The advancement of TCP, which at the beginning involved the engagement of TCP and IP at the 1970s addressed the issue through giving a convention which is in support of webwork, that utilizes a wide range of advancements while also possessed with various associations. The phrase "the Internet" was utilized to allude to the arrangement of every TCP and IP web works with an of all TCP/IP based internetworks with a familiar address. The TCP and IP convention engineering started taking root and shape in the 1980s which had also turned into the convention ARPANET standard. All through in the 80s, system frameworks of TCP/IP rose that joined colleges and registering focuses, and furthermore crossing point to the current ARPANET. The NSFNET system built by the National Science Foundation turned into ARPANET's heir as the Internet's central foundation. In the late 1980s, numerous provincial and worldwide TCP/IP based systems associated with the NSFNET, and made the establishment for the present worldwide Internet framework in the 1980s. Recently, the web comprises of numerous thousand, for the most part, business, joined together and gives system administrations. The sensational development of the web.

The Internet Framework

The Internet Framework The framework of the Internet comprises of an organization of associated systems that are each independently overseen. The systems are composed in a loose-fitting order, where the quality "free" alludes to the way that the progression isn't needed, yet has developed to its current structure. At the bottom layer in the chain of importance are concealed systems, which are either campus or corporate systems, as well as nearby internet specialist organizations (ISPs). Regional systems are in the next layer which involves the inclusion of one or a few states. At the top degree of the order are spine systems which range whole nations or even mainlands. The regional networks, ISPs, as well as spine systems are additionally named, individually, Tier 1,2 and 3 network specialist organizations (NSPs).

In the United States of America, Local ISPs, corporate systems, and ISPs are commonly associated with at least one regional network or, less frequently, to a spine organize. There are less than twenty tier-1 NSPs, fewer than 100 tier 2 NSPs as well as thousands of tier-3 ISPs. Point-of-Presence (POP) is the area where a corporate network gets admission into the net. On the other hand, where spine systems and regional networks join to trade. Peering is supposed to be accessible either as open peering or private peering. Open peering often happens at devoted areas, named Internet trade focuses (IXPs), and these are where a huge number of systems change their traffic. On the other hand, in private peering, two systems build up a straight connection to one another. The inward

system and gear of every system of the Internet are self-sufficient. The system topology of a nearby ISP may comprise just of few routers, a couple of modem banks for the dial-in clients, and an entrance connect to a local system. The internal structure of a spine system is essentially increasingly perplexing and delineates the system topology. Every hub of the system topology is a network by itself, with an enormous arrangement of systems administration gear. The depicted gadgets are a switch or different bits of system gear, and every bolt speaks to an outgoing system interface.

Just a few connections associate with different hubs of the same backbone system, and most connections interface with different systems or to clients.

Organization and Standard Bodies of the Internet

Organization and Standard Bodies of the Internet Numerous managerial bodies regulate and deal with the development of the internet. Based on the foundation of the internet, the organization of the Internet depends on collaboration and illustrated by at least focal control. The Internet Society (ISOC) is a universal philanthropic expert association that provides regulatory internet assistance. ISOC was established in 1992 and serves as the hub for the institutionalization of the internet assortments. Internet Architecture Board (IAB) involves a specialized warning gathering of the Internet Society, it gives architecture supervision of the architecture to the conventions and the institutionalization procedure. A gathering to organize the improvement of fresh conventions and gauges is called the Internet Engineering Task Force (IETF). The IETF is sorted out in gatherings of work which are distributed to a particular theme. These work gatherings record their effort in statements, which are named Request for Comments (RFCs), which also are the for internet benchmarks. Everything about the internet conventions is distributed as RFCs. An example, instance, IP is indicated in RFC791, TCP in RFC 793, ARP in RFC 826, and much more. The little division of the distributed RFCs is aligned to progress toward becoming Internet principles. Web measures are said to be experiencing a lot of phases, ranging from the draft to the accepted standard, draft standard, and finally the standard of the internet. The endorsed RFCs Internet guidelines are doled out with the STD record. Currently, there include as much as 61 designated standards of the internet. A significant Organization of the internet piece comprises of the task and for seeing of one of a kind identifiers. These incorporate area terms, IP addresses, the port numbers such as the web servers, protocol numbers which are used for demultiplexing. Since the start of ARPANET till the part of the arrangement organization of identifiers was finished by a solitary individual who is Jon Postel. The privatization of the internet has prompted an arrangement where identifiers are overseen by associations with wide universal support. Currently, Internet Corporation for Assigned Names (ICANN) accepts the accountability for the work of specialized convention factors, distribution including the spread of IP address space, the board of the area name framework, and others. The administration of IP

address and space name allocation isn't finished by ICANN itself, yet by associations that are approved by ICANN. The ICANN has conceded minimal Regional Internet Registries (RIRs) which is the expert to assign IP addresses inside specific land zones. Currently, RIRs are three in number. They include; Asia Pacific Network Information Center (APNIC) which is for the district of ASIA, the Reseaux IP Europeens Network Coordination Center (RIPE NCC) which serves Europe and surrounding areas. The third is American Registry for Internet Numbers (ARIN) which is for the sub-Saharan Africa and Americans. The spread of area terms is finished using an enormous private association, that is authorized by ICANN. An important assignment of ICANN in the location term is the starting of new to level spaces like Edu, US, and JP.

Advantages and disadvantages of the internet

Current life has turned out to be simpler and the individuals of the world need to gratitude to the huge commitment of web innovation to correspondence and data sharing. There is no uncertainty that the web has caused our life to end up simpler and progressively helpful. We can utilize the web to speak with individuals around the globe, working together by utilizing the web, make another companion and know various societies, scanning for data, examining and so on. The web takes into consideration correspondence through email as well as guarantees simple accessibility of data, pictures, and items in addition to other things. Consistently the web keeps on giving another office, something new that is enormously helpful and that makes life simpler for web clients. In any case, the web likewise contains some undesirable components or detriments. Coming up next are the focal points and inconveniences of the web. The internet has brought about numerous advantages in the world. We list them below.

Advantages

Initially, the web can give an individual a chance to speak with individuals in essentially any pieces of the world through the web or email, without leaving his room. Email enabled people groups to speak with at least occasions. It is presently possible to make an impression on any pieces of the world through a basic email address and the message is conveyed in merely seconds. Each organization is utilizing email in business. The accommodation of email has enabled organizations to grow and speaks with their merchants and clients found everywhere throughout the world in records times. Individual correspondence has likewise turned out to be simpler gratitude to email. Talk rooms, video conferencing are the absolute most recent augmentations in this innovation and these have enabled people groups to visit continuously. Additionally, there is a great deal of errand people benefits in advertising. With the assistance of such benefits, it has turned out to be exceptionally simple to build up a sort of worldwide companionship where you can share your contemplations and investigate different societies. The web additionally enables individuals inside an association to effectively impart and share data.

Second, data is most likely the greatest favorable circumstances that the web offers. The web is a virtual fortunes trove of data. Any sorts of data on any point under the sun are accessible on the web. The web indexes like Google, Yahoo are at your administration through the web. There is a tremendous measure of data accessible on the web for pretty much every subject known to man, running from government law and administrations, exchange fairs and meetings, showcase data, new thoughts, and specialized help, the rundowns are perpetual. We can utilize these web search tools, sites committed to various subjects and countless articles and papers are accessible for examination in a matter of a couple of moments.

Gatherings on various destinations enable people groups to talk about and share their considerations and data with others situated at better places everywhere throughout the world. Regardless of whether this data is the most recent news happenings on the planet or data about your preferred VIP, everything is accessible readily available. An immense reserve of information is accessible on the web on every subject. With this storage facility of data, individuals can expand their insight bank as well as can do as such without burning through their time through customary methods, for example, visiting libraries and directing comprehensive research. With the web, understudies can spare their occasions to scan for data and utilizing their opportunity to do different works.

This is especially pertinent for understudies who can utilize this abundance of data for their school undertakings and furthermore adapt new things about the subjects they are keen on. Truth be told, this web is for some schools and colleges that are presently ready to dole out activities and work to the understudies and pursues their advancement which can be effectively posted on the school or college inside sites. Online training has developed at an exceptionally quick pace since the web permits the advancement and employments of imaginative instruments for giving instruction. College understudies and teachers can convey through the web. Moreover, a few colleges are likewise contributions far separations courses to cause concentrate to turn out to be progressively wasteful and accommodation. The web turns into an entryway for the individuals who need to adapt however can't bear the cost of the living charges at remote nations.

Thirdly, excitement is another well-known motivation behind why numerous individuals want to surf the web. Truth be told, the web has turned out to be very fruitful in catching the multifaceted media outlet. Downloading games or simply surfing the VIP sites are a portion of the utilizations individuals have found. Indeed, even VIPs are utilizing the web viably for limited time crusades. Other than that, various games can be downloaded for nothing. The business of web-based gaming has tasted emotional and extraordinary considerations by game darlings. The web has likewise reformed the diversions business. Individuals these days no compelling reason to go to a film corridor to watch your preferred motion picture. Rather than watching motion pictures at the film presently have organizations offering their administrations where you simply can download or arrange your preferred motion picture and watch it with a quick web association. Other than that, you additionally can download other significant programming or your preferred music in a matter of a couple of minutes. Various shareware programs enable you to share and download your preferred music and recordings. The web additionally permits individuals from various societies and foundation to associate with one another. Web gaming is a tremendous business and enables excited gamers to contend with one another in games notwithstanding when they are situated far separated. Moreover, dating has additionally enabled individuals to locate their forthcoming perfect partners.

Through the web, shopping has likewise got a total makeover because of the commitments of the web. You have numerous sites selling an assortment of items on the web and one simply need to choose or offer for the ideal item and whole money related exchanges can be led through the web. Online business has an office given the web and whole worldwide business arrangements can be directed over the web. The move of cash is additionally no longer multiple times devouring occupation and with only a tick of a catch, you can undoubtedly move assets to wherever you wish. A portion of these administrations of courses include some significant downfalls. The web has made life exceptionally helpful. With various online administrations, you would now be able to play out the entirety of your exchange on the web. You can books tickets for a film, move reserves, pay service bills, charges and so forth, and appropriate from your home. Some movement sites even arrangement a schedule according to your inclinations and deals with carrier tickets, inn reservation, and so forth by utilizing the web, shoppers can think about the costs of the item before settling on choices to buy.

Individuals who accept that the effects of the web on understudies are positives said that web help understudies by giving them convenient material and assets for their investigations. It is a major reality that now understudies takes a great deal of assistance from the web. Understudies have any issue in regards to their examinations or the day by day life they can discover heaps of answers for that issue from the web. There they can discover articles of researcher and other expert individuals which would be useful for them. They can take addresses from various scholastics on various subjects.

One of the most significant advantages of the web is that understudies can acquire from the web through bloggers. Understudies can check out gaining through the web. It would be an incredible wellspring of salary for them and furthermore, it would give them a major encounter of composing. The understudies who are keen on media and needed to be an essayist, later on, must do this work. This would expand their expert abilities which would lead them towards an incredible future.

Understudies can likewise utilize the web for social availability and there are bunches of internet-based life sites which for the most part understudies use for interpersonal interaction. For example, Facebook, Twitter, Weibo and so forth are the celebrated person to person communication site. Understudies can get in touch with themselves with remote understudies and talk about them on the diverse issue to improve their abilities and learning. By utilizing web astutely, understudies can get much data to enhance their insight.

Disadvantages of the internet

Be that as it may, for every one of its preferences and positive viewpoints, the web has its dull and terrible side as well. The ongoing bits of gossip that mongering about racial uproars in Kuala Lumpur which in made a tumult, just demonstrates how this apparatus, with its unparalleled notoriety as data deaths and friends notorieties, can endure if web offices are manhandled, particularly by those with a grievance.

Other than that, a few understudies will invest an excess of energy in the web. Understudies are probably going to disregard their investigations. On the off chance that the motion picture has too solid a hold, even old individuals are probably going to disregard a portion of their significant work. Understudies may lose focus on their examinations since they invested a lot of energy on the web. Some of them cannot even separate their opportunity to do schoolwork yet they invested their energy in viewing a motion picture or talking with their companions through the web.

While the web has made life simpler for individuals from multiple points of view it is additionally mirroring an uglier side to its reality through various issues that it has hurled for its clients. With a lot of data uninhibitedly accessible on the web burglary and abuse of this data is a reasonable plausibility. Over and over you see instances of individuals utilizing another person's data and research and passing it off as their own. Kids these days appear losing their capacity to speak with others. They are utilized to speak with others utilizing the web however they can't speak with others face by a face familiar. It was an abnormal sight that the web needed to make individuals losing their capacity to convey. It is because individuals presently are over-relying upon the web.

Another issue or impediment of the web is that it has enabled a lot of namelessness to countless individuals who may get to the various sites, gatherings and visit rooms accessible. This has enabled distorted people to on occasion exploit blameless individuals and misuse their trust. We can generally get notification from the news that con artists utilized the web to make wrongdoings. The con artists will warm up to single women and cheat them by utilizing sweet words. Forlorn single women in all respects effectively get in the snare of these con artists. These miscreants regularly will swindle these women to bank-in cash to them. A portion of the con artists attempts to acquire cash from these women.

There are a large group of games that are accessible on the web and this has made most youngsters evade all outside action. Without physical movement, youngsters can undoubtedly fall prey to many ways of life-related infections, for example, stoutness, aside from neglecting to create relational abilities. Aside from these elements, sitting consistently before a PC screen can genuinely harm our eyes, and put a strain on our neck and shoulders. Youngsters are in their creating years and these elements can make deep-rooted issues for them. Kids will turn out to be more viciousness because influenced by web games. There are such a large number of web games that contain viciousness substance and it might influence a negative impact on kids.

Another weakness of the web is destructive to little kids. Youngsters these days are investigated to the web and they are utilized to keep up the web as their day by day life. This is perhaps the best danger web postures to kids. The web has given a simple medium to kids to access sex entertainment and this can make them either become explicitly freak or explicitly addictive. This wonder has additionally caused another issue, and that is the expansion in the pervasiveness of explicitly transmitted sicknesses (STD) in kids. As indicated by reports, one out of each four adolescents gets tainted with an STD consistently. The grown-up substance that is available on the web advances flippant sex and makes false thoughts in the psyches of understudies.

If you have been following news of late, at that point, you should comprehend what we are alluding to. Kids have been baited by pedophiles acting like great Samaritans and have been physically mishandled and attacked. The web has additionally made it simple for deceitful components to connect with kids and this has prompted an expansion in the instances of capturing and character burglaries. About 60% youthful adolescents in the United States have confessed to reacting to messages from outsiders. This sort of conduct is amazingly dangerous and has made youngsters incredibly helpless against becoming casualties of digital wrongdoing.

Conclusion

The focuses referenced above have presented new difficulties to educators and guardians. There are requests from different quarters that there ought to be a type of guideline to check this issue. In any case, we accept that as opposed to making the web an unthinkable, we ought to instruct youngsters to utilize it for their advantage. It is fitting for guardians to screen how much time their youngsters spend on the web, and if conceivable set a period point of confinement till which they would be permitted to utilize the web. Having the PC in the parlor rather than a tyke's room can likewise guarantee control on what they are getting to on the web. It is likewise significant that you converse with them about 'sexual intimacy supposing that you don't converse with them, they will go to their companions and web for answers which may not give bona fide data. Guardians assume a significant job in this substance and they need to focus on their kids in spite of them get influenced by the web.

Despite the fact that reviews on this issue are in fundamental stages, it has been built up that youngsters who invest a large portion of their energy in the web, demonstrate a curious sort of conduct which is set apart by a desire to be on the web constantly, so much that the kid may demonstrate all exercises and become inundated in the virtual world. Studies led throughout the years have discovered that a great many people who experience the ill effects of Internet dependence issue are youthful grown-ups, who effectively fall into the draw of investigating everything accessible on the web. In America alone, it has been assessed that around 10-15 million individuals are experiencing web compulsion issue, and this is expanding at the pace of 25% consistently. The web had controlled some of them who are depending on the web in their life exercises. A large portion of them will get distraught if they can't interface with the web. It turns into a sort of physiology affliction around us.

The web concentrated on the negative impacts, it not the slightest bit implies that we are undermining the significance of web in our lives. We have composed this article for the web group of spectators, and you are understanding it through the web, which itself clarifies the positive side of web use. It is for us to choose whether we use innovation for the advancement of our lives or put it to unabated maltreatment. Youngsters may not be developed enough to get this, yet us as guardians, educators and watchmen need to guarantee that we instill the correct conduct in our kids. In conclusion, we need to take the duties to guide out kids to utilize web carefully and guarantee them to get the right data from the web.

Addresses and Numbers

While at the systems administration model where we experienced many various location systems: such as port numbers, MAC addresses and domain names. It is good to understand that space terms, the IP locations, as well as and MAC locations have not been redirected to switches, however, it is done in their system edges. And because many clients chip away at the host including a solitary system edge, the qualification among the system and host is sometimes not important. This becomes distinctive during working with switches. The addresses of Media Access Control (MAC) are usually utilized to assign arrange edges at the information connection level. The casing of header to differentiate the source and goal of an edge is done by MAC addresses. Utilization of addresses is not a must for every information connection layer. Example, in case two switches are joined at each point connection, for example, a fast sequential connection, there would be no compelling reason to make use of addresses in an edge to recognize the goal. Each edge that is broadcasted at the far end of each point connection goes to the gadget at the opposite part of the bargain. Along these lines, the propelling from one point to another in a frame connection is aware of where the edge is heading to, as well as point to point connection recipient of a casing realizes that the casing propeller is the gadget at the opposite part of the arrangement of information connection levels for point-to-point connections, of which don't utilize addresses for network interfaces.

Within a neighborhood, numerous system interface gets to communicate broadcast channel, where it assumes the job of a mutual connection. Every broadcast on the mutual connection can be gotten through all organized borders joined to the common connection. Accordingly, each system interface must have a one of a kind location, and each broadcasted edge must convey a goal source address. With the goal, the address is required with the goal that a system interface that gets an edge within the shared connection can decide whether it is the expected recipient of the edge. The outline header is the host of the source header. Many neighborhoods embrace a location conspire that was created by the IEEE 802committee, an institutionalization body that has characterized numerous gauges for the neighborhood, token ring, Ethernet and Local area networks. A piece of the MAC level is the location plan. In this plan, MAC addresses or equipment locations are 48 bits in length.

The show for MAC documentation will in general use the hexadecimal report, whereby each byte is a colon or a dash confined. 01110001. The address for the MAC framework interface card is interminable and is apportioned when the card is made. Every framework interface card gets a globally unique MAC address. Right when the system interface card of a host is displaced, the host is come to through the other MAC address. Since starting late, some framework interface cards enable to modify the MAC address of a framework interface card. In any case, changing the MAC address of a framework interface card may achieve area duplication. Thusly, when the MAC address is a balanced assurance that the doled out MAC address is unique in the area organized. The errand of the MAC address space is coordinated by the IEEE. Every association that produces organize interface cards gets address discourages from the IEEE as an a24-bit prefix. The producer uses this prefix for the underlying 24 bits of the MAC locations of its organizing interface cards. The last 24 bits are apportioned by

the maker, who must guarantee that the bits are consigned without duplication.

At the point when the area square is drained, the producer can request another area discourage from the IEEE. Note, in any case, that one24-piece prefix continues for

$224^{\underline{a}}$ 16.7 million interface cards. A captivating aftereffect of this task plan is

that the MAC address can be used to recognize the creator of an Ethernet card. For the MAC addresses in Section 1, we can affirm that the organize interface card of Argon and

Neon were created by the 3COM Company, since the prefixes 00:21:af is consigned to the 3COM Company, and that the Ethernet interface of the switch with MAC address 00:e0:f8:24:a9:20 was made by Cisco Systems. Apart from than recognizing the creator, the area space of MAC areas is level, implying that MAC areas try not to encode any pecking request or other structure that can be abused for the transport of edges. There are two or three one of a kind areas. The area ff:ff: that is, the location with every one of the 48 bits set to '1', is appointed as conveying address. A packaging where the goal address is the conveyed area is sent to all framework contraptions on the close by region arrange. For example, the Ethernet traces that pass on the ARP request packs have the objective location set to the conveyed location. Addresses where the underlying 24 bits are reset to 01:00:5e is multicast MAC addresses.

Port numbers

Port numbers At the drive layer, TCP and UDP use 16-piece port numbers to perceive an application procedure, which is either an application-layer show or an application program. Each TCP area or UDP datagram passes on the port number of the source and the objective in the bundle header. The IP address, the vehicle show number (0x60 for TCP, 0x11 for

UDP), and the port number of a group strikingly perceive a methodology on the Web. Right when a bundle is gotten by the vehicle layer, the vehicle show number and the port number give the demultiplexing data to enable the data to the correct technique. Since the amount of the vehicle convention is used in the demultiplexing decision, a host can have ports for TCP furthermore, ports for UDP with a similar number. For example, a UDP port 80 and a TCP port 80 are segregated ports, which that can be bound different application forms. Most framework organizations and application programs on the Web have client assistance communication. When allocating port numbers the server tasks of the client-server applications are allocated to without a doubt comprehended port number, inferring that all hosts on the Internet have default port numbers for their server programs. For example, the eminent port number for an HTTP server is port 80, and the extraordinary port amounts of various applications are port 21 for File Transfer Protocol (FTP) servers, port 25 for the mail servers that run the Simple Mail Transfer Protocol (SMTP), and port 23 for Telnet servers. All extraordinary port numbers are in the range from 0 to 1023. The errand of unquestionably comprehended port numbers to the server undertakings of utilization layer conventions is, generally, set away in a record on a host. The errand can be found in RFC 1700 (STD2). The advantage of using comprehended port numbers is that client ventures of utilization layer conventions which need to get to a server program can get the port number of the server essentially utilizing an area query. The errand of port numbers 1024 and higher isn't coordinated. Port numbers in this range are utilized by client tasks of framework organizations. All things considered, client undertakings apportion a port number just for a brief time allotment furthermore, release the port number when the client program has finished its task. Due to the transient circulation, port numbers at least 1024 are called transient port numbers. At the point when making programming for application undertakings and application layer shows for the Internet, engineers, for the most part, use the connection application programming interface. A connection provides for the application designer a reflection that resembles that of a record. An application program can open a connection, and a while later read from also, stay in contact with an attachment, and, when a task is done, close a connection. My accomplice (definitive) a connection to a port number, an application program gets to the Internet address space.

IP Addresses

The identifier of a framework edge at the system level is known as the IP address.

At the point when the net crossing point is associated with the Internet, then there should be an all-round IP address special inside the location position of the Internet. Then this means that there are no two system interfaces on the Internet that can own similar IP addresses. Every gadget associated with the web has an extraordinary identifier. Most systems currently, which include many PCs on the web, utilize TCP/IP as a typical to impart the system. IP Address is one of a kind identifier within the TCP/IP. The two sorts of IP Addresses areIPv6 and IPv4. IPv4 versus IPv6 IPv4 utilizes 32 parallel bits to make a solitary remarkable location

on the system. four numbers isolated by spots communicate an IPv4 address. Every number is a base 10 for the decimal portrayal in an eight-digit parallel (base-2) number, additionally called an octet. IPv6 utilizes 128 twofold bits to make a solitary one of a kind location on the system. An IPv6 address is communicated by eight gatherings of hexadecimal (base-16) numbers isolated by colons. Gatherings of numbers that contain every one of the zeros are regularly discarded to spare space, leaving a colon separator to stamp the hole. IPv6 space is a lot bigger than the IPv4 space due to the utilization of hexadecimal just as having 8 gatherings. Most gadgets use IPv4. Be that as it may, because of the approach of IoT gadgets and the more noteworthy interest for IP Addresses, an ever-increasing number of gadgets are tolerating IPv6.

Protocols of the Application layer

The importance of transfer reports between the computers, have access to resource enrollment and assist customer correspondence at separate hosts, was looked at by the first of internet apps from the late 1960s and mid-1970s. The apps that discussed the following problems: In the integral countless extended periods of the Web, FTP, Telnet, and Email were the mind-boggling programs. The World Wide Web's rise in the mid-1990s rapidly produced the most normal Internet application browsing the internet. Lately, applications for streaming audio and video, interaction across the Web, and suitable exchanging of files have once again changed the names of Online apps. This chapter describes information on the online functionality of apps and also how apps manipulate the web to provide service-clients with context organizations. This is based on the surface of the Earth, along with area and ocean areas, which are approximately 196,935,000 square miles in size. Multiple Web apps which are centered on application-layer displays that the IETF has institutionalized them. Around it, we quickly undoubtedly portray the most common app layer on the net, in which we focus onto the application protocols used in the Website Lab. Because this manuscript and the Online Lab core demonstrates on web errands, and thus less on how apps use web, we wouldn't address it all about the apps and application layer displays. But at the other side, we may give a template which the usage layer reveals strategy, concentrating onto the communications among app initiatives and what the app layer demonstrates, as well as between what app layer shows and transport layer. Taking a look for at this goal, we find a few resemblances that what different application layer displays.

File Transfer

Amongst the most proven application layer displays is the File Transfer Protocol (FTP) for recurring documents between PC systems and it was created prior to the actual TCP / IP display suite. FTP is a client server that shows where the Ftp server receives the FTP server. The Ftp server justifies itself for setting up an FTP meeting with a client name and a hidden phrase. Enticing the verification results in the establishment of an FTP meeting in which the Ftp server can upload and exchange files and record documents. FTP recognizes the possession and access benefits of the records when transferring the documents. Most of them had a service system, all things regarded, just like FTP, that provides a smart query row functionality to operate an FTP session. This service system is used in all parts of the Online Lab. FTP customers can participate distinct apps, such as internet projects, in the same way. Ambiguous FTP is a notable type of record transfer regime that encourages the system to record on an FTP server. The Ftp server can set up a unique FTP meeting by providing the client name "dark" and an obligatory secret word (the FTP server, as a rule of thumb, asks to provide a mail address as a secret phrase).

FTP utilizes TCP because its car shows to ensure a reliable exchange in transferred data. With each FTP meeting, two TCP allegiances are created, called command membership and data membership. Power membership can be used for user captions and client emails. The information association will be used for the register unit. The Ftp client utilizes the influential TCP harbour 21 for power association, and the noteworthy TCP gateway 20 for information association, and the Ftp server selects the accessible temporary port figures. The power allegiance is arranged across the start of the FTP meeting and will remain awake throughout the meeting's life time. The command membership will be used by the Ftp server for checking, for establishing unique meeting variables, and for downloading or transferring files. The information allegiance is opened and closed for each movement of a file or report. The information membership is shut at the stage where a paper or document review has also been transferred. The information affiliation will be certainly-opened when there is another file move. As usual, the information affiliation is created by the Ftp client upon request. The Ftp server begins a TCP server that conveys the port code of this device to the command linked to the FTP server for a connection on a fleeting port. Once the signal is received by the Ftp client, it can demand the FTP client associated information. FTP safety pressure has been that the title of the client, as well as the secret key displayed by the FTP client in the power partnership across the start of the FTP session, are not encoded. Consequently, anyone with the capacity to capture requests from the Ftp server can have the title of the client as well as the hidden name used by Ftp server. The Ftp server puts wheels to both the FTP server, and the Ftp client responds with such a three-digit reaction system and an explanatory message. The Ftp server handles as well as the Ftp client answers are transferred as ASCII characters. The portion of the action query as well as the part of the agreement reaction is discussed by the part of the agreement, that involves the ASCII outstanding personalities Carriage Return (ASCII10) followed by Row Feed (ASCII 13). Essentially once the TCP connection with the TCP harbour 21 of the Ftp client is created, the Ftp client gives an obvious indication that it will be set up to join forces for the next FTP meeting. In the meantime, the client provides the title of the client and the description of the puzzle. When the verification is efficient, the client will submit the IP address as well as the container code of the temporary ship to the information membership. The Domain name and the submission quantity is sent to the affected citation record, in which the preceding four digits indicate the IP address and last two digits show the transaction amount.

The Trivial Transfer protocol (TFTP)

The Trivial File Transfer Protocol (TFTP) is an unimportant display for shifting documents without identification without packet headers as in FTP. TFTP is regularly utilized by devices without an unchanging limit with regards to recreating a fundamental memory picture remote server bootstrap when the systems are checked. In the absence of any safety, that use of TFTP is usually limited. TFTP utilizes a hazardous vehicle to display UDP for information conveyance. Every TFTP text is transmitted in an alterative UDP packet headers. The two bytes underpinning the TFTP signal show the type of message that can be a permission to upload an file, a purchases to migrate a history, a information text, or a assertion or amble text. A TFTP meeting is started if a TFTP user starts sending a request to leave or install a record from either a short UDP station to the (excellent) UDP harbor 69 of both the TFTP server. The TFTP provider selects its special vaporous UDP channel right after the application is received and utilizes this channel to speak to the TFTP server. In the same way, the temporary devices are used by both client and client.

Because UDP may not retrieve lost or demolished information, TFTP is responsible for maintaining the exchange of information integrity. TFTP transfers information in 512 byte blocks. A 2-byte lengthy collection amount is assigned to each square and is transferred in an alternative UDP packet headers. Once sending the associated space, a circle must be viewed. The block is transmitted electronically just when accreditation is not obtained before a countdown ends. Just as the agency receives a block that is below 512 lines of code long, it considers the deal's piece to arrive.

Remote Login

To execute captions on a distant server, Remote Login Telnet is a remote login display. The Telnet conference keeps running in a customer-server manner and utilizes the data transfer TCP display. A customer starts a Telnet meeting by reaching a distant user on a Telnet server. Such as FTP, Telnet's manifestations returned to the early ARPANET throughout the late 1960s. Coming early, Telnet's use in accessible structures has also been weakened as Telnet will not give amazing affirmations to strangers who can view ("snoop") communications between a Telnet user and a Telnet server. A personality produced on the comforting does not appear on-screen on the Telnet server, irrespective of it being transcribed as an ASCII personality and distributed to a distant Telnet server. The character ASCII is viewed on the server just as a client produced the character on the distant machine's convenience. Throughout the event that the mouse click notices any return, this output is represented as a product (ASCII) and sent to the Telnet server on their screen. The output can only be the formed feature (resonance of the) or it could be the output of a display performed on a distant Telnet server. For transactions, Telnet utilizes a simple TCP connection. The Telnet server utilizes the outstanding TCP harbour 23 as well as a transitory TCP port is used by the Telnet customer. The Telnet server and user assembles a ton of variables for the Telnet meeting in the aftermath of setting up the TCP membership, such as node type, line velocity, at any point characters can or can not reverberate to the customer, etc. However the Telnet user puts one TCP part of each created character if by any possibility that a Telnet session is expressly organized to not do so. Telnet provides some chance by tracing information from the distinction of equipment and programming in servers and regards a virtual contraction called Network Virtual Terminal (NVT). The Telnet user and Telnet server trace engagement to the ASCII file name from a reassurance and return to a display. It is now encrypted as an ASCII character when a personality is sent through the structure. In addition, the friendly host converts the personality and deciphers it into community personality layout whenever an ASCII image is passed on to the TCP panel. Rlogin is an optional distant login software that runs the Unix operating system for servers. Rlogin abuses the manner the user and server operate an equal working structure and is clearer than Telnet in this sense. Surge is an app system on distant Unix to execute a single request. Similarly, there is also an app program called RCP for file transfers around Unix. In either scenario, this social occurrence of uses includes bad safety and is therefore frequently weakened. The Safe Casing display package provides application layer services for distant check-in and file movement organizations comparable to FTP, Telnet, rlogin, rsh, and RCP, yet guarantees safely recorded communications between unreliable organizations. All Safe Shell parts provide identification, safety and authenticity of information, using a range of estimates of encoding and authentication, and ensure the safety or reliability of intersections among users against normal ambushes. Safe Casing continues to operate over a TCP membership on the Web as a client-server convention, and Safe Shell applications using the notable TCP interface 22.

WEB

Developed in the mid-1990s, the World wide web is another Internet-based application for access to the substance. Within a couple of years, the Web became the most influential Web apps, and web apps have outmatched users on the Net. The Web is a dispersed framework of html that is understood as an implementation for customer support. Domain controller transactions are recovered and displayed by a web client scheme called an online program. By use of Hypertext Markup Language (HTML), the stories give an indication occasionally that the websites are structured. HTML documents are substance reports containing HTML marks that show how the content should seem in a web program's UI. A hyperlink is a tag of a distinctive kind. It is a connection to the next document that can be set up on an alternative Browser. Hyperlinks could be prompted with such a keyboard shortcut straight once appearing in a system. The system reinvests the record mentioned in the link when it starts. A internet system supports a mixture of documents on distinct servers that allude to each other via links, thus providing clients a sense of researching a global study library. Analogous to a Uniform Resource Locator (URL), the territory of a study is transmitted onto the

Internet. A URL shows a beautiful region for just a internet study. It can mention an HTML document, but it is contiguous to whichever distinct documents a internet system can get to.

HTTP

The Hypertext Transfer Protocol (HTTP) is the Web app element display. HTTP is indeed a reaction display of concern in which an HTTP user provides requests to such an HTTP server and the HTTP server reacts with status data, potentially requested by an HTML file. HTTP employs TCP for information motion and an exceptional TCP interface 80 is used by the HTTP server to recognize TCP registration requests. HTTP is a self-governing display because the HTTP server may not maintain customers executable code about such a query. Every HTTP server treats a user requests publicly, owing little attention of whether a comparable client makes different resulting requests. So there is no meeting thinking like in Telnet and FTP. An HTTP client starts one TCP connection for each sale to the HTTP server in progressively ready kinds of HTTP that are still being used currently. Only when the user asks the HTTP server differently, the amount of TCP connection between the HTTP user and the HTTP server can increase enormously. In order to bring down the number of TCP associations, HTTP/1.1, the current variability of HTTP, the licensing of various HTTP sales and the reaction to a comparison TCP association abandon the TCP affiliation open until the application has been made. Before issuing fresh requirements, the HTTP user doesn't need to keep up until sales are completed. As with different many web software layer displays, HTTP signals are transferred as ASCII material using action development bit to display the strategy section. A customer's only well-known HTTP posts are HTML applications or different accounts. Whether the client reacts with a message containing the quoted record or, if the requesting can't be satisfied, with a mix-up code.

Chapter 2: Storage Architecture

A few strategies for putting away information have developed to adapt to the prerequisite to save data. Here are four key stockpiling models:

Server-joined capacity

System joined capacity

Capacity zone systems

Tape libraries

Server-appended capacity

Server-appended capacity is the most widely recognized kind of capacity and has maybe turned into somewhat unfashionable.

As the name suggests, the majority of the circles and gadgets used to store the information are introduced in the server itself, as opposed to in a different gadget. That makes server-appended capacity financially savvy, particularly for little and moderate size organizations (SMBs), because they won't have to purchase some other gadget or framework. This method is increasingly reasonable for little servers that help access to petition for a few PCs or clients in a little office arrange. It is additionally a dependable method to give stockpiling to an application that keeps running on a server. Be that as it may, one test organizations face with server-appended capacity is versatility, as a server can just help such a large number of hard drives. This means, on the off chance that you come up short on space and need new capacity, the main option is to utilize greater plates. Be that as it may, when your organization begins utilizing greatest circles, the movement or redesign way to a greater stockpiling system turns out to be progressively unpredictable.

Network Attached Storage (NAS)

The essential distinction among NAS and server-joined capacity is its utilization of a committed apparatus to house circle drives. NAS boxes, as they are known, associated with a system and can be gotten to by numerous customer gadgets, for example, PCs or servers. These containers are presently accessible in different sizes extending from single drive units costing a few hundred dollars each, to million-dollar frameworks each pressed with many plates. NAS became a force to be reckoned with in the late 1990s as an approach to enable servers to run applications quicker, easing the server from conveying information documents to clients. This type of capacity design additionally enables organizations to keep documents and information they need now and again in a committed machine. NAS is likewise well known for its capacity to hold different circles, which enables the reflecting of information to guarantee unwavering quality and information security. NAS machines have multiplied into numerous expert structures. In smaller-scale or independent ventures, NAS units are regularly utilized as a substitute for a server. In enormous organizations, master NAS gadgets speed access to information, for example, databases or email chronicles.

Bigger organizations use NAS as a spot to store information they use oftentimes, as opposed to producing system traffic that courses through other capacity machines, for example, stockpiling region systems.

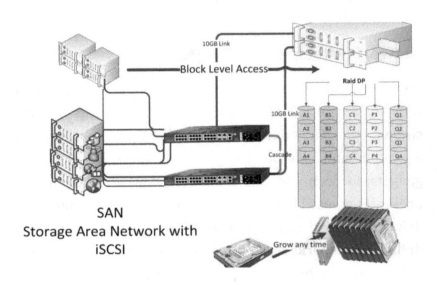

SAN
Storage Area Network with
iSCSI

Storage Area Network (SAN)

The present most progressive stockpiling choice is a capacity region to arrange (SAN). These capacity systems can include at least one stockpiling gadgets, however, are seen by applications and servers as a solitary wellspring of information. This is significant for clients who need a ton of capacity limit because by joining gadgets into a solitary legitimate substance, SAN bolsters the utilization of various gadgets with various abilities to store information of various significance. These capacity systems are likewise incredible because they enable organizations to more readily control their capacity costs by mixing various kinds of capacity equipment in a solitary coherent unit. Records that are utilized each day, for instance, can be put away on quick, costly plates so clients can get to them instantly. More seasoned information that is just gotten to once a month can be moved off to more established, increasingly slow capacity gadgets. Access to the information here is slower however since the documents are utilized less now and again, client desires can be better overseen. Since these capacity choices live in a solitary SAN, which the working framework oversees as one single unit, organizations can blend and match stockpiling to accomplish higher execution and value proportion. One significant component organizations must remember is that, with SAN, they should send and deal with a system to associate their capacity gadgets. This system can be executed dependent on Fiber Channel, a convention that is full-grown and broadly conveyed and gives quicker, progressively complex access to information. Be that as it may, this type of system is more costly to obtain and work than an Ethernet arrange. Fiber Channel is all the more expensive because such arrange frameworks sell at much lower volumes than Ethernet. All things considered, there are less prepared specialists fit for working a fiber channel system and this drives up work and in general costs for such organizes. An opponent Ethernet-based standard Internet SCSI (iSCSI), has since developed, giving paces moving toward 10Gbps, contrasted with Fiber Channel's 8Gbps. Whichever stage an association picks, it ought to recall that speed is significant if its representatives frequently get to bigger documents - an undertaking for which SANs are perfect on account of their entrance speed capacities.

Tape and tape libraries

Any of the capacity advancements referenced above are more than equipped for making reinforcements for an organization's information documents. All can be conveyed with Redundant Arrays of Inexpensive Disks (RAID), an innovation that permits the coordinated utilization of at least two hard drives so organizations can achieve better repetition, and henceforth, more prominent execution and information unwavering quality. Be that as it may, long haul information stockpiling on the circle is not a typical practice since plate stockpiling is still nearly more costly than tape. Moreover, plates work inside servers so NASs or SANs expend control at whatever point they are being used, and this can be an exorbitant domain for SMBs to keep up - just as a situation that isn't eco-accommodating for its high vitality utilization. Another contention against the utilization of plate as reinforcement is its cumbersomeness. The tape is, in this way, regularly pushed as the most ideal approach to store reinforcements and long haul documents. Tapes are commonly less expensive than plate since they can be put away on the rack, rather than inside a circle exhibit, and devour less power. Tape additionally has the benefit of being inactive when not being used, which means they break less regularly than plates. An amazing cluster of tape drives is accessible in the market today, going to top-end tape library frameworks that mechanize the capacity and recovery of tapes, making it simple to get to the tape- -

and information - organizations need to recover. Getting to information from tape, notwithstanding, accepts somewhat longer as organizations still need to distinguish and find the suitable piece of tape to recover specific information they need. Circles, on the other hand, take into account the recovery of any record or information inside minutes.

The staff in Internet technology send machines that are a virtual great rate, they unavoidably arrive at the presentation furthest reaches of the turning plates, surpassing most extreme stockpiling IOPS before arriving at the greatest limit. Accordingly, there is a lot of unutilized limits. There are four principal segments of virtualization;

The central processing unit (CPU)

Memory

Circle stockpiling

System

The work of the CPU power is that it keeps on expanding as per Moore's Law, multiplying roughly like clockwork by giving a consistently expanding number of handling centers and clock speeds. We likewise observe memory sizes expanding quickly attributable to ease RAM modules and quicker network, for example, here are 10 gigabit Ethernet, fiber channel 8gb, and Infiniband 40gb.

The majority the said permits, the VMs that are to be sent at expanded degrees of execution. Whilst we take a gander at plate innovation, in any case, great turning circles stay restricted by their involuntary parts, compelling IOPS in this manner the quantity of VMs they can bolster. Even though the SSD innovation may change this association, it is probably not going to move toward becoming standard as essential stockpiling for quite a long while as a result of cost/limit imperatives and unwavering quality concerns. Along these lines, as the IT business' hunger for more noteworthy quantities of VMs develops, it puts a huge weight on the capacity framework an issue that must be tended to by progressively effective plan.

At what time did capacity become so basic?

When you make servers virtual clients, they can separate them in between equipment quickly and with no vacation, while excluding the seen machine for them to be viewed as little than the CPU with the memory and I/O. On the other hand, in a VM domain, the capacity framework develops insignificance, as it turns into the supporting of the whole foundation. In a virtualized domain the customary framework circles are provisioned from the focal stockpiling, including load as well as adding to the randomized information access design the same number of virtual servers simultaneously fight for plate assets.

Think about this model: Admin A requires to solidify and make virtual the framework Let us say they own 25 window servers, MS Exchange, Linux servers, two little SQL databases, ERP framework and also client host indexes. The overseer in this situation will frequently put resources into a few new servers which have radically expanded CPU centers and give memory required yet may disregard to measure the capacity framework appropriately. The issues begin here because numerous elements, including limit, sorts of the RAID levels, and that of drivers as well as irregular execution of I/O should be taken into consideration.

Execution versus limit

Within the exemplary plate coerce showcase, huge limit increments happen at regular intervals. Be that as it may, we don't see a critical increment in turning plate execution. Execution outcomes continue as before. Back then, it might have displayed a test, as circle limit stayed down in that many SAN arrangements involve of 50+ plates to give any helpful limit. This numerous plates gave a lot of IOPS for every GB of limit. In the present innovation atmosphere, a pervasiveness of savvy SATA drives could give a similar limit of a fifth or sixth of the required number of plates contrasted and also SAS drives. The quantity of IOPS diminishes with the utilization of SATA drives which whenever utilized in a requesting irregular I/O condition like an exceptionally value-based file or enormous servers that are virtual, the SATA circles and their IOPS ability will block well prior to as far as possible is come to, except if they are led with strong condition reserve, where it can expand the framework's arbitrary in I/O execution by many times. It's additionally of value taking a gander with the rough manageable cost purposes of various circle innovations: During the IOPS run of 100-3000 run, the SATA drives give a very financially savvy stage, with estimating as a rule given in terms of per GB dollars. The SAS are generally in automatic innovation, as arriving at this SATA exhibition needs countless shafts or measure of SSD reserving. Elite plates are normally estimated up cost for each GB. In the 10,000+ IOPS run, SSD starts to bode well, as just a small amount of clients general stockpiling requires such degrees of execution. Be that as it may, the best utilization of blaze is as a reserve.

The I/O data Patterns

The example where the request or the host' server peruses information can essentially influence the presentation of the capacity framework. Information examples are normally alluded to as either arbitrary or successive. An irregular information example suggests that the information is composed of arbitrary regions of the circle platter. With these, there are two fundamental impacts on a RAID exhibition framework. First, there is decreasing of the controller reserve viability, with which depends on examples to 'surmise' which information squares will be perused or composed straightaway. In irregular information design, this is beyond the realm of imagination, since an arbitrary grouping of occasions can never be 'speculated' and, accordingly, stored, however, 'hot information' tends to float into the reserve. The second pivotal impact of arbitrary examples is an expanded number of 'looks for': the time when a plate head must move to the following mentioned information square. If this square is haphazardly set, the plate's head and implementor have to go a huge separation in search of the square for every compose. In the circumstance includes overhead that is huge and also lessens execution. For instance, SATA drives, which utilize bigger circle platters, endure under arbitrary outstanding tasks at hand, as they just turn at 7200rpm and also have an extended look for and entry times. There are more qualified SAS drives just for the reason that they have platters that are littler and turn at the rate of 15000rpm, which also they look for in a moment of a fraction of the selected time (3.3ms by and large). Due to lack of moving parts, SSD is an option in the outrageous elite apps which makes it non-existent to look for times.

With an irregular remaining task at hand, turn rate and right to use time are usually vital to turning circle execution. The quicker a circle turns, then the IOPS will be more. On the other hand, one of the structures is successive information and consistency: an instance, information reinforcement as well as video gushing. Within these apps, then the records are normally enormous and also kept in touch with the plate in nonstop squares and areas. Given this, the RAID controller and plates can all the more effectively 'surmise' and additionally store the looming information squares to expand execution. Moreover, there is no need to move the header and actuator arm of the plate in an incredible separation to look for the mentioned square. Such successive apps are generally planned when within MBs. This structure is infrequently constrained by plate speed and all the more ordinarily restricted by the controller and interconnect. Along these lines, in a capacity structure for consecutive applications, such as SATA, SSD and SAS circles give fundamentally the same as execution levels. The fast decide guideline is that consecutive examples are those with huge or gushing records and are most appropriate to SATA drives. Arbitrary remaining tasks at hand are commonly those with little documents or capacity demands that have no steady structure (virtual servers, virtual work areas, value-based databases, etc) and are most appropriate to SSD or conceivably SAS.

The RAID Effect

The comprehending of information examples, as well as plate kinds, are urgent during planning to stockpile for explicit applications, however, RAID level/type should likewise be considered. The capacity idea of 'equality punishment' alludes to the exhibition cost or effect of securing information through RAID. This punishment is only available on composes, therefore it is essential to recognize whether the earth is composed or perused escalated. These are the RAID insurance equality punishments: Peruses In light of these compose overhead costs, think about the accompanying: SSD drives are intended for irregular outstanding tasks at hand, so they ought to ordinarily be arranged as RAID1+0 to augment execution (except if a domain is 100% perused). SAS drives are additionally gone for execution. Along these lines, there ought to be the utilization of RAID 1+0 or RAID 5.

Enormous limits of SATA drives are usually gone for limit with throughput ought to be arranged as RAID6. RAID6 likewise gives extra security and true serenity during remakes for reinforcement apps where SATA the drives are liked. There can be viewing of RAID 5 when utilizing 2TB drives or littler. RAID1+0 can likewise be believed in exceptionally top-ranked virtual frameworks of about 2000 machines.

Structuring the capacity framework

The good way of structuring a productive stockpiling arrangement is getting application and condition necessities. Building up the information to plan the correct engineering can emerge out of specialized gatherings and talks, remote examination, on-location expert administrations and contemplating apps good practice IOPS control necessities for the SQL, VMware View, Exchange, or different apps explicit to nature. For each situation, the fundamental objective is to decide whether the earth/application is consecutive or arbitrary. Next, find the necessities for limit, IOPS, and MBs. However, there could be necessities used for capacity capacities, for example, depictions and duplication. In any case, the information full detail is inaccessible, basically with knowledge in the working framework and apps will provide you with guidance within the structure. The I/O stat can be used for requesting servers within the client condition can be checked utilizing (Unix) or Perfmon (Windows). At the point when utilized accurately, these implicit instruments can give every one of the information required. Another alternative is to utilize outsider observing applications, for example, VMware Capacity Planner. Such applications will accumulate nitty-gritty execution data and produce stockpiling reports. At last, you may assemble execution measurements from your current stockpiling framework. This information offers a beginning stage for planning the capacity arrangement. In an irregular condition, you will require to adjust and limit IOPS. In a successive domain, the structure will concentrate on limit and throughput or MB/s. Significantly, consecutive stockpiling frameworks are a lot simpler to design, as the MB/s appraisals quite often surpass the prerequisites.

Importance of Data storage

In the beginning, it is necessary to discuss the significance of data. The sheer volume of information combined with the improved investigation abilities accessible today implies that organizations currently can show signs of improvement comprehension of how their clients act in the at various times just as potentially what's to come. This veritable abundance of information can be mined and controlled into noteworthy data that can help take care of key business issues, sell more items or administrations, and everything in the middle. Information examination has turned into a significant focused separation from which most any business can profit.

Importance of storage

Because of its supreme volume, how and where organizations store this consistently developing pool of information has turned out to could easily compare to ever. The IT foundation must most likely scale with development and keep on giving reliable degrees of execution.

However, the truth for some is that server farms are coming up short on space in offices with premium expense per square foot. Moreover, inheritance circle based capacity can't convey reliably against new execution necessities. Putting away information isn't just about how and where, yet also, the speed wherein it very well may be gotten to, controlled, and introduced. For instance, getting to information in 5-10 ms is simply unreasonably delayed for an information-driven business that is reacting progressively to worldwide business openings on a 24×7 premise.

Because of its characteristic innovative favorable circumstances, an flash storage arrangement can illuminate a considerable lot of the present information development and availability issues in a denser, progressively productive, and littler structure factor. This empowers a higher level of capacity combination inside each 42U rack, sparing enormously on server farm space. This expanded rack thickness is balanced by power and cooling investment funds of up to 80% along these lines empowering server farms to remain inside their capacity envelope for each rack on the floor. Also, with progression in glimmer innovation, the descending value bend implies that every single blaze arrangement would now be able to be procured at a similar expense as customary endeavor plate stockpiling.

Simultaneously, streak based capacity conveys higher I/O execution, which is by and large 10-15x quicker than heritage stockpiling. Blaze can recover information in microseconds, as opposed to milliseconds, which is fundamental for constant or other execution delicate remaining burdens. Along these lines, glimmer conveys higher thickness and execution at the practically identical expense.

Virtualization Architecture

The term virtualization extensively depicts the detachment of an asset or solicitation for an administration which comes from the hidden seen conveyance of the administration. Using virtual memory as an example, PC programming accesses large memory chunk than what is initially introduced, using the foundation exchanging of information to circle stockpiling. Additionally, the virtualization strategies can be connected to other layers of the foundation levels which also include systems, stockpiling, PC or server equipment, working frameworks, and apps. The sending of the virtual foundation is non-problematic since the client encounters are to a great extent unaltered. In any case, the virtual framework gives heads the upside of overseeing pooled assets over the enterprise, enabling IT supervisors to be increasingly receptive to diverse authoritative needs and also all the more likely influence foundation speculations. Utilizing virtual framework arrangements, for example, those from VM ware, venture IT supervisors should be able to attend to difficulties that comprise: Consolidation of server, and also sprawl containment using framework sending which act as virtual machines. This is VMs that can securely run and go straightforwardly crosswise over communal equipment, as well as increment server usage speed which ranges 5-15 to 60-80.

The test and development optimization quickly provides test and improvement servers which include reusing of prearranged frameworks and also upgrading designer joint effort and standardizing advancement situations. Advancement of Business- Decreasing of the expense and intricacy of business progression which includes high accessibility and calamity recuperation arrangements) by typifying whole frameworks into single documents that can be imitated and reestablished on any objective server, accordingly limiting vacation. Undertaking the work stations and Desktop Securing unmanaged PCs, where there is no trading off end client self-rule by leveling a safety approach in programming around work area virtual machines.

Virtualization Approaches

Whilst virtualization is a piece of the IT scene for quite a long time, it is as of late that the advantages virtualization were conveyed by VMware to the industry value set stages, which currently structure most of the work area, workstation as well as shipment of servers. A key virtualization advantage involves the capacity to run different working frameworks on a solitary physical framework and offer the fundamental equipment assets known as parceling. Hypervisors can be intended to stay firmly combined with the working frameworks or else rationalist to working frameworks. Additionally, the last approach furnishes clients with the capacity to execute a nonpartisan of an OS administration worldview, consequently giving further legitimization of the server farm. The parceling of the level of application is yet another methodology, where numerous apps share a solitary working framework, yet this offers less seclusion (and higher hazard) than equipment or programming dividing, and constrained help for heritage applications or heterogeneous conditions. Be that as it may, different dividing methods can be joined, but with expanded unpredictability. Thus, virtualization is a wide IT activity, of which apportioning is only one aspect.

Different advantages incorporate the detachment of the virtual machines and the equipment autonomy that outcomes from the virtualization procedure. One outstanding advantage is the compactness of the virtual machines which can also be shifted and copied to any acceptable standard in the industry equipment stage, paying little heed to the make or model. In this way, virtualization encourages versatile IT asset the board and more noteworthy responsiveness to changing business conditions. To give favorable circumstances past parceling, a few framework assets have to be virtualized and overseen. This includes the Central processing units, I/O and principle memory notwithstanding having a between segment asset the board capacity. While parceling is a helpful capacity for IT associations, a genuine virtual framework conveys business worth well that has past that.

The Virtualization for the Server Consolidation and Containment- Virtual framework activities regularly leap from server farm server union tasks, which spotlight on decreasing existing foundation "box tally", resigning more seasoned equipment expanding inheritance apps. The solidification of server advantages come from a decrease in the general number of frameworks and related repeating costs which involve control, rack space, cooling and so forth. Whilst server solidification tends to the decrease of the present foundation, server control takes a progressively key view, server regulation takes an increasingly vital view, server containment leading to an objective of framework unification. Server containment utilizes a gradual way to deal with outstanding burden virtualization, where new ventures are provided with machines that are virtual instead of the servers that are physical, in this manner conceding equipment buys. It's essential to take note of that solidification nor repression ought to be seen as an independent implementation. Either way, the most noteworthy advantages come about because of embracing an all-out expense of-proprietorship (TCO) point of view, with an attention on the progressing, repeating backing and the board costs, notwithstanding onetime, direct costs. Server farm conditions are winding up increasingly mind-boggling and heterogeneous, with correspondingly higher administration costs. Virtual foundation empowers increasingly powerful improvement of IT assets, through the institutionalization of server farm components that should be overseen. Apportioning alone does not convey server union or control, and thus solidification does not liken to full virtual foundation the board. Past segmenting and fundamental part level asset the board, a center arrangement of frameworks the board abilities are required to adequately actualize sensible server farm solutions. These the executive's capacities should incorporate exhaustive framework asset observing (of measurements, for example, CPU action, circle get to, memory usage and system data transmission), mechanized provisioning, high accessibility and the remaining task at hand relocation support. These administration capacities should incorporate extensive framework asset observing (of measurements, for example, CPU action, circle get to, memory use and system data transfer capacity), mechanized provisioning, high accessibility, and outstanding burden relocation hold.

The complementing of virtualization New Generation Hardware Extensive 'scale-out' and multi-level application models are ending up progressively normal, and the appropriation of littler structure factor edge servers is developing significantly. Since the change to edge designs is commonly determined by a longing for a physical combination of IT assets, virtualization is a perfect supplement for cutting edge servers, conveying advantages, for example, asset enhancement, operational effectiveness, and quick provisioning. The most recent age of x86-based frameworks highlight processors with 64-piece augmentations supporting memories with large space. With this, there is the improvement of their ability to have huge, serious memory apps, just as permitting a lot increasingly machines that are virtual to be facilitated by a server that is physically conveyed inside a virtual system. The consistent abatement in the cost of memory costs will further quicken this pattern. In like manner, the approaching double center processor innovation altogether benefits IT associations by drastically bringing down the expenses of expanded execution. Contrasted with conventional single-center frameworks, frameworks using double center processors will be more affordable since just a large portion of the attachments numbers which are to be needed in a similar number of CPUs.

Essentially, by bringing down the multi-processor expense frameworks, double center innovation will quicken server farm union and virtual foundation ventures. Past these upgrades, the VMware is additionally toiling intimately to guarantee that the technology of the processor of intel and AMD highlights virtual framework to the furthest reaches. Specifically, the new virtualization equipment assists in supporting Intel and AMD and will empower powerful CPU virtualization usefulness. In such equipment virtualization backing does not supplant virtual foundation, however, enables it to run all the more productively.

Paravirtualization - Even though virtualization is quickly getting to be standard technology, the idea has pulled in an enormous measure of premium, and upgrades keep on being explored. One of these is paravirtualization, whereby working framework similarity is exchanged against execution for specific CPU-bound apps which run on frameworks even without virtualization equipment help. There is possible performance in the para-virtualized model and gives advantages when a visitor working framework concerned that it is working inside a virtualized domain, and also adjusted to misuse this. One potential drawback of this methodology is that such adjusted visitors can't ever be relocated back to keep running on physical equipment.

Before actualizing virtualized frameworks, you have to decide the sort of virtualization engineering to use in your datacenter. There are two noteworthy sorts of virtualization engineering: facilitated and exposed metal.

Facilitated Architecture

In facilitated design, a working framework (OS) is introduced on the equipment first. Next programming, a hypervisor or virtual machine screen is introduced. This product is utilized to introduce different visitor activity frameworks, or virtual machines (VMs), on the equipment. Applications are then introduced and kept running on the virtual machines similarly as on a physical machine. Facilitated virtualization engineering is increasingly helpful for programming advancement, running inheritance applications, and supporting distinctive working frameworks.

Exposed metal Architecture

With the exposed metal design, the hypervisor is introduced straightforwardly on the equipment instead of over a hidden working framework. VMs and their applications are introduced on the hypervisor similarly as with facilitated design. Applications that give constant access or information preparing advantage from uncovered metal virtualization desi

Chapter 3: Transmission control protocol (TCP) and IMPLEMENTATION

The Transmission Control Protocol (TCP). It's the system model utilized during the present web engineering also. Conventions are a set of principles which administer each conceivable correspondence over a system. These conventions portray the development of information in between the foundation as well as the goal. They additionally offer straight forward giving the names and also tending to plans.

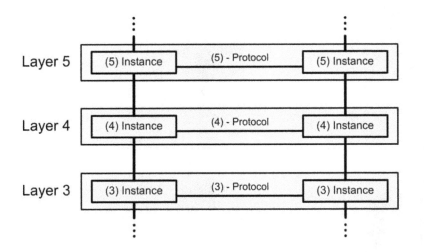

Overview of TCP

The department of defense project research agency(ARPA, which changed to DARPA) created Transmission Control Protocol and Internet Protocol as a piece of an examination venture of system interconnection to interface remote machines. The highlights were outstanding during the exploration, which prompted making the TCP/IP reference model were:

• Sustaining adaptable engineering. Additional more machines in the system were simple.

• The system was powerful, and the associations stayed unblemished until the host and goal mechanisms were working.

The general thought was to enable each app on the PC to spread information on another PC. Various levels of TCP/IP reference Model Beneath have talked about the 4 layers that structure the TCP/IP referal model:

Hardware layer

The Hardware layer is in charge of precisely that equipment. This incorporates links, the repeaters and interface documents. It acknowledges the information go to it through the Network edge layer and prefixes what is referred to as the Preamble, where there is a notable succession bit utilized for management. And when the work is complete, it creates a sign to give to the electronic media link as a rule. The Hardware layer additionally forces the most extreme exchange

component utilized by the level of the internet to guarantee the hardware doesn't get frames3 that are excessively enormous or excessively little. There involve two equipment gadgets in which they work at this level: This includes Repeaters and speakers

A repeater is a gadget with various ports normally that is equipped for accepting sign, sifting through clamor (marvels not identified with the current correspondence), and rehashing the sign to each port aside from the entrance (approaching) port. Speakers play out a similar

assignment, then again, actually they don't channel clamor. Thusly, repeaters are utilized in electrical correspondences conditions and intensifiers are utilized in light-based interchanges situations. These gadgets are frequently called center points or concentrators.

The Network Interface Layer

The addition of drivers of the gadgets is regarded to the network Interface layer. It has to set up the information from the internet level to the flagging. This is done by prefixing the header, affixing the datagram by adding CRC and also spreading this data into the gadget interface, motioning which is termed casing. Specifically, this level comprehends seen locations regularly termed to as the Media Access Control [MAC] addresses. During the utilization of Ethernet, it is frequently termed as an Ethernet address. The physical locations are neighborhood and just should be remarkable inside the nearby arrange. There are 48 chipsets of the Ethernet addresses for all time composed into readable programs. This layer involves the goal and the foundation location in the header in epitome. Thus, at this level deep capsulation, beginning choices are made about whether to keep preparing an approaching edge up the stack. A switch is the one gadget that is well related to this layer. The Switches look particularly like repeaters, a bit of equipment within any event two system ports, yet are shrewd than the repeaters. Since they work at the Network Interface layer, they can settle on choices dependent on physical locations. Switches are here and there called center points or scaffolds or layer two switches.

The Internet Layer

The Internet layer is in charge of an assortment of undertakings. To achieve these assignments it utilizes three head conventions. The IP is in charge of directing and discontinuity. The ICMP creates blunder messages, helps directing through redirection, may execute simple stream control, bolsters the ping order, underpins switch disclosure, and may produce time stamp and net cover inquiries and reactions. The IGMP underpins the Internet Layer multicasting. Every one of the professional tools has double accessible forms four and 6. The gadget that works at this level is a switch. Switches are hubs that actualize the knowledge of the net level conventions and forward information grams to the fitting systems or sub-systems dependent on IP addresses and the directing calculation. Switches are in some cases called layer 3 switches. Lamentably, switches are additionally in some cases called center points. The Internet level delivers or peruses the Internet level header. It involves great deal of data and, specifically, incorporates the host and goal of the IP address related to the bundle. There involves two renditions of the protocols in this level: adaptation four and variant six. These are worldwide locations, implying that all hubs all through an accumulation of systems that are interconnected (web) must be exceptionally recognized by this location. Information is gone through such a web by the way toward directing. Steering is carried out by analyzing a segment of an IP address to decide to which system the information should be sent (adequately the reason for the directing calculation). Linux frameworks can go about as switches.

The Transport level

It is responsible for the start to finish

stream of information. It chooses if information transmission ought to be in a parallel way or single way.

1. Functions, for example, multiplexing, sectioning or parting on the information is finished by vehicle layer.

2. The applications can peruse and keep in touch with the vehicle layer.

3.Transport level positions in header data to the information.

4. Transport level splits the information hooked on little elements with the goal that they are

taken care of all the more productively by the system layer.

5. The Transport layer additionally masterminds the parcels to be sent, in succession.

The Application Level

Every application lives in the Application layer. The applications are accountable for being aware of the information group just as translating the information. The sample apps incorporate the Dynamic host configuration protocol (DHCP), The network file system (NFS), Domain Name Service (DNS), Electronic email, Samba, the document move convention(FTP), and also telnet utility. One of the gadgets that work on this level is the entryway. Tragically, the passage is a term, to some degree like center, that is utilized from multiple points of view. We, for the most part, characterize it to mean a connection among unmistakable and additionally extraordinary PC systems. Frequently, it is used to allude to a framework that is equipped for changing over starting with one system protocol stack then onto the next, for example, a framework which is linked into TCP/IP and also net ware. The door is frequently utilized to allude to a framework that links an inner web work and an outer system, for example, the Internet. Different employments of the term portal are portrayed as they emerge.

The TCP/IP model Benefits

1. It worked autonomously.

2. It is adaptable.

3.Client/server The design of client/server.

4. It holds up various steering conventions.

5. Can be utilized to build up an association between two PCs.

Disadvantages of TCP/IP

1. Usually, the vehicle level doesn't ensure conveyance of bundles.

2. this model cannot be utilized in another app.

3. Substituting the convention isn't simple.

4. It has not isolated its administrations, interfaces, and convention

Since the ascent of TCP Reno, a few TCP options in contrast to Reno have been built up; every endeavor to administer the apparent Reno inadequacy. Whilst a large number is quite certain endeavors in dealing with the high bandwidth issue which was considered the High Bandwidth TCP issues, a number of them concentrate principally or totally on the shortfalls of TCP Reno. Such a problem is TCP Reno's "avarice" regarding line usage; another is the lossy interface issue experienced by, state, Wi-Fi clients. As a rule, the usage of TCP reacts to clog during the bluff which can react to bundle misfortunes or else react when there is a blockage, it can distinguish the expansion in RTT related with the filling of the line. These methodologies are some of the time alluded to as misfortune with the basis of the delay based separately; the last term as a result of the ascent in the RTT. The TCP implementers can have changed in both the misfortune reaction the multiple reductions of the TCP Reno and furthermore how TCP expands its CWND in the non-attendance of misfortune. There involves an assortment of the high value of choices accessible. The idea of observing the RTT maintain a strategic distance from blockage at the knee was first presented in TCP. The one outstanding element of the TCP Vegas is, without rivalry, the line can never fill, and accordingly there could be no congestive misfortunes. The TCP saw tooth, at the end of the day, isn't unavoidable. At the point when misfortunes do happen, the greater part of the components explored here keep on utilizing the TCP New Reno recuperation methodology. As the greater part of executions here are moderate, later senders can, by and large, be expecting the end will bolster SACK TCP, which permits increasingly fast recuperation from different misfortunes.

High bandwidth

One objective of the TCP usage that endeavors in attaching the High transmission capacity issue are to be unreasonable in the TCP Reno: general-purpose involves permitting CWND in expanding further forcefully than what is allowed by Reno. Past that, we can survey what another thing the TCP rendition ought to do. The first one is the regressive similarity imperative: A new TCP is needed to display sensible decency with TCP Reno at lower data transfer capacity defer items. Specifically, it ought to not have a fundamentally lesser cwnd than what a contending TCP Reno would. Yet, also, it ought not to take data transfer capacity from a TCP Reno association unreasonably. The remark above on the shamefulness to Reno, in any case, the original TCP, when contending with the TCP Reno, can shift the Reno association with a similar transmission capacity it would have on the off chance that it was rivaling another Reno association. This is conceivable because at higher bandwidth-delay items TCP Reno does not effectively utilize the accessible transmission capacity; the new TCP ought to the degree conceivable confine itself to devouring this already inaccessible data transfer capacity as opposed to eating essentially into the data transmission of a contending

TCP Reno association. There is additionally the self decency issue: different associations utilizing the new TCP ought to get comparable data transfer capacity assignments, at any rate with comparable RTTs. For disparate RTTs, the data transfer capacity extents ought to in a perfect world be no more terrible than they would be under TCP Reno. In a perfect world, we additionally need the moderately fast assembly to decency; reasonableness is something of an empty guarantee if just associations moving at the rate of a gigabit will profit by it. In the case of the TCP Reno, two associations divide the distinction in their separate funds at each mutual misfortune occasion; more slow intermingling is conceivable. It is more enthusiastically to seek after decency between contending new executions. In any case, at any rate, on the off chance that new executions tcp1 and tcp2 are contending, at that point neither ought to get not as much as TCP Reno would get. Some new TCPs utilize cautious RTT estimations, and, as we will see beneath, such estimations are liable to a significant level of commotion. Any new TCP execution ought to be sensibly strong even with mistakes in RTT estimation; an unassuming or transient estimation blunder ought not to cause the convention to carry on seriously, with either heading of less cwnd. At long last, another TCP ought to in a perfect world attempt to keep away from groups of different misfortunes at every misfortune occasion. Such various misfortunes, for instance, are an issue for TCP New Reno with no SACK: normally, one RTT is needed to every bundle that is lost. Indeed, when having SACK, numerous misfortunes confound recuperation. However, on the off chance that another TCP increases cwnd by a sum N>1 on each RTT, at that point, the system roof can be passed because the system has the ability while making N group misfortunes sensibly prone to happen. The misfortunes could be circulated among all associations, not simply the new-TCP one. All TCPs tending to the high- transmission capacity issue will require a cwnd increase N that is genuinely enormous, probably a portion of the time, clearly clashing with this no- various misfortune perfect. One stunt is to decrease N when bundle misfortune has all the earmarks of being approaching. There are instruments of TCP Illinois and cubic which are set up to decrease various misfortunes.

Round Trip Time (RTT)

The accurate exhibition of a portion of the quicker TCPs we consider so far as that is concerned, the careful TCP Reno presentation is impacted through the RTT. This usually influences singular TCP execution and furthermore rivalry between various TCPs. For mention, here is a couple of average RTTs from Chicago to different spots:

• Southeast Asia 100-200 ms

• The United states west coast 50-100ms

• The Europe 100-50ms

We begin with the High-speed TCP, which is a pioneer and moderately straightforward endeavor to deal with the high transfer speed TCP issue. The activity that follows is the TCP Vegas, TCP Westwood, TCP Fast, and compound TCP gathering. These all include supposed postponement based blockage control, in which the sender cautiously screens the

RTT for the moment builds that sign lining. TCP Vegas, which dates from 1995, is the most punctual TCP here and in certainty originates before across the board acknowledgment of the high-transmission capacity TCP issue. Its objective at that point and now was to demonstrate that one could fabricate a TCP that, without rivalry, could move subjectively long surges of information without any misfortunes

and with complete block interface usage. The next gathering, comprising of TCP Veno, TCP Hybla and DCTCP, speak to specific reason TCPs. While TCP Veno might be a sensible high- data transfer capacity TCP up-and-comer, it's essential objective is to get better TCP execution on bad connections, for example, the Wifi. The satellite internet uses TCP Hybla with extended RTTs whereas DCTCP is used for inside associations inside an information center which has RTTs that are short. The final set of three speaks to more up to date, no delay endeavors for tackling the elevated transfer speed TCP issue: HTCP, TCP Cubic, and TCP BBR. TCP Cubic has turned into the TCP on Linux default.

High-Speed TCP

The proposed repair for TCP high transfer speed issue is the high-speed TCP, which is reported by Floyd in 2003. The High-speed TCP is usually here and there termed HS-TCP, however, there is utilization the more drawn out name her to stay away from perplexity with the disconnected H-TCP, beneath. High-speed TCP alters the added substance increment and multiplier decline structures in order, for bigger estimations of cwnd, the pace increment among misfortunes is a lot quicker, therefore the cwnd decline at misfortune occasions is a lot littler. This permits effective utilization of all the accessible transfer speed for enormous delays in the band with items. Consequently, when cwnd is in the variety where TCP Reno functions admirably, TCP throughput High speed is just unassumingly bigger than the TCP Reno's, therefore both contend moderately decently. The limit for High-speed TCP separating from the TCP Reno includes a misfortune rate under 10–3, which for TCP Reno happens when cwnd = 38. Past that point, High-speed TCP step by step expands and diminishes. The general impact is to beat TCP Reno by a factor N = N(cwnd) as per the table beneath.

TCP VEGAS

The Vegas was presented in BP 95. It is the basic TCP adaptation that is we believed to be from the past century. The objective was not meant to legitimately to deal with the high transmission capacity issue, yet rather to improve TCP throughput by and large; surely, in 1995 the high data transfer capacity issue had no focus on pragmatic alarm. Eager TCP Vegas objective is basically to kill many misfortunes and also to attempt to store the blockage connect fully used consistently. Review from the TCP indicates that, with an enormous line, the normal bottleneck interface usage for the TCP Reno usually sums to less with up to 75%. The TCP Vegas accomplishes the development while perceiving TCP blockage at the center wherever the bottleneck connection has turned out to be soaked and additional cwnd expands outcome in RTT increments. A TCP Vegas propeller unaided rivalry just joined with the rest of TCP Vegas associations will only here and there if at any point approach the "precipice" where parcel misfortunes happen. To achieve this, no uncommon switch participation or significantly recipient collaboration – is essential. Rather, the sender utilizes cautious checking of the RTT to monitor the quantity of "additional bundles" (ie parcels sitting in lines) it has infused into the system. Without rivalry, the RTT will stay consistent, equivalent to no-load of RTT, in anticipation of cwnd when it expands to the moment that the bottleneck connection has turned out to be soaked and the line starts to fill. By checking the data transfer capacity too, a transmitter can decide on the genuine bundle's numbers in the bottleneck line, as transmission capacity. TCP Vegas utilizes this data to endeavor in keeping up consistently a little yet an optimistic number of parcels in the bottleneck line. The technique on TCP Vegas is presently frequently alluded to as postponement supported clog control, instead of TCP Reno's misfortune based blockage control. TCP Reno's occasional misfortunes pursued by the dividing of cwnd is the thing that prompts the "TCP sawtooth"; TCP Vegas, be that as it may, has no saw tooth. A TCP sender can promptly gauge the throughput. One of the easiest estimations is cwnd/RTT as in RTT Calculations; this adds up to averaging throughput over a whole RTT. Give us a chance to signify this transmission capacity gauge by BWE; until further notice, we will acknowledge BWE as precise. TCP Vegas gauges the no-load RTT using the base RTT experienced in the period of the association. Among the "perfect" cwnd that just soaks the bottleneck connection is BWE_RTT load. Note that BWE will be considerably more unpredictable than RTTmin; the last will commonly arrive at its last esteem right off the bat in the association, while BWE will vary here and there with clog (which will likewise follow up on RTT, yet by expanding it

Chapter 4: Planning a Network

Organization set up

The business client of information correspondences frequently applies the specialized material in this book to the arranging and structure of an information interchanges framework, or the activity and the board of the example of the framework. As a focus in this section, there is the bargain with arranging as well as the plan of information correspondence frameworks. First, we concentrate on the huge issues involving how the hierarchical technique, traditions, and approaches influence the arrangement and structuring of information correspondence frameworks. Next, we take a gander at orderly methods for arranging and plan. Arranging and structuring of information correspondence systems are massively complex. In the first place, we usually confine to arranging as well as de-marking medium-size systems.

With these, they are most habitually claimed by the firms due to their very personal utilization; which is, private systems. This prohibits the enormous web works, particularly the open systems actualized by correspondence administration sellers with an example of the phone organizations, and also the huge Internet specialist organizations. Finally, we don't consider systems that are little to the point that they can be purchased out of the container" and for which the arranging, plan, and execution can all be carried out by not very many individuals, maybe just one. We center essentially around the network planning and plan issues of client associations with noteworthy coordination issues; this normally implies wide zone systems. Before an information correspondences venture even gets to the formal plausibility thinks about that piece of the improvement philosophy that is advocated in this segment, it is important to list down, subjective assessment of accepted information interchanges arrangement. In that assessment, there is no need for consuming a lot of time or assets and this can lead to an outcome of hasty endeavors in the beginning. With this assessment, there needs to begin from an unmistakable comprehending of the systems approaches, and also the association tradition which will be using the framework. One's business for the recommended app should likewise be comprehended.

For example, someone ought to make certain that the undertaking isn't implemented because some progressed or innovation appears to be fascinating. Also, a person should be careful and cautious in that concentrating too barely on business should not put boundaries or mislead the specialized methodology. Because information activities occur in a domain of quick mechanical progression, it is useful to intently look at innovative hazard. At long last, outside elements, for example, government strategy and guideline, the focused circumstance, and accessible technological services and items must be considered.

Strategy and Culture

Strategy and Culture In a perfect world, any information correspondences undertaking ought to be arranged with regards to an organizational data methodology and strategy.

Formal and casual approaches in regards to re-appropriating, turnkey obtainment, purchasing of administrations, and in-house development are significant. Once in awhile approaches influence the utilization of open over with the private networks. The measure of the human and specialized assets in the information correspondence purpose of the association additionally emphatically influences these decisions. Building up touchy mindfulness of the hierarchical traditions getting into a task helps stay away from upcoming despondency. For instance, it is critical to be aware of the association you want on putting centrally administration range. For the most part, however not generally, the executives of an association's system which is incorporated by whether the general administration organization is concentrated. Regrettable, electronic correspondence is so omnipresent in present-day business that it is difficult to build up a by and large vital vision that is far-reaching and at the same point by point enough to be helpful. Be that as it may, an unassuming exertion can yield a procedure to guide the advancement.

PLANNING

It's essential to own up professional arranging system for the nontrivial venture. As much as there are many venture arranging techniques; nonetheless, most are comparative. Numerous organizations have their own, "favored" variants, however, the mapping from the methodology we propose here to different systems ought to be sensibly clear. In most times, contended that most ventures include changes in living frameworks, hence professional framework arranging is usually tedious and gives pitiful advantageous. The contention is regularly not true for a reason as well as the end. The exponential growth of Web-based interchanges, especially online business utilizing the new systems Internet calls and upgrade of the systems that are already there, not an evolutionary change from past systems. In any case, regardless of whether the proposed venture is a seemingly straight forward improvement to existing frameworks, an arrangement of incremental changes without a well-considered system directing the advancement outcomes organizes which is dark to the client also hard to direct. Most of the techniques comprise of various steps to be carried out in the mission improvement progression. In whatever strategy, usually, it is fundamental that at the stage finishing the executives settle on an unequivocal and composed choice whether to abort the undertaking, continue to the following stage, or return to the past stage and resolve specifically characterized issues. While planning a network, it is necessary to look at the scope and the main objectives of the project. You will frequently be given a casual portrayal of the task to reach here and there casual. A fresh, unambiguous, composed characterization is important now. This portrayal ought to outline the consequences of the kind of vital, abnormal state investigation depicted toward the start of the last segment. Most of the problems to be attended to include; the one speaking and with who? Is the expert ject intended to help interchanges in the organization, correspondences with merchants and clients, interchanges with the clients, or also a blend all? What needs to be imparted? What is involved in the business functions of the system support? What, when all is said in done named, is usually the business proportion for the task? What is the period for the proposed venture?

Feasibility study

In the feasibility analysis for an undertaking is significant due to the typically the last operation opportunity to roll out real improvements in the venture before considerable assets are expended. Now quantitative cost/advantage examinations are needed to enhance undertaking has an exclusive standard of achievement. Some portion of the possible analysis is to enhance certain that the spending limit, as well as time stipend, is adequate on behalf of the destinations that are explained the underlying procedure. The practicality analysis is founded on suppositions which should be expressed, recorded as a hard copy. In the case of, during the venture, at least one of these assumptions winds up invalid, a quick evaluation of the task ought to be made to check whether modifications are expected to look after achievability. Another examination required at this point is of mechanical hazard. Picking precisely which age of technology to use is major. Lamentably, fitting innovation is a progressive objective. In many ventures, accessible innovation will look up fundamentally in the time of realization. The most prevalent pointer of the outstanding development of PC tech is Moore's law, where, in one of its signs, reveals the work of the computer chips as estimated using the quantity of the transistor pairs each 18months. Regardless, a venture, particularly a gradually creating one, will discover technology developing below its feet.

Analysis

The objective in here is to sharpen and make equally the objectives of the first step;

This starts with deciding the direct organizations to be used, for instance, voice, data, Web organizations, virtual business, and various types of blended media. To the rate possible, future organizations must be suited as well. For every organization, one must assess the recent traffic and adventure this clog into what is to come. Particularly irksome is traffic showing for new or foreseen organizations for which there is no present traffic to use as a benchmark. One of the most unreasonable traffic for such a framework is what you foreseen. Either the framework misses the mark and you get less traffic, maybe none of the framework/app success, in the case you should take quick dares to thwart being overwhelmed.

Nature of organization is likewise a critical issue in the present-day important assessment. Shifting organizations require contrasting execution guarantees. For example, video and voice require stringent deferral guarantees, while data affiliations award no data setback or degradation. In this way, traffic volumes must not only be portrayed by their sources and objectives however by their inclination of organization essentials also. The dynamic idea of the traffic in like manner offers perplexities. Traffic rates have patterns and cyclic assortments that must be considered. The pile-on most data correspondence systems create with time. Likewise, traffic levels waver when of day, weekday, and the time of the year. Gathering traffic data and lessening it to a structure that can be used in the setup is very dull and slip-up slanted. The information is consistently fragmented and regularly started from various and conflicting sources. Necessities must be proficiently addressed. Each need can be addressed as a once-over of information senders, a summary of data recipients (these two records routinely include one entry each, at the same time, for the model, multicasting applications have longer ones). For every one of these prerequisites the kind of correspondence organization voice, data, various types of sight and sound must be demonstrated. For every organization, the traffic volume is required. Normally a powerful detail of the volume is basic reflecting the step by step, consistently, month to month, and yearly traffic structures and whole deal designs. Nature of-organization essentials should be shown moreover. These fuses concede impediments (both in degree and variety), the probability of pack hardship necessities, and guaranteed point of confinement, accessibility, and immovable quality (e.g., different directing). Yet again, while we portray the strategy of social occasion essentials as being self-ruling of the arrangement, in reality, the method is iterative. For the model, the use of the area supports a couple of sorts of multicasting. At the point when these headways are joined into the structure, unexpected necessities frequently appear. Luckily, present-day mastermind the board systems and rules offer sup-port for requirements examination. For example, the Management Information Base(MIB) of the Simple Network Management Protocol (SNMP) offers much valuable pattern information for the articles in existing frameworks—has, ranges, switches, and focus focuses, similarly as transmission workplaces. RMON, a remote checking standard, permits orchestrating a wide assembling of framework watching data, particularly from Ethernet LAN divides. RMON (RFCs 2021 and 1757) makes it possible to gather programmed accounts of traffic estimations, for instance, use and clog. At long last, some overall essentials must be tended to. These consolidate insurance/security issues and framework the officials' abilities.

Black box specifications

The objective is an information/yield portrayal of the framework from the client's perspective. How does the framework look at all things considered? What do clients see? What would they be able to do? Cautious thought of human variables is basic. The results in this phase include, one might say, a concurrence with the customer system describing what the correspondence framework will achieve for them. For the legitimacy of the undertaking, it is fundamental to have objective (and in a perfect world quantitative) centers for organization execution, unwavering quality, reaction, and so on with the objective that gives support to the customers and can be looked upon. To the degree conceivable, the system should consolidate modified checking of these organization destinations measures.

Options Analysis

Now, with a better than average handle of the objectives and necessities of the undertaking, one can go to the ID and appraisal of open use activities. One way to deal with do this is to use the information so far collected and prepare a Request for Information (RFI) to send to merchants to build a general thought of the hardware, workplaces, and organizations they can give that applies to the goals and necessities. In any case, you need to efficiently accumulate data on the gadgets, transmission workplaces, programming, and organizations that may be useful. For each situation, you need to know the features, costs, financing decisions (lease, buy, etc.), advantage limit, reliability of the trader, and merchant customer support.

The network architecture

The key endeavor is to browse the options perceived in the assessment of the decision the net-working approaches to managing to be taken to support the necessities. Furthermore, the verifying framework should in like manner be recognized: what components to develop, what to buy, and what to redistribute. Standards expect a huge activity in planning correspondence systems. They normally choose whether you have the prosperity of elective shippers. So you ought to pick which standards to require in your plan. In the current state of quick inventive change and uncertain prerequisites, a basic objective is to take care of flexibility: lease, don't buy; utilize acknowledged benchmarks; don't get rushed into one merchant's things or organizations. Pick innovations and structures that scale; that is destined to be, that can be agilely adjusted to help in-wrinkling demands without requiring an extreme update.

RFP

In this level, there is a build-up of the documentation where against which purchases, execution, contracts, and other cash related obligations will be made. We ought to decide in a practically stunning focal point how the structure of the correspondence is to be executed. Emissary needs and dealers may help, yet the owner is finally careful. The customers of the framework must be recognized. The territories of the equipment must be demonstrated. The applications that will be maintained must be point by point. The utmost and execution of the systems must be estimated. Security and faithful quality necessities must be introduced. The costs of equipment, transmission, and organizations (checking support and upkeep) must be explained. Organization and cutover (progress from old to new structure), together with installment plans, must be set down. The cutover plan must make courses of action for a fall back if the new structure does not execute similarly true to form with the objective that central tasks are kept up. On the off chance that possible, the new and old systems should work in standard allele until the new structure is exhibited latency. Affirmation testing should be executed as a formal procedure to find that the improvement is finished. Game plans for a customer getting ready must be made. For systems including specific hazard or various vulnerabilities, a pilot undertaking might be called for. Backing for insurance and security must be resolved. Framework the board instruments to help the movement of the framework must be shown specifically.

Implementation

This is the certified utilization of the framework. The basic activity of the coordinator/originator is to set up an intentional overview system to audit adherence to the de-pursued setup chronicle. If there ought to emerge an event of certifiable divergences, it may be essential to cycle back to earlier walks in the improvement technique and make changes. The course of action ner/organizer, generally, expect a noteworthy activity in the affirmation testing as well, which closures this progression.

Preparing and Cutover-A detailed schedule should have been set up for customer setting up that will be finished before the cutover. In case a pilot is a bit of the improvement plan, it is consistently valuable to test the arrangement structures too. A fundamental decision here is when to empower the fall-back workplaces to be disposed of.

Evaluation

After the system has been inertia for a long time, it is basic to have a planned and formal evaluation of the structure in light of operational experience. A portion of the components that should be considered is, Did the structure achieve its operational targets? Do the customers find the system responsive and trustworthy? What was/is the budgetary show? Did the endeavor come in inside spending plan? Are the operational expenses inside the spending plan? Were the cash related points of interest of the undertaking made sense of it? How does the authentic weight on the system appear differently about the master jected loads?

Redesigning/Modifications/Replacement

In basically all cases, the evaluation step will perceive various awes, much of the time unsavory. These will normally ought to be tended to by changes following the framework. Besides, it is never too early to start envisioning the redesigning or overriding the framework. A noteworthy mistake is to see system arranging and structure as an occasion rather than a procedure. Alterations, overhauls, and substitution will occur continuously. There won't be a time when triumph can be articulated and the project declared complete.

The Model

The setup methodology starts with a model of the system, consistently numerical. The model incorporates components, goals, and arrangement goals. The maker attempts to pick regards for the elements with the goal that the prerequisites are satisfied and the objective improved. We, all things considered, acknowledge that building is given and that it is only the sizes, numbers, and territories of its components similarly as their interconnections that stay to be resolved. The model of the entire trades system is involved models of traffic and solicitation, models of correspondence workplaces, and models of the terminal and exchanging gadgets. There may be various components, yet they can be parceled into two or three classifications. There are factors that measure; (a) price and return, (b) execution and unwavering quality, and (c) traffic.

In most arrangement models, the costs are disengaged into beginning costs and repeating costs. There are various

246

variables portraying execution. Deferral, blocking, percent package disaster, throughput limit, interim among frustrations, and accessibility are models; there are various others. These variables portray the idea of administration. Describing traffic is normally the most dreary and expensive piece of the design procedure. The principle issue is that most ideal situation, you simply acknowledge what traffic there was beforehand and not what traffic there will be over the future lifetime of the proposed system. Especially in the current state of quick mechanical change, you now and again are organizing a structure for applications that did not beforehand exist or, in case they existed, were managed as of now in such an in a general sense unprecedented route from the proposed strategy that past data is of little use. Web structures to sup-port Web traffic, intelligent media, just as electronic business are typical models. The following issue is that traffic requirements must be demonstrated for each sender of data to each recipient or social affair of beneficiaries. This ideas to climb to a combinatorial impact on the required data. For instance, on the off chance that we have 100 clients, there are 9900 potential to-from sets of clients; with 1000 clients, there are 999,000 conceivable pairs. Obviously, for real frameworks, the clients must be combined into gatherings. Be that as it may, fittingly doing this isn't inconsequential. The third trouble is managing the dynamics of traffic. Traffic levels change in arbitrary courses for the time being; frequently have daily, week after week, month to month, and yearly designs. The suitable method to manage traffic dynamics relies upon the utilization of the correspondence framework. For instance, numerous retailers make the stunning bit of their arrangements in the Christmas season, and an enormous number of their correspondences structures must assistance the extraordinary traffic during this time, which could be significantly more critical than the typical weight or the store at different occasions of years. The selection of relations as objectives or the objective is somewhat subjective. Regularly one is excited about the trade-offs between these relations. For example, in one setting you might be excited about restricting ordinary deferment of messages, con-worried by the need of a given breaking point. In various settings, you may wish to boost the farthest point given an upper bound on the typical deferral as an objective.

System Design Tools and Algorithms

Network configuration devices **are** frameworks worked **around suites of** structure calculations. **The apparatuses bolster the counts with straightforward graphical UIs. They** additionally master vide arrange to alter offices with the goal that systems can be effectively changed to

produce multiple "imagine a scenario where" situations. Regularly the apparatuses additionally include a type of adaptation **control to monitor all of these circumstances. Databases for data, for instance, traffic, device, and duty data are** additionally given. In particular, the devices give integration among the different calculations in the suite. The

common calculations for explaining the models can be described as exact fast calculations, accurate moderate calculations, **also, construed counts. Notwithstanding**

these descriptive strategies, discrete event reenactment is in the like manner normal. Careful brisk counts, for example, most brief way, least spreading over the tree, and arranging algorithms are

instructed in starting software engineering calculation courses [CORM01]. They can be actualized in all respects just and run proficiently even on exceptionally huge problems. Shockingly, they are delicate as in apparently unimportant modifications to the hidden model can make the calculations improper; the

calculations are not hearty as for model developments. There are various problems for which realized estimations are moderate, here and there very little superior to savage power specification. These are frequently not valuable for commonsense measured issues. The traveling salesman issue (which has noteworthy interchanges applications) is an outstanding case of this sort. For issues without any known gainful calculations, rough just as heuristic techniques can be used. Discrete event diversion, which is a reenactment technique that is acclaimed for exhibiting correspondence structures, is another likelihood. It is the most versatile approach to manage to illustrate. In any case, it tends to be in all respects expensive computationally, especially for huge frameworks. The wide assortment in the trademark times of a correspondence framework makes a united reenactment impracticable. Procedure terms of automated switches and bit times of fiber optic directs are evaluated in nanoseconds, bit times for remote transmission are estimated in microseconds, human response times are in seconds to minutes, and interim between frustrations of specific devices goes upward from months. This makes recreation pursuing all intents and purposes estimated frameworks. Additionally, the size of present-day arranges their high data rates, and the modestly little sizes of ATM cells on other data units makes reproduction restrictively tedious for general use. However, the method is valuable for displaying singular gadgets and complex protocols on little nets. Every single business apparatus that utilization discrete occasion simulation utilizes crossbreed techniques that blend diagnostic and discrete occasion reproduction. The algorithms for entire systems by and large are systematic, while nitty-gritty conduct of switches and different gadgets might be reproduced.

Network Design tools

Net Rule, Analytical Engines, a Java-based instrument for WAN based systems. It has all the earmarks of being exquisite and generally easy to utilize and utilizes primarily scientific algorithms. OPNET Technologies offers a product suite planned to support system specialist organizations. The examination and configuration apparatuses underline integration of expository and reproduction procedures to give exact outcomes in a reasonable time to huge, complex networks.

Network Topology

Topology is the programming of a network. It is the game plan of hubs typically switches, programming switch/switch highlights and associations in a system regularly spoke to as a diagram. The topology of the system and the overall areas of the source and goal of traffic streams on the system decide the ideal way for each stream and the degree to which repetitive choices for steering exist in case of a disappointment. There are two unique methods for portraying framework geometry: the physical topology and the insightful (or sign) topology. The seen topology of a framework is the configuration of hubs and physical associations, including wires (Ethernet, DSL), fiber optics, and microwave. There are a few basic physical topologies, as depicted beneath and as appeared in the delineation.

Sorts of physical topologies

In the transport organize topology, each hub is associated in arrangement directly. This game plan is discovered today fundamentally in link broadband appropriation systems.

In the star arrange topology, a focal hub has an immediate association with every other hub. Exchanged neighborhood (LANs) in light of Ethernet switches, including most wired home and office systems, have a physical star topology.

In the ring system topology, the hubs are associated in a shut circle design. A few rings will pass information just one way, while others are fit for transmission in the two headings. These bidirectional ring systems are stronger than transport systems since traffic can arrive at a hub by moving in either heading. Metro systems dependent on Synchronous Optical Network Technology (SONET) are the essential case of ring systems today.

The work arranges topology joins hubs with associations so different ways between probably a few points of the system are accessible. A system is said to be completely fit if all hubs are straightforwardly associated with every single other hub and halfway coincided if just a few hubs have various associations with others. Lattice to make various ways builds flexibility under disappointment, yet expands cost. The Internet is a work organize.

The tree arranges topology, additionally called a star of stars, is where star topologies are themselves associated in a star setup. Numerous bigger Ethernet switch systems including server farm systems, are arranged as trees.

Logical topologies

A consistent topology for a system more often than not alludes to the connection among hubs and legitimate associations. A coherent association will vary from a physical way when data can take an undetectable jump at the middle of the road focuses. In optical systems, optical include drop multiplexers (ADMs) make consistent optical ways because the ADM jump isn't unmistakable to the endpoint hubs. Systems dependent on virtual circuits (or passages) will have a physical topology dependent on the genuine association medium (fiber, for instance) and a coherent topology dependent on the circuits/burrows.

Once in awhile the legitimate topology will allude to the topology from the's perspective, which means the availability of the system. IP and Ethernet organize, the two most generally utilized today, are completely coincided at the association level because any client can interface with some other - except if a few methods for blocking undesirable associations, similar to a firewall, is presented.

This full availability is a property of the system conventions utilized (IP and Ethernet), not of the system topology itself. Any system topology can seem, by all accounts, to be completely fit its clients.

Ring Topology

This is termed ring configuration because it forms a ring, because each PC is linked with yet a fellow PC, the other one being connected with the first. Just two neighbors for every gadget.

Highlights of Ring Topology Various signal boosters are often used for Ring Topology with such a large amount of hubs provided that somebody needs to send a few information to the last hub in the ring topology with 100 hubs, at that point the information should go through 99 hubs to arrive at the 100th hub. Subsequently to avert information misfortune

repeaters are utilized in the system. The transmission is unidirectional, be that as it may, it might be made double directional by having 2 affiliations among each Network Node, it is called double

Ring Topology.

In double Ring Topology, double ring frameworks are confined, and the data stream is a reverse route in them. Likewise, on the off chance that one ring comes up short, the subsequent ring can go about as a reinforcement, to keep the system up. Information is moved in a consecutive way that is a little bit at a time.

Information transmitted needs to go through every hub of the system, till the goal hub.

Pros of Ring Topology

Transmitting system isn't affected by heavy traffic or through along with more core stations, merely because the core stations with coins are capable of transmitting information. Unobstructive to introduce and expand

Cons of Ring Topology

Investigation in ring structure is unpleasant.

Eliminating PCs is pestering the system exercise.

The inability of one PC is irritating to whole structure.

Transport Topology

Transport Topology is a system form where every Computer and system piece of equipment is linked to a lonely link.

If it has two data sources properly, it's termed the Linear Bus Topology.

Characteristics of Bus Topology Information is transmitted in one manner only.

Each device is linked to a unique

Bus Topology Link Strong points.

At the very least, the necessary relation emerged separately with respect to many other context topology.

For use in small organizations It's immediate. Difficult to make to combine two of the junctions.

Shortcomings of Bus Topology

Links the arrows and now the whole structure misses the point. In the event that perhaps the template traffic is friendly or the middle lines are more visible, the structure decreases.

The link has a limited duration. It's lighter than that of the structure of the ring.

Showcases of Star Topology Each core has some kind of connection with an inside point. Concentrate spot is a transmitter for the data flow.

Can be used with distorted pair, Optical Fiber or coaxial connection

Advantages of Star Topology

Quick execution with two or three centers and low framework traffic

Focus can be updated viably.

Easy to examine.

Straightforward to the course of action and alter.

Simply that center is impacted which has failed, rest of the center points can work effectively.

Weaknesses of Star Topology

The Price of the framework is high price to be used in the unlikely event that the emphasis point misses the mark, by then the whole structure is halted because all center points rely on the inside.

Chapter 5: WIDE AREA NETWORK

A wide territory organizes (WAN) is a media communications arrange, normally utilized for associating PCs, which traverses a wide land region, for example, between various urban communities, states, or even nations. WANs normally are utilized by partnerships or associations to encourage the trading of information between their PCs in scattered workplaces. Overall enterprises, most enormous organizations with offices at different areas use WANs, and even free organizations with just two local areas logically use WANs. Most WANs interface at any rate two neighborhood (LANs) and the Internet is on a very basic level an immense WAN.

Even though WANs fill a need like that of LANs, WANs are sorted out and worked out of the blue. The customer of a WAN as a general rule does not have the correspondence lines that interface the remote PC frameworks however rather buys into an administration through a media communications supplier. In contrast to LANs, WANs normally don't connect singular PCs, however rather are used to interface LANs in what are known as internetworks, using devices called switches and remote augmentations. WANs in like manner transmit data at considerably more moderate velocities than LANs, most ordinarily at about 1.5 megabits consistently (Mbps) or less, as opposed to the tens, hundreds, or even a large number of Mbps achieved by LANs. WANs are fundamentally similar to metropolitan region frameworks (MANs), in any case, are regularly increasingly slow correspondences joins for separations more noteworthy than 50 kilometers.

WANs have existed for quite a long time, yet new advances, administrations, and applications have created throughout the years. WANs were initially created for advanced rented line administrations conveying just voice, instead of information. In that capacity, they associated the private branch exchanges (PBXs) of remote work environments of a comparable association. WANs are up 'til now used for voice organizations, notwithstanding, are used most strongly for data and, as of late, likewise for pictures, for example, video conferencing. WAN usage is creating, as more associations have presented LANs and as continuously moderate internetworking apparatus has ended up being open.

Even though WANs fill a need like that of LANs, WANs are organized and worked unexpectedly. The client of a WAN, for the most part, does not claim the correspondence lines that associate the remote PC frameworks yet rather buys into an administration through a broadcast communications supplier. In contrast to LANs, WANs ordinarily don't interface singular PCs, yet rather are utilized to connect LANs in what are known as internetworks, utilizing gadgets called switches and remote scaffolds. WANs additionally transmit information at much more slow speeds than LANs, most regularly at about 1.5 megabits every second (Mbps) or less, rather than the tens, hundreds, or even a huge number of Mbps accomplished by LANs. WANs are basically like metropolitan zone systems (MANs), yet are ordinarily increasingly slow interchanges joins for separations more noteworthy than 50 kilometers.

WANs have existed for a considerable length of time, yet innovations, administrations, and applications have created throughout the years. WANs were initially created for advanced rented line administrations conveying just voice, instead of information. Accordingly, they associated the private branch trades (PBXs) of remote workplaces of a similar organization. WANs are as yet utilized for voice administrations, however, are utilized most vigorously for information and, as of late, additionally for pictures, for example, video conferencing. WAN utilization is developing, as more organizations have introduced LANs and as progressively moderate internetworking hardware has turned out to be accessible.

Even though WANs fill a need like that of LANs, WANs are sorted out and worked out of the blue. The customer of a WAN normally does not have the correspondence lines that interface the remote PC structures anyway rather gets tied up with an organization through a media interchanges provider. As opposed to LANs, WANs normally don't associate particular PCs, yet rather are used to interface LANs in what are known as internetworks, using contraptions called switches and remote frameworks. WANs moreover transmit data at significantly more moderate rates than LANs, most for the most part at about 1.5 megabits consistently (Mbps) or less, as opposed to the tens, hundreds, or even a considerable number of Mbps achieved by LANs. WANs are in a general sense like metropolitan zone frameworks (MANs), be that as it may, are conventionally progressively moderate trades joins for partitions more unmistakable than 50 kilometers.

WANs have existed for an extensive timeframe, yet developments, organizations, and applications have made consistently. WANs were at first delivered for cutting edge leased line organizations passing on simply voice, rather than data. Therefore, they related the private branch exchanges (PBXs) of remote work environments of a comparative association. WANs are so far used for voice organizations, nonetheless, are used most seriously for data and, starting late, also for pictures, for instance, video conferencing. WAN use is creating, as more associations have presented LANs and as progressively moderate internetworking equipment has ended up being available.

Point to Point services

The fundamental sort of point-to-point WAN development in North America is TI, which relies upon a strategy for disengaging a propelled line organization with a pace of 1.544 Mbps into 24 channels of 64 Kbps each. By recent rules, this rate is respectably moderate appeared differently concerning LAN advancement and stood out from the extending corporate solicitations set on LANs. The cost of setting up and leasing a TI (or the snappier T3) addresses a sizable expense for associations. In the mid-1990s pretty much all WANs used Ti or other leased lines, which are leased from a media correspondences transporter, yet this changed rapidly as more affordable and faster alternatives rose. Various onlookers have guessed the sharp lessening of leased line benefits once the system is set up to all the more probable assistance the more exceptional, increasingly moderate alternatives. Other point-to-point organizations open consolidate fragmentary Tl, T3, information telephone automated organizations, traded 56 Kbps, composed organizations propelled framework (ISDN), and digressed propelled endorser line (ADSL). ADSL and practically identical DSL developments drew a great deal of thought from corporate framework chairmen in the late 1990s since they were widely more reasonable than leased lines—as much as 60 percent less and passed on relative or better execution.

Despite their average amazing costs, another drawback to point-to-point arrangements is that they aren't fitting to oblige convenient customers, e.g., business voyagers. Since the organizations are associated exceptionally to unequivocal territories, associations must find elective techniques for framework access for versatile customers. Group traded frameworks organization gives this limit, among various points of interest.

Group Switched Services

WAN advancements that rely upon open frameworks utilizing package trading, a system for encoding data into little, amazingly recognized pieces known as groups, have been logically renowned over the earlier decade. Two of the most noteworthy pack based developments are edge hand-off and non concurrent move mode (ATM).

Packaging move is the more prepared of the two, coming into general use in the mid-1990s. It was in the colossal segment a substitution to the slower X.25 standard that had been around since the mid-1970s. Most packaging hand-off WANs are encouraged by business sort out chairmen that charge level rates subject to the speed of organization or volume of data required. Supported by decently modest frameworks organization hardware, diagram handoff relies upon structure up a predictable or virtual circuit over a framework with another PC. In packaging hand-off, the groups, or edges, of data may change in size, and no undertaking is made to address botches. This keeps going part relies upon the assumption that packaging move is continued running over the commonly high gauge, automated frameworks, and the data is less weak to botches. This is like manner improves speed since the framework show isn't endeavoring to address the data. The reliability of this affiliation licenses packaging move master centers to guarantee a particular least level of organization. The close to insignificant exertion and high bore of the organization made edge move one of the most noticeable WAN developments during the 1990s.

ATM organizations, which were introduced monetarily in the mid-1990s, contingent upon relative gauges. Many have touted ATM as a jump forward development, anyway as of the late 1990s it had only an unassuming impact on the WAN market. ATM uses a thought called cell to move to transmit data. Cells are reliably evaluated, little packages of data; by ATM, just 53 bytes each, including a 5-byte header. Then again, a packaging hand-off bundle may range up to a couple of thousand bytes. Correspondingly, similarly as with edge hand-off, ATM moves data over a portrayed virtual path as opposed to empowering groups to seek after any number of approaches to their objectives, as occurs in TCP/IP shows used in Internet applications. This particularly relentless affiliation fits video and various applications that require a reliable, obvious movement of data. The weaknesses to this sureness are that the enduring level of organization may below stood out from various decisions, an ATM may not be all around arranged to regulate transient spikes looked for after for framework resources.

Fiber Optic network

Fiber-optic accessibility for WANs is another huge innovative work in an area. Fiber optics, which incorporates sending light banner through glass or plastic fibers, can reinforce brisk and incredibly astonishing data move. Most fiber-optic frameworks use some sort of group trading advancement, for instance, ATM.

One creating a standard in this field is a synchronous optical framework (SONET), a lot of shows grasped by the American National Standards Institute (ANSI) for high-transmission limit fiber-optic frameworks organization. The all-inclusive easy to SONET is known as the synchronous modernized pecking request (SDH). While its specific advantages have been recognized by a couple of, others note that the monetary issues of SONET are less captivating. It has exhibited expensive to execute, and a couple of critics promise it wasn't organized properly to manage overpowering data traffic that associations need such benefits for. Regardless, gigantic associations with generous throughput necessities have begun to connect to SONET-based organizations.

A battling, and even more fiscally persuading, standard is thick wavelength division multiplexing (DWDM). DWDM is a system for capably sharing give up the fiber by changing the piece of the light go for each phenomenal stream of data. By using each fiber even more capably, DWDM allows inside and out higher exchange speeds for data than SONET, which relies upon time-division multiplexing (TDM) or conveying time to each unique stream of data on a fixed rotate. This proselyte into extensive cost speculation assets on gear as well. DWDM development was overall rapidly sent by different framework overseers because of such focal points. While the Internet and different frameworks organization progressions have changed the quintessence of WANs and have bargained some progressively prepared kinds of WAN development, different authorities acknowledge they will end up being increasingly huge instead of less, as examples can envision globalization and telecommuting make new enthusiasm for high control long-partition arranging. Enthusiasm for framework information move limit will continue swelling. One advancement measure saw corporate WAN traffic climbing by as much as 30 percent a year through 2002, and a lot of this traffic will dynamically be coordinated through open frameworks using virtual private framework development rather than the shut private previous frameworks.

Advantages of WAN

Brings together IT framework-Many think about this present WAN's top preferred position. A WAN takes out the need to purchase email or record servers for every office. Rather, you just need to set up one at your head office's server farm. Setting up a WAN additionally streamlines server the board, since you won't need to help, back-up, host, or physically secure a few units. Additionally, setting up a WAN gives huge economies of scale by giving a focal pool of IT assets the entire organization can take advantage of.

Lifts your security -Setting up a WAN enables you to impart touchy information to every one of your destinations without sending the data over the Internet. Having your WAN scramble your information before you send it includes an additional layer of insurance for any secret material you might move. With such huge numbers of programmers out there simply kicking the bucket to take delicate corporate information, a business needs all the security it can get from system interruptions.

Expands transmission capacity-Corporate WANS regularly utilize rented lines rather than broadband associations with the structure the foundation of their systems. Utilizing rented lines offers a few pluses for an organization, including higher transfer speeds than your run of the mill broadband associations. Corporate WANS additionally commonly offer boundless month to month information move limits, so you can utilize these connections as much as you can imagine without boosting costs. Improved correspondences increment proficiency as well as lift profitability.

Disposes of Need for ISDN-WANs can slash expenses by wiping out the need to lease costly ISDN circuits for telephone calls. Rather, you can have your WAN convey them. If your WAN supplier "organizes voice traffic," you likely won't perceive any drop off in voice quality, either. You may likewise profit by a lot less expensive call rates when contrasted with calls made utilizing ISDN circuits. A few organizations utilize a half and half approach. They have inbound brings come over ISDN and outbound brings go over the WAN. This methodology won't set aside you like a lot of money, yet it will even now bring down your bill.

Ensured uptime-Many WAN suppliers offer business-class support. That implies you get a particular measure of uptime month to month, quarterly, or yearly as a component of your SLA. They may likewise offer you nonstop help. Ensured uptime is a major in addition to regardless of what your industry. Let's be honest. No organization can bear to be down for any time allotment in the present business condition given the stringent requests of current clients.

Cuts costs, increment benefits-notwithstanding taking out the requirement for ISDN, WANs can enable you to cut expenses and increment benefits in a wide assortment of different ways. For instance, WANS kill or altogether decrease the expenses of social occasion groups from various workplaces in a single area. Your promoting group in the United States can work intimately with your assembling group in Germany utilizing video conferencing and email. Saving money on the movement costs alone could make putting resources into a WAN a reasonable alternative for you.

Technical support-Notwithstanding offering help for a wide assortment of utilizations and countless terminals, WANs enable organizations to grow their systems through module associations over areas and lift interconnectivity by utilizing portals, scaffolds, and switches. Besides, by bringing together organize the board and observing of utilization and execution, WANS guarantee the greatest accessibility and unwavering quality.

Disadvantages of WAN

High arrangement costs — WANs are confused and complex, so they are fairly costly to set up. Clearly, the greater the WAN, the costlier it is to set up. One reason that the arrangement expenses are high is the need to associate remote zones. In any case, by utilizing open systems, you can set up a WAN utilizing just programming (SD-WAN), which diminishes arrangement costs. Remember additionally that the value/execution proportion of WANs is preferable now over 10 years or so back.

Security Concerns — WANs open the path for particular sorts of inward security breaks, for example, unapproved use, data robbery, and malignant harm to documents. While numerous organizations have some security set up with regards to the branches, they send the majority of their security at their server farms to control and oversee data sent to their areas. This technique decreases the executives' costs yet restrains the organization's capacity to manage security breaks at their areas. A few organizations additionally experience serious difficulties compacting and quickening SSL traffic without fundamentally expanding security vulnerabilities and making new administration challenges.

Support Issues-Maintaining a WAN is a test, no uncertainty about it. Ensuring that your server farm will be up and working every minute of every day is the greatest upkeep challenge of all. Server farm supervisors must most likely distinguish disappointments before they happen and decrease server farm personal time however much as could reasonably be expected, paying little respect to the reasons.

Chapter 6: Configuration Windows servers

The accomplishment of an established development undertaking depends upon wary orchestrating got together with cautious execution. You need to start by portraying the degree of the errand with the objective you know where you're going to have to spin up. By then, you just have to develop an effort plan that includes prototype testing to adjust to the new organization and to see any future problems which may occur during most of the motion technique. In addition, a thorough assessment of your current situation is crucial to guarantee that no curve balls come in. A technique should be used to relocate current computers and professions. Eventually, once development is in progress, continuous experimentation should be carried out to guarantee that all is done as a mastermind.

Migration situations

Relocation errands including servers can be requested in different ways, dependent upon whether you are passing on another structure, refreshing or joining a present framework, or executing another establishment model, for instance, dispersed processing. In addition, advances may vary based on whether you move your entire premise or just part of it; paying little attention to whether you intend to reuse current equipment or move to fresh hardware; whether your situation is monitored or uncontrolled; regardless your current structure is large or small, bound together or encircled, heterogeneous or homogeneous; and whether it is different. With the such tremendous quantities of different strategies for envisioning and checking establishment migration stretches out, there is no single method to manage how such exercises should be masterminded and executed. In any case, there are a couple of stages and examinations that are ordinary to all relocation broadens, and observing such endorsed systems and completing They can assist guarantee the success of the excursion. I will start by describing the six necessary migration conditions for affiliates who need to overuse the latest characteristics and capabilities discovered in Windows Server 2012.

Greenfield

So far as the institution is concerned, a greenfield scheme is such that there is currently no building at all. Presume, for instance, that company X Is yet another organization beginning up which requires an on-site institution sent to work quickly. Greenfield carries on a framework that is dependent on Windows Server 2012 will join developments such as: constructing, gathering and understanding the vital context for setting up contacts, segments and distinct organizational processes. Buying the framework equipment which has been secured for Windows Server 2012.

Performing a prototype allows you to choose if the orchestrated framework will satisfy your company requirements and to guess any future problems that may arise during the carry-out. Showing your education scheme using any strategy tools you've been using. The normal favourite position of a startup motion is that it gives you the chance to get what needed to be done right from the beginning. Organizations are constantly making strides and are stationary, so giving little attention to how you are carefully considering future enhancement, you can, however, be confronted with difficulties in propelling your institution to deal with occurrences such as partnerships, purchases and sub-venture claims to reputation divisions. In conjunction, as a dose of reality, almost all of the customers of this quick start guide who are intending to update their capacity for intervention are likely to enter into company with organizations that have, in any case, one of the current Active Directory trees established and are talking about shifting them to Windows Server 2012, which is the associated implementation situation.

Boondocks update

Managers of Active Directory circumstances have by and large Be wary, or even shaky, of conducting maps updates using Adprep.exe order line utility. Introduction of each different type of Windows Server, a further instance design arises in the same way, but before that, the attempt to introduce land controllers operating a type of Windows Server for your current Active Directory has taken that you also set up your Active Directory by upgrading the system. The willingness of managers to make such changes relies, metaphorically speaking, on three issues: the method of upgrading a woodland instance using Adprep was most of the moment a stumbling block on previous variants Windows Host includes the use of a broad range of certifications to log onto unmistakable space servers, copy Adprep documents, and operate Adprep from the request line with different parameters. The more incredible the approach, the further recognizable the description of the botch is.

There is a likelihood that anything was going on may turn out severely during the mapping overhaul process, achieving degenerate timberland that anticipates that you should play out a woodlands recovery, which can be an irksome and repetitive methodology.

There was the probability that the arrangement redesign may go off well yet realize indications, for instance, adventure applications that break and never again work suitably. The endorsed approach to manage to keep up a vital good ways from such issues is to make a test circumstance that mirrors your creation condition the extent that its Active Directory design, arrange organizations, and business applications. By upgrading the organization of your test boondocks using Adprep, you would then have the option to all the more probable imagine any issues that may arise when you update the development of your age timberland

Mixed condition

As you found in the past development circumstance, existing associations that need to abuse the new limits of Windows Server 2012 can do thusly without removing their system and superseding it with another. They should just Implement computers running on Windows Server 2012 to their status and progress them as room processors. Doing it now usually recharges the recipe, and management can increase the woods and room minimalist standard to Windows Server 2012 with little fear of adversely affecting their current apps and organization. Having to pay little character to that one, however, ensure you last test your growth update and useful adjustments in the test situation that reflects your birth situation just to ensure that there will be no problems that can affect your company. In either case, many features of Windows Server 2012 can be performed in the same way as existing content taking off basic upgrades to the present boondocks, for instance, overhauling the mapping or raising the forest or space valuable levels.

Essential steps of configuring a new server

Client Configuration

The absolute first thing you're going to need to do, on the off chance that it wasn't a piece of your OS arrangement, is to change the root secret word. This ought to act naturally obvious, yet can be shockingly disregarded during a standard server arrangement. The secret word ought to be in any event 8 characters, utilizing a mix of upper and lowercase letters, numbers and images. You should likewise set up a secret word strategy that indicates maturing, locking, history and unpredictability necessities on the off chance that you are going to utilize neighborhood accounts. By and large, you should cripple the root client totally and make non-favored client accounts with sudo access for the individuals who require raised rights.

System Configuration

One of the most fundamental designs you'll have to make is to empower arrange network by doling out the server an IP address and hostname. For most servers, you'll need to utilize a static IP so customers can generally discover the asset at a similar location. On the off chance that your system utilizes VLANs, think about how disengaged the server's portion is and where it would best fit. On the off chance that you don't utilize IPv6, turn it off. Set the hostname, area and DNS server data. At least two DNS servers ought to be utilized for repetition and you should test and look up to ensure name goals is working effectively.

Bundle Management

You're setting up your new server for a particular reason, so ensure you introduce whatever bundles you may require if they aren't a piece of the dispersion you're utilizing. These could be application bundles like PHP, MongoDB, Nginx or supporting bundles like the pear. Similarly, any incidental bundles that are introduced on your framework ought to be expelled to recoil the server impression. The majority of this ought to be done through your conveyance's bundle the executives' arrangement, for example, yum or adept for simpler administration not far off.

Update Installation and Configuration

When you have the correct bundles introduced on your server, you should ensure everything is refreshed. The bundles you introduced, yet the piece and default bundles too. Except if you have a necessity for a particular variant, you ought to consistently utilize the most recent creation discharge to keep your framework secure. More often than not, your bundle the board arrangement will convey the most up to date upheld rendition. You ought to likewise consider setting up programmed refreshes inside the bundle the executives device if doing as such works for the service(s) you're facilitating on this server.

NTP Configuration

Arrange your server to match up to its opportunity to NTP servers. These could be inside NTP servers if your condition has those, or outside time servers that are accessible for anybody. What's significant is to avoid clock float, where the server's clock slants from the genuine time. This can cause a lot of issues, including confirmation issues where time slant between the server and the validating framework is estimated before allowing access. This ought to be a straightforward change, yet it's a basic piece of a solid foundation.

Firewalls and iptables

Contingent upon your circulation, iptables may as of now be secured and expect you to open what you need, yet paying little mind to the default configuration, you ought to consistently investigate it and ensure it's set up how you need. Make sure to consistently utilize the guideline of least benefit and just open those ports you completely required for the administrations on that server. If your server is behind a committed firewall or some likeness thereof, make certain to deny everything except for what's vital there too. Accepting your firewall IS prohibitive as a matter of course;

remember to open up what you require for your server to carry out its responsibility.

Verifying SSH

SSH is the fundamental remote access strategy for Linux circulations and all things considered ought to be appropriately verified. You should cripple root's capacity to SSH in remotely, regardless of whether you handicapped the record with the goal that just if there should arise an occurrence of root gets empowered on the server for reasons unknown despite everything it won't be exploitable remotely. You can likewise confine SSH to certain IP ranges on the off chance that you have a fixed arrangement of customer IPs that will interface. Alternatively, you can change the default SSH port to "darken" it, yet truly, a basic sweep will uncover the new open port to any individual who needs to discover it. At long last, you can impair secret key validation through and through and use declaration based confirmation to lessen considerably further the odds of SSH abuse.

Daemon Configuration

You've tidied up your bundles, but at the same time, it's critical to set the correct applications to auto-start on reboot. Make certain to mood killer any daemons you needn't bother with. One key to a safe server is lessening the dynamic impression however much as could be expected so the main surface territories accessible for the assault are those required by the application(s). When this is done, outstanding administrations ought to be solidified however much as could be expected to guarantee versatility.

SELinux and Further Hardening

On the off chance that you've at any point utilized a Red Hat distro, you may be comfortable with SELinux, the portion solidifying apparatus that shields the framework from different activities. SELinux is extraordinary at ensuring against unapproved use and access to framework assets. It's likewise extraordinary at breaking applications, so ensure you test your setup out with SELinux empowered and utilize the logs to ensure nothing real is being blocked.

Logging

At long last, you should ensure that the degree of logging you need is empowered and that you have adequate assets for it. You will wind up investigating this server, so help yourself out now and manufacture the logging structure you'll have to tackle issues rapidly. Most programming has configurable logging, however, you'll require some experimentation to locate the correct harmony between insufficient data and to an extreme. There are a large group of outsider logging instruments that can help including collection to perception, yet every condition should be considered for its needs first. At that point, you can discover the tool(s) that will enable you to fill them.

Every single one of these means can set aside some effort to actualize, particularly the first run through around. Be that as it may, by setting up a daily schedule of beginning server design, you can guarantee that new machines in your condition will be versatile. Inability to make any of these strides can prompt truly genuine results if your server is ever the objective of an assault. Tailing them won't ensure wellbeing - information breaks occur however it makes it undeniably progressively hard for pernicious on-screen characters and will require some level of ability to survive.

Advantages of having servers

A server offers you a mess of dependability. A server, then again, is a powerful answer for such a significant issue. Server equipment keeps up excess equipment to handle these issues at minute's notice.

In such cases, the disappointment of one gadget doesn't ensure the disappointment of the whole server framework. In this way, it can keep on serving your business with full zeal even after the disappointment of an unimportant little related gadget, in contrast to your interlinked PCs. Dependability you needed, the unwavering quality you'll get.

A server furnishes your business with system security

This can be viewed as truly outstanding and most critical advantages of a server. By making the recognized gathering and individual records, an individual right can be relegated to clients dependent on the nature and measure of information they can access based on their necessities. This can cut down unapproved information access, all things considered and can give your system extra security that you had hungered for previously. On the off chance that you have a business group and an HR group in your organization, both would not have the option to get to the information of each other regardless of whether the whole information is available on a solitary server.

A server gives your business a consistent remote openness

A Windows 2008 server would give you the alternative to have 2 remote clients on its system simultaneously of course. What's more, it likewise offers you the chance to include the same number of remote clients you need sooner rather than later through Remote Desktop allowance. Hence, land boundaries stop to be an issue any longer. Your laborers will most likely work remotely and access records on your server at whatever point they need any place they are. They would likewise have the option to get to their organization messages from any internet browser on their particular gadgets at whatever point they need from anyplace on the planet.

A server furnishes your business with a brought together reinforcement office

Information misfortunes happen generally in working environments for a few reasons running from machine disappointments to indiscretion. These things make tremendous issues particularly when the work environment works without a server. A server can be viewed as a gift in this angle since it helps a great deal in smoothing up your information reinforcement process. You will almost certainly back up the entirety of your information including your messages to unified capacity on your server and lessen every one of the problems related with information misfortunes subsequently, improving your work environment efficiency simultaneously.

A server framework helps in legitimate infection the board

Perhaps the best danger looked by your system is a conceivable infection or spyware disease. Consequently, an antivirus framework is an outright need nowadays. A server framework can help a ton in advantageous infection the executives. The framework director will almost certainly send the counter infection programming from a solitary PC to every workstation PC associated on the system, run a system-wide filter in general (counting the gadgets associated on the WiFi system) and evacuate a wide range of infections assuming any. So you can see that this accommodation is fundamentally unrivaled. Because of the minimized server framework, the whole infection the executives' procedure should be possible from a solitary PC itself. Continuously recollect that costs caused in making a server-based system aren't only an expense. It's speculation; a contribute having high ROI particularly when your independent company adventure is concerned. It's certainly going to profit you over the long haul.

Disadvantages' of having a server

1. High Costs

The most evident point about having a Server-based system is the expanded expense. Servers are substantially more costly than PC's to gain and you should become accustomed to expanded costs for Server-based programming as well.

Servers don't keep going forever and are commonly repetitive following 5 years for everything except the most essential of capacities. Windows and Mac Servers are authorized 'per client' so as you increment the quantity of staff, these organizations will need their offer as well! Servers do require ordinary checking, refreshing, and observing. All things considered, you should attempt changes in clients, consents, email locations and this may require some itemized IT information. Also, if Servers turn out badly, they will be in all respects expensive to fix. While producers regularly offer sensibly estimated equipment guarantees, they will wash their hands of any issue with the Software (regardless of whether brought about by the equipment issue) and as specially appointed IT to bolster will rapidly include, numerous associations structure some sort of agreement with their Server providers/installers. This bodes well as the organization that introduced your framework ought to be in a decent position to have the option to look after it. Hope to pay a noteworthy sum may be significantly more than you paid for the establishment - for a complete help contract.

2. Single-purpose of disappointment

In concentrating your documents and programming in the way portrayed above, you can't abstain from making a solitary purpose of disappointment in your system. If somebody takes or loses the way to your sparkling new

'focal file organizer' your work will endure colossally. While a critical level of the expense of procuring a Server goes towards enhancing the dangers of disappointment, the probability of noteworthy 'down-time' is consistently there. A consistently observed reinforcement framework, RAID cluster, and an uninterruptible power supply (UPS) ought to be considered as an absolute minimum, however and, after it's all said and done blackouts of different sorts can and do occur.

3. Progress

The procedure of progress from a non-server system to a Server-based one can be inconvenient what's more, is sure to include disturbance to PC clients just as changes in the manner they work. This is particularly the situation with a Windows-based Server, as the connection among PC's and Servers in a Windows domain rotates around a client account which will be not quite the same as the one you at present use. At the very least, this involves moving work area settings just like records, top picks and perhaps email to the new account and may even include reinstalling or reconfiguring printers, antivirus programming, and different projects as well. When getting ready for another Server at that point, it is imperative to separate the highlights and programming you should have in this new condition. The disturbance caused to your staff and different clients is best limited by keeping them educated on how things may change. This can be a significant tedious and needs somebody inside your association with some IT learning to deal with it effectively.

4. Nature of help

Disengaging the reason for a given issue is one of the most troublesome parts of ICT support. When an individual from staff can't get an email for instance, would they say they are accomplishing something incorrectly? Is there a major issue with their PC? Is there a system issue? Is it an issue with the

Server? Maybe the ISP is to blame? Or then again even the facilitating organization? Adding a Server to your system includes layers of multifaceted nature and is sure to befuddle these issues. It is essential then that you approach great quality, far-reaching and educated ICT support. The provider ought to be equipped for diagnosing and settling issues at any of these levels to stay away from the bad dream of 'buck-going' between various organizations. Such help can be costly and laden with hazy areas where duty is vague. Ensure you read the agreement!

Conclusion

Thank you for making it through to the end of the Computer Networking course. I hope that it was informative and able to provide you with all the basic tools you need to achieve your goals.

The next step is to take note of what you read and put it into practice. In this case, you will now be able to explain and tell what needs you may be required in terms of networking. You are now able to explain the terms and also knowledgeable about how things work. Some of the things that you have learned include the Wireless networks, system models and also Addresses and IPs. You have further learned on the internet, including the history of the internet, and also the pros and cons that it has brought about in the world.

Did you know the details on storage architecture? Well, now you know more on these and also network-attached storage, storage area network, as well as, tape and tape libraries. Further, you have been enlightened about data patterns and virtualization architecture. This book has given you great and detailed content on TCP and implementation. This include's, layers of TCP, the benefits and also details on the Round Trip Time.

The author has taken you through the details of planning a network. In these, you have gotten the skills on; Organization set up, strategy and culture, options analysis as well as implementation. Network topology has been broken down as well as the design tools.

I believe that this book has enlightened you on the WAN. This includes the point to point services, bundle switched services, the fiber connectivity, and you have also learned the advantages and disadvantages of WAN.

Finally, the author has discussed on the configuration windows server. You have learned step by step the essential steps of configuring a new server.

Finally, if you found this book useful in any way, a review on Amazon is always appreciated!

Computer Networking Beginners Guide

What is the computer network and how to learn it in a simple way?

The Easy step by step Guide for beginners

Introduction

Congratulations on purchasing this book, Computer Networking Beginners Guide: What is the computer network and how to learn it in a simple way?

The Easy step by step Guide for beginners, and thank you for doing so.

The internet has turn into a crucial part of our life in the 21st century. The technology has been integrated with our means of living. For most of us, we start our day by checking e-mails and reading or streaming the news on websites, pay bills through our smartphone's apps and we can navigate our bank accounts better now more than ever with online banking. E-commerce has come a long way. As consumers, we now have the ability to purchase almost anything within our fingertips. We also have the ability to research products, read and provide reviews, and look for the best possible deal. For businesses, this means that they now have the ability for a farther reach. Through e-commerce, small businesses now have a better chance of competing with bigger companies, in getting their products to their target market.

Most schools have incorporated the internet to everyone's advantage. Aside from online portals where students can access school-related materials, teachers can now also communicate with the parents or guardians through email, bridging more connections instead of missed phone calls. A good number of universities, colleges, and trade schools are now offering Distance Education; which is focused on non-traditional students (mostly students who, for any reason, cannot physically attend a class at all times), classes are done via web-stream and student web portals. The end result ranges from a class credit to a certificate, diploma, a bachelor's degree, even a post graduate degree.

Perhaps the most influential contribution the internet has provided is social media. Through it, it somehow made our world a bit smaller, most of us closer. Facebook has reconnected us with our childhood friends, dear relatives we haven't seen in a while, and it has given most of us a way to be connected to our line of interests through groups. Twitter started with only 160 characters per post, since we have the choice on who to follow, we can curate our timeline and be informed of what interests us. The symbol # is WAS more commonly known as the number sign, or pound sign. Today's generation can recognize the sign better as "hashtag". A symbol that has the ability to catapult a topic or a person to the limelight or at least to people's online radar. Social media has become an industry on its own.

Gone are the days when the internet was thought was viewed to be a luxury or a "craze that will fade away". The technology has become so integrated with our lives that the United Nations made a declaration on 2011 that internet access as an important component of a basic human right.

Computer networking is an essential framework for the internet to work for most of us. The tech term can be overwhelming for some, but it exists in almost every home, offices, businesses and establishment that is connected to the internet.

In this book, we will discuss the most basic principles behind computer networking without the complexities of technical jargon (technical terms will be explained). Visual representations will be provided to expound on the technical concepts.

This book is written for anyone who wants an introductory course on computer networking, which is basically what is needed if you want to create a simple home network or office computer network.

Chapter 1: What is Computer Networking

What is networking?

The term "networking" is, by all means, to exchange information or the action or process of interacting with others.

What is Computer Networking?

Computer Networking may sound intimidating or can be overwhelming at first, but the advancements in technology have gone a long way. The graphical user interface (GUI) has become simpler for most operating systems (OS) making it easier to understand and navigate through.

Network is a set of computers connected together with common objective of sharing resources and those resources can be the internet, a printer, or a file server.

Computing is the process of utilizing computer technology to complete a task and the task can be as simple as swiping a credit card or making a call or sending an email. Computing involves the use of computer systems like a laptop, a smartphone, a desktop computer, or even an ATM, basically almost any other smart electronic device.

Computer network involves the use of computers for computing and telecommunication technology like telephone lines, wireless radio links for transmitting the processed data over long distances so the computer network is said to be evolved at the interface of telecommunications and computing.

The first computer that appeared was a TA (terminal adapter) network in a joint geographically distributed computers to each other that word area network is now more commonly known as the internet.

Network is a collection of computers linked together with the goal of allocating resources and those resources can be the internet, a printer, or a file server.

Computing is the process of utilizing computer technology to complete a task and the task can be as simple as swiping a credit card or making a call or sending an email. Computing involves the use of computer systems like a laptop, a smartphone, a desktop computer, or even an ATM, basically almost any other smart electronic device.

Computer network involves the use of computers for computing and telecommunication technology like telephone lines, wireless radio links for transmitting the processed data over long distances so the computer network is said to be evolved at the interface of telecommunications and computing.

The first computer that appeared was a TA network in a joint geographically distributed computers to each other that word area network is now more commonly known as the internet.

Wi-Fi

The word Wi-Fi is derived from the term "wireless fidelity". This type of connection is particularly useful for laptops, smartphones, and other mobile devices that may come and go. Wi-Fi networks rely on a wireless access point through which all traffic must flow the Wireless Access Point creates an area around it known as a hotspot. The Wireless Access Point is effectively a substitute for the backbone cable. If the wireless access point is connected to another network. For example, a much larger wired network or even the internet then it is known as a router.

Local Area Network (LAN)

The computers and other devices are geographically close together with this . This means that computers are usually are in the same town or the same city. In fact, computers in this kind of setup are usually on the same site. For example, all of the computers in an office or all of the computers on campus. Desktop computers in a LAN are usually connected via cable but if there are laptop users as well, then it can possibly connect using W-Fi. One of the biggest advantages of using LAN is it can be used only by the people who are allowed to use it. It is private and secure.

Wide Area Network

This type of network works on a much bigger scale than a LAN. The computers are geographically remote. The network might span an entire city, a country. The devices on the web are usually connected using leased telecommunication lines or satellite links. Signals on WAN will probably be encrypted but it is still less secure than a LAN.

Servers

These are the most powerful computers on a network. They allow the users to share files, applications and peripheral devices. Servers authenticate users to the network when they log on, they have to type in a username and password. Servers can provide email services, can also host private websites known as intranets.

What is not a Computer Network?

Stand-alone computer, which is not connected to any other computers

May have peripheral devices connected like a printer but it cannot communicate with any other computers.

Computers on a network are often referred to as workstations.

For a setup like a peer-to-peer network the ensemble of computers have equal status or no server or if all the workstations share files and peripheral devices, they can all be thought of as servers.

Connections between devices on a network can be made using radio signals, this is known as Wi-Fi network.

Advantages of stand-alone computers
· No reliance on servers for files and peripherals
· Faster access to local files
· No need to logon

- More secure than network computers
- Cheaper than network computers

Advantages of networked computers
- Can share files, peripheral devices and even applications
- Communication services such as email and web pages
- Easy to install software onto workstations from a central location
- Easy to set up new users and peripheral devices
- Roaming users can access their own files and settings from anywhere
- Users can have different levels of access to shared resources

Disadvantages of networked computers
- Can be expensive to set up and manage
- Requires specialist skills to keep running
- If the network stops, it may not be possible to access shared resources
- Difficult to secure from hackers or even industrial espionage
- Performance degrades as traffic increases, unless well designed

Chapter 2: History of the Internet

It can be mind-boggling, and anyone can get curious easily as to how we have arrived at a present time where almost countless number of computing devices are all linked together via this extraordinary framework that we all know as the internet. Starting at the initial efforts at organizing computers to function together up to the contemporary inventions like social media networks and video conferences that can be accessed easily, the history and journey of the internet has come a long way.

The design and process making stage took decades to achieve a balanced nature of both software and hardware technology, so this part of the discussion is not going to focus on each single influential inventor and apparatus but we will focus and shed more light on a number of essential design proposals and pivotal moments that have taken the internet technology to this day.

It has been 75 years since World War II and the public has been trying to facilitate to have computers to work together since these days.
This is during a period when computing devices are described to be as huge and awkward - looking equipment that was only capable of solving complex mathematical problems, nothing more than that.

Richard Feynman, a physicist, led a team that was able to formulate an avenue to solve a big batch of mathematical problems simultaneously. Efficiency was also being advocated during this period, whenever a computing device is not at work, they had it use and delegate it to work on a separate section of a different problem. One mathematical problem might take months to get solved but at the same time, they could also finish multiple math equations in the same period. Whenever they are faced with a critical calculation, they utilized the systems concurrently to do the same problem numerous amounts of times.

This was their means of quality control and be certain of the final answer, even a couple of computing devices are capable of having mistaken once in a while.

Colleges have begun segregating their computer terminals during the early 1950s and 60s. This is when some would experiment programs onto the computers directly. By separating their computer terminals, it made it almost effortless for some to play around and do some trials on new computing devices while safeguarding the circuits and tubes off from tampering.

It can be compared or somehow similar structure of our present day's cloud computing, complicated tasks are being sent away to be worked on by computing machines that are located somewhere else. In order for the modern cloud computing to function, it is essential to have an internet connection for it to work unlike in 1960 when it wasn't the case.

ARPA or the advance Research Project Agency was created by the Department of Defense of the US (today the agency is called Defense Advanced Research Project Agency or DARPA), its goal is to retain its advancement of technology more advanced than the Soviets. Joseph Licklider, who is a renowned American psychologist and computer scientist, took an important role by helping to persuade ARPA to allocate budget for computer network research by bringing together engineers and computer scientists across the country. A number of colleges signed on with the project and in 1969 the construction of the framework was initiated by ARPA. The name ARPANET was given to the technological infrastructure. The network was first of its kind during this period. Though it started small-scale, it functions as a means of messaging service across computers at various universities like the University of Utah, UC Santa Barbara, Stanford University and UCLA.

Engineers kept on increasing the features and their ability to solve problems as the ARPANET continues to expand over the next few decades. Some of these innovations have influenced the manner of what we do online to this day. Packet switching is one of the first major modification done by ARPANET.

[Backstory: In the old days, as you can also see in movies set in the olden times, whenever a person wants to get in touch with somebody via the phone, the first step is to dial and reach a switchboard. Phones during this period could only work because of circuit switching - only when there is a single uninterrupted circuit available can a signal get from one point to another; this is the reason why operators were needed for this form of communication to work. An operator is responsible to move and connect cables from one phone's port into the wire from another one. The idea behind circuit switching is good only if two points are connected for an extended period of time, most landlines still work through this method except today there is no need for operators since circuit switching can be done automatically.]

It would be unwise and unattainable for the internet to perform as how circuit switching did decades ago. If this were the case today - it would take an enormous amount of time for a computer to connect to another digital device and to repeat the process all over. Fortunately, websites of today are capable of connecting a user to computers across the group, up to 10 computers at a time. Simultaneously while monitoring and connecting countless of visitors all at once, it is important that all of these computers respond immediately whenever a user clicks on it. So, in this made-up scenario, it just would not work because of the circuits that are scattered all over the place, it would always be jerking around and connecting to a point for a millisecond before getting disconnected and be misplaced and connected somewhere else.

Computer engineers were made aware as early as the 1960s that computers are capable of sending messages in a far speedy way in order for circuit switching to be practical. Engineers found a way to solve this and invented a substitute way: packet switching, where various computing devices can dispatch messages within the constant set of wires rather than obtaining each separately.

A message called the packet is dispatched within the wires is the method of how to communicate with each other. The address label was assigned to each and every packet.

A set of numbers characterizing the computer where it was going to. The computing device where it began would search the address on a table that contains all the addresses within the network and then dispatches the packet to the nearest computer to the destination. That second computer would receive the packet, search the destination address, and again dispatch the packet to the correct path. This process would be repeated until the packet ultimately reaches its destination. In this process, there was no need to move circuits or wires, it was simultaneous.

The packets of ARPANET moved through phone lines and have utilized packet switching since the beginning. The technology performed as to how it was designed. However, as the year progresses, there were challenges that were encountered along the way.

The number of computers across the country that has joined was surprising. Every computer was somehow required to keep up with the updates list of computer addresses, this is the result of how the packet switching was initially designed. If a computer has failed to update its list, it might receive the packets but may not know the correct patch where to dispatch or forwards it to an address that does not exist anymore. As time went by, it was no longer surprising as to how the network structure kept getting vaster by the minute. There were instances when a computer's address might possibly be altered if it temporarily detaches itself from the network or there was a malfunction within a connection. If the updates were not done fast enough, some computers could end up with different and incorrect address books.

Stanford University was selected by the ARPANET's engineering team as a formal record-keeper of addresses back in 1973. ARPANET has resolved to move on from the problematic system and wanted to keep it more organized. The effectivity of ARPANET's solution has resulted in an increase, with only sixty computers before 1975 that number grew to more than a hundred computing devices by late 1977.

ARPANET was able to stretch its reach to Hawaii from California via satellites. This was remarkable since Hawaii was once considered to be an isolated place at time. ARPANET went further its reach by extending its infrastructure and placed networks in Norway and England.

Comparable networks began to appear across the world, some became more competitive since some had more computing capabilities on them. Around the mid-seventies, the market share was no longer solely owned by ARPANET. During this period, the packets were formatted differently by each company, as a result even though a user could connect and work with various networks together, it was not functioning as it was originally planned.

The problem at hand was not ironed out until 1974, however, it wasn't until the first part of the eighties when

ARPANET and the majority of the networks began utilizing it.

A series of rules named Transmission Control Protocol / Internet Protocol or TCP/IP, which is still being utilized up to this day was the solution that was designed.

The Transmission Control Protocol is a means to standardize how packets were being formatted, in order to have uniformity with how everyone was communicating using the same "language". Internet Protocol is the definitive method of allocating addresses, this is to avoid any error on where the packets should be directed. By the time when both networks began using TCP/IP, communicating and connecting across networks became uncomplicated. The entire existing networks in operations were interconnected, as a result, forming what became recognized as the - INTERNET, with ARPANET as the backbone of it all.

The record-keepers at Stanford began getting overwhelmed with the workload as a result of how fast ARPANET was thriving and needing to connect to various networks at the same time. There was a constant need to update the address book and download its most recent version because of the ever-changing addresses brought by number of hosts that repeatedly joined. In some cases, there were botched communication across the network as a result of the errors in the Stanford list.

In 1971 another form of communication was invented, the email. Two years after it was invented, seventy-five percent of ARPANET's entire packets were comprised of emails. Computers had various email programs during this period, a table of every computer it would pass through across the sender and the receiver; were sometimes required.

During this period, computer users had to have an up to date map of the entirety of the network handy with them. It was necessary for them to key in the path of the email in order for them to send it. The growing number of computers that were on ARPANET, at this point within hundreds and over a thousand that were on the internet, sustaining the most recent maps and its information were becoming a hopeless task.

The engineers of ARPANET have figured out that the total infrastructure of the internet had to be systematically coordinated. The Domain Name System was a part of their solution. The hosts were classified into domains, rather than dichotomizing every host and saving its address in a casual order.

Initially, the domains that were classified as top-level arrived. Email addresses are now ending with either ".com" and ``.edu" . Before there was DNS, the way to send an email was just to type in "sam@example" but the new top-level domains meant in order to send an email, the address should be written with an extension like "sam@example.com". Second-level domain was called within each host, for example, "ucla.edu" means the second-level domain is ucla" while the top-level is ".edu". The domain infrastructure has standardized and coordinated all those various hosts across the globe in such a manner that computers could deal with. The DNS's sole responsibility is to keep an account of all addresses and connections; this adds an entirely different network to the internet.

How it works is a computer that lies on the new network adequately saves all the addresses within the dot-com top-level domain. A separate computer has all the dot-edu addresses. Another independent computer houses all the dot-org, and that is how the system works. Other computing devices have the ability to jointly charted out the complete network. As a result, whenever a user wants to send an email, it is no longer required to refer to the map and chart out all the required connections by the user. That has been the purpose of the DNS.

At the onset, they just preferred a couple of dependable interconnected computing devices, but it resulted in performing as the foundation of a universal network of a high number of companies, government, and universities all communication with each other. It was determined to put a closure on the ARPANET project, it was a necessity for them to discover a replacement that will take charge of all the infrastructure, someone to manage the internet.

Big questions came up immediately:
With all this power, can anyone be trusted with it?
Can the general public still have access to the internet which by itself is a massive and perplexing system?

A few companies began to market access to the networks by the 1970s, this is almost the first glimpse into the future of internet use.

The users had the ability to do almost everything; from sending emails, to playing games, chatting on instant messaging programs, and even checking weather reports. However, these were standalone networks and were not attached to the main network that was the internet. It was as good as it gets.

On some that works like Compu Serve, Micronet users had the luxury of reading the news at the comfort of their home via their computers.

During that period those networks were as great as it could for its end-users. However, it still had its limitations, the availability of Micronet was only during the nights and weekends - this is when most businesses that usually utilize the CompuServe's networks are not in operation.

Since they were not precisely interconnected with each other or to the wider internet, it was comparable to being isolated islands.

During the eighties, regardless of the size or expansion of the privatized networks, they were still restricted to be "on the internet".

ARPANET and other founding networks consist of the foundation of the internet was funded and managed by the government, hence any other organizations like universities and private businesses that were permitted to use the network were not authorized to conduct any commercial traffic within the network.

The internet was permitted to be used to download data or send an email of a thesis or a report to your cohorts, but it was not permitted to use for the promotion of a new product and certainly were not permitted to demand payment from the general public to come online. The internet was initially meant for research and development and not for commercialization.

It came to appear that the National Science Foundation's huge network - NSFNET to be the best option to take over the responsibilities from ARPANET and be in charge of the internet. It began in 1986 and expanded rapidly following the connection to ARPANET that within that year, it warranted a considerable number of upgrades to manage all the new traffic.

By the year 1990, NSFNET formally took over ARPANET as the internet's foundation, along with it came its approximately half a million end users. Prior to ARPANET being removed from the scene, a few private companies were connecting members of the general public to the internet.

Initially, NSFNET had a procedure in place regarding forbidding commercial traffic on its network. This policy has changed by 1988 when they have concluded to allow a number of private network's email server to connect to the NSFNET.

In 1989, the first commercial email could be sent across the internet by the users of Compu Serve and MCI Mail - an email service.

In the same year, the first Internet Service Providers (ISP) came to the scene. These were private companies that typically do not own any network, they just facilitate the connection of their customers to the internet and to a local network.

In between the late eighties and early nineties, there were a number of internet service providers that presented various service options from one another; there was an option available that just offers email service, some other options were their privately-owned network that was partially connected to the internet and some presented internet access but with the absence of their own online community. By 1995, ARPANET has ceased its operations for good and transitioned the entire operations to the ISPs.

In the first part of the nineties, for someone to connect to the network, the computer needs a modem in order to place a phone call to the network, the job of the modem is to translate or decode the signals being used by the computer an by the telephone. Computers were utilizing digital signal whilst the landline phone was working on analog signals. The next step is the computer would try to communicate with another set of computers that are on the network by means of the phone lines connecting them. This method of getting online is better known as the dial-up connection. In comparison to how fast our internet works today, the dial-up connection can be described as extremely slow. However, during that time when this was the only method of getting online, it does the job pretty well. Phone lines were active and had a broad coverage across the country when ARPANET came to the scene, it became a logical and cost-efficient decision to utilize the existing phone lines rather than attempting to create something entirely new or invent something else from the ground up. A major factor as to why the dial-up connection was ultra-slow is the existing limitation of how fast a user can compress data down into a phone line. To be able to dispatch and transmit a good amount of data, what is needed is a signal with a categorically high frequency, this means it can quickly change. An extreme high-pitched sound is needed in order for a signal to be sent down through the phone lines. When phone lines were first invented and engineered, it was meant for the phone communications - phone calls. It was not designed to manage the type of signal that the dial-up connection does have. Whenever a modem establishes a connection to a network, its first task is to monitor the signal with the highest frequency that the wires could possibly manage to handle, then it decelerates the channel of ones and zeroes heading from the computer down to that speed.

When the first batch of internet service providers arrived on the scene, the internet could be described as a bit different than it is today. A major reason behind this is the fact that in 1989 the Web was not in existence yet, more so as a single website. Though a lot of people today have been using the terms "internet" and "web" interchangeably, these two words actually are different from one another. It was a decade later until the Web was introduced to the market.

The term "internet" is derived from "internetworking", the word came about during the seventies to specify the connecting of the tangible cables and computing devices altogether. The concept behind the internet originated with it being designed as a method of accessing computers, sharing files and programs remotely.

It was getting more challenging to maneuver and move across the network despite knowing where you are supposed to go, this was a direct result of the growing internet community. In 1989, Tim Berners-Lee, a scientist, along with some assistance from his cohort Robert Caillou began on a more efficient avenue to organize all that data. Tim Berners-Lee is frequently attributed as the one who invented the web. Berners-Lee had a big concept to systematize and somehow deflate the multi-branch structure. Rather than having each file being placed separately on its own remote branch, any file could direct the user to other similar or related data files in other for the user to seamlessly navigate one place to the next. There was only one tool that Berners-Lee had in mind that could take this task and it was the - HYPERTEXT.

In the sixties, a protocol called the Hypertext was invented as a means of navigating from one section of a document to a different part, when more users began to utilize it to connect various documents. By the eighties, it was assimilated into majority of programs being used. Berners-Lee incorporated the hypertext in the web developing process and made it the primary method of navigating the web which was later referred to as the "World Wide Web".

Because of hyperlinks' ability to connect and ease the navigation through web pages, the web was definitely a sensation at CERN (the European Organization for Nuclear Research). In 1993, web technology was made available to the general public; the last crucial piece of the internet technology of today was put in place.

The concept of utilizing the hypertext protocol is the basis behind most websites having URL that begins with "HTTP" or "HTTPS" (its secured version). HyperText Transfer Protocol is the set of rules, standards, and procedures that are being utilized to inspect and decode files that contains a hyperlink.

The ::// is a method of presenting to the system what is coming up next and "www" is sign that tells the user that the page is a part of the World Wide Web.

New assortments of programs have emerged to open these contemporary hyperlinked web pages. The specifics of each program rely on what the user needs or wants - these were the previous versions of web browsers. The year was 1994 and a browser called - the Netscape was initially launched. The code for this browser was ultimately integrated into another browser which most internet users of today might be familiar with - Firefox. During this time, both the internet and web ultimately partnered up and became easily available and attainable for the public; as a result, the tally of computers utilizing the internet has surged exceedingly.

Due to the sudden increase of computer users in the nineties, during this decade, investments worth billions were cascaded into internet-based startup enterprises.

Investors riled up behind companies like eToys.com, govWorks and WorldCom - a majority of these companies took a hard fall and had to file for bankruptcy by the end of the decade, this is around the same time when ".com bubble" have popped and went out.

The web of the mid to late nineties was a bit like the Wild West, it was a huge new world of people and companies popping up everywhere you looked, and it seemed like there was plenty of room for everyone to have a piece of the pie. A lot of wealthy investors started piling money into companies without worrying about whether they were making a profit or even if they had many customers. The mentality of some during this period was: that being on the internet, old rules for being cautious about investing in young companies did not apply and more, and that all anyone needed was a good idea and enough money to reach an audience.

This period did not last as long as everyone wanted, and what is known as ".com bubble" started bursting in March of 2000. Stocks in tech companies plummeted for the next couple of years, over half of them declared bankruptcy, eventually losing trillions of dollars in total as an industry.

A couple of famous court cases against Microsoft and the music-downloading service Napster put new boundaries on what companies could do with the internet. Napster had been one of the fastest-growing businesses in the tech history, but it went bankrupt paying back musicians for copyright infringement. Microsoft, on the other hand, narrowly avoided being dissolved after violating antitrust laws.

Another one of the ".com bubble" casualties was GeoCities, one of the first social networking sites. Today's web is flooded with social networking, most of us would not be able to imagine going through a day or at the minimum a week without checking at least one social media site. Today, just about every website constantly encourages everyone to use their personal profiles and share everything they see with everyone they know. But things were different back in 1994, when GeoCities first came online. The first websites of the nineties mostly had a clear divide between creators and users. Creators - they wrote the computer code and assembled different documents and files and hyperlinks and pictures that made the website what it was. Users - they just visited the website and looked at whatever the creators had put on there. GeoCities worked on a different model. Anyone and everyone could make a GeoCities account and create their own website, with all their own stuff and formatting and backgrounds and interests. GeoCities mixed together users and creators because everyone with an account was both at the same time. Its users could also send each other messages and joins communities of pages with similar topics and interests, creating a whole section of the site that focused on just about everything imaginable. Its 19 million users made GeoCities the third most popular site on the web in 1999 behind AOL and Yahoo!. The latter bought GeoCities that same year for 3.6 billion dollars, but it fell on hard times during the ".com bubble" crash and has never managed to regain its former glory again. Yahoo! finally shut down most of GeoCities back in 2009 when it had long-since been surpassed by other sites that took the idea of social networking and ran with it. GeoCities gave way to some sites that pretty much everyone can easily recognize today. Friendster launched in 2002 giving each user their own profile and a way of seeing different networks of friends on the site. It quickly became popular, with three million accounts in its first three months. But it was plagued by technical troubles and after a couple of years, it had fewer users than Myspace, which was itself passed in 2008 by Facebook. The number of active users of Facebook has reached almost 2 billion and that number just keeps going up. But it is far from being the only social media site out there today - there's Reddit, Twitter, Tumblr, LinkedIn, YouTube, not even counting all the Disqus comments sections and Digg share buttons and WordPress blogs all over the web - all of these sites, big or small are descended from GeoCities: the first site mix users and creators in a completely new way of using the internet.

Most people still use dial-up to get online in the heydays of GeoCities and Friendster. By the time Myspace took over around 2005, there was something new on the market. Instead of using dial-up, most people had switched over to broadband. Since dial-up has a built-in speed limit, because of how phone lines were made, the fastest dial-up connection could only receive or transmit about 56 kilobits per second. To put that into perspective, that's about 56,000 ones and zeros in or out of the computer every second. With a dial-up speed, downloading a sing song off Napster would take about ten minutes, even at top speed. Downloading a whole movie could take days. Even just loading a site with a few images took a long time. Since the internet was getting more and more popular, companies came up with better ways of getting online that were not so limited.

Like DSL, which transmits digital data along phone lines instead of analog signals like dial-up does; and cable internet, which uses the wires for a cable box to connect to the internet. These newer technologies came to be known as broadband, which is really a broad term for all the ways of getting online that are not dial-up. Depending on the type of broadband, the connections can be tens or hundreds or even thousands of times faster than dial-up is. People started using broadband in the early 2000s, and in 2005 it overtook dial-up as the most popular way Americans got online.

With more people on faster connections, it was no longer a big of a deal for sites to have lots of images or even video being displayed. However, all the data on those sites needed to be stored somewhere. Another legacy of the ".com bubble" is the place of Data Center in today's internet, where hundreds of computers work together for a single company to give users a better and faster experience. The earliest computers could be big enough to take up entire rooms, but those dedicated computer rooms stuck around in a lot of places even as computers for smaller and faster. A sample set up would be like - ten computers, all connected together to act like one big computer with the combined speed and memory of all ten. Lots of the earlier startups needed computer space to store all their data and computer speed to handle all the user traffic in their websites - data centers were perfect for this job. Instead of owning, powering cooling, and maintaining your own computers, and reliably connecting all of them together and to the internet, you could just pay a data center to manage this job. Today's websites have more than a hundred and fifty times as much data on them as they did in 1995, and a lot of that information comes from these data centers that could be in a room or building or whole complexes full of computers. Today's web relies on these huge collections of computers to work like we all expect it to. Because of all the speed and storage available today, websites can now do things they could never have back in 1995.

After the ".com bubble" have gone away, the incident has paved the way for a tamer and steadier web in its wake. Few well-run companies could quietly become empires.

Startups like Google, Amazon, and Facebook began to grow as giant corporations and have started to dominate the market, they have their hands on just about everything you can do online - from search, to advertising, to storage, just to name a few. These websites get about 600 million visitors a year, with hundreds of millions more seeing their ads or using their apps.

Whenever you browse a website like YouTube, even if you're not signed in, you're the only one in the world who sees that exact same YouTube homepage, with those exact recommended videos. This is probably because no one has watched the same video you have, in the same order, for the same amount of time, from the same places in the world - all the stuff that YouTube uses to choose what to recommend. This is similar to when you see banner ads everywhere for products you were just looking at Amazon. Just about everywhere on the web has this sort of algorithmic filtering, where the website decides on what you are probably interested in and shows you more stuff like that. Data centers don't just store all the website's data; they run special programs to look through that data and use information that they have saved about you to decide what you want to see, buy or whatever you might be interested next. Figuring out what you want to see can involve tracking you around the internet. A lot of people have been worried about their privacy - especially because some companies are not shy about selling what they learn about people to the highest bidder. It seems like every day there is another news story about people being tracked around the internet in a similar way.

In a little over fifty years, the internet's grown from four computers to billions. From having connected just within the United States now onto every continent and even into outer space. We can say it is still new and it is still evolving. One thing is for sure, it is exciting what the technology of the future holds for us.

Chapter 3: Components of a Computer Network

Internet Technology

Broadband Cable Internet

Cable internet is a high-speed access technology which utilizes a cable modem with an attached coaxial cable which provides a link to the internet service provider (ISP). Broadband cable is commonly furnished by the same provider that lends cable television to their customer. Because it is provided by cable television providers, broadband cable leverages on the existing infrastructure from cable TV to cover large geographical areas, especially here in the United States. Most cable providers offer different packages vary in speed. Download speed can vary from anywhere from 25 megabits per second all the way up to 400 megabits per second.

If you were to order cable internet for your home or even home office, your cable internet provider would send you modem but more recently they have been sending a modem with a Wi-Fi router combo which is often referred to as a gateway. A device could be a modem with built-in switch and Wi-Fi router, all in one. This modem requires the user to attach a coaxial cable that is routed to the home and then it needs to be attached to the back of the device. The modem is what delivers the internet into a house, the switch and the Wi-Fi router is there so the user can connect multiple wired wireless devices such as computers, laptops, tablets, and smartphones and provide it with the internet access.

Cable broadband does have a downside, because the houses in the same neighborhood will all have to share a pull of bandwidth that is being provided by the cable provider with that specific area. It means that during peak hours, time when a lot of devices are online and using bandwidth, users may experience a slowdown in the internet speed.

DSL Internet

The DSL or Digital Subscriber Line is a popular technology, used by most homes and businesses to access broadband data over the internet. DSL can carry both voice and data at the same time over phone lines. It uses a modem where a common telephone line (rj45) to carry its data. Since this technology uses phone lines, it is far-off in comparison to the older technology - dial up connection. DSL is a high-speed connection that is faster than dial up connection, and in this technology the user can go on the internet and talk on the landline phone at the same time. In case you're not familiar with dial up connection, you can only do phone call OR be on the internet but can never do both at the same time if using the same connection.

DSL is not as fast as cable internet, but it is more affordable from the price point. There is no need to share bandwidth within a neighborhood or block, everyone who is using DSL has their own dedicated connection. It is not a shared line.

In terms of availability, DSL is widely accessible to users because it uses common telephone lines which are nearly everywhere. The internet speed on DSL can vary depending on the area, but on average it can offer download speeds anywhere from 5 megabits per second up to 100 megabits per second. The DSL modem typically comes as a modem and Wi-Fi router combo, it requires the user to plug a standard phone line with a phone jack at the back of the DSL modem.

Asymmetric Digital Subscriber Line (ADSL)
·   The download speed is considerably faster than the upload speed
·   This is ideal for home-use. Typically, home users download a lot more than upload
·   Most affordable form of DSL

Symmetric Digital Subscriber Line (SDSL)
·   As the name implies, the download and upload speeds are the same level
·   Ideal for business-use

Very High Bit Rate Digital Subscriber Line (VDSL)
·   Fast form of DSL that also runs over copper wire
·   Since it uses copper wire, it is more effective for short distance
·   VDSL is roughly three times faster than ADSL

Fiber Internet
This type of internet technology offers the fastest internet speeds available today. It has download and upload speeds that can reach as fast as 1,000 megabits per second. The

reason why this type of connection is extremely fast is because it uses light to send data running through fiber optic cable. Fiber optic cable is what is already being used as the backbone of the internet.

Aside from speed, fiber internet can also travel much longer distances than DSL or cable. The reason behind is; DSL and cable transmit data using electricity over copper cable and signals in copper cable can be affected by electromagnetic interference as it travels which can weaken the signal, especially over a long distance. Fiber internet, on the other hand, uses light to transmit its data through a thin glass cable which makes it less vulnerable to interference.

Physical Components of a Computer Network

Internet is but a network of computing devices allowing us to send messages, make voice calls, video calls, online shopping, and other similar tasks online, but what are the physical components of this computer network which are helping us to perform all these activities?

- **End Points** - includes personal computers, phones, tablets, printers, servers, or any other devices that users need. Servers are data centers used to sort it out that can be shared with other devices. Servers also provides information while other devices retrieve information. End Points can both provide or retrieve information

- **Network Interface Card (NIC)** - To retrieve information of you Facebook account from the Facebook server, you will need to type www.facebook.com in your web browser. This request is first converted to a format which can reach facebook.com; The server device which carries out this conversion process is called network interface card. Port to which to connect a LAN cable in our computers is embedded in a network interface card. All endpoints have a network interface card, either wired or wireless. The NIC of an endpoint can convert data to electrical signals, light signals, or radio signals.

- **Network Media** - It provides means through which data from a NIC of one device is transmitted to and NIC of the other device and it can be a LAN cable for transmitting electrical signals, optical fiber for transmitting light signals, or air in case of radio signals.
- **Connectors** - Connectors provides connection points for a network media.
- **LAN Cables** - are connected to network interface cards of computers using rj45 connectors. All devices in the internet are connected to each other using connectors and network media.
- **Switch** - Network switch is a multi-port device which assures data will go to the right destination within the local area network.

  For a local area network, various equipment and gadgets are linked to each other using another network component called Switch. A SOHO network or small office home office network typically uses single network switch to connect multiple devices.
- **Router** - To access internet networks which is further connected to a device called a router.

The internet is consisting of a large number of interconnected routers and all of these routers perform two basic functions. First is to connect different networks, second is to provide the best path to access the requested content.

A typical computer network may include endpoints, network interface card, network media, connectors, switches, and routers as physical components.

Pretty much all computer networks these days are using Ethernet, it is a system by which devices can exchange data on a network. Data is broken up and packaged into small pieces by the sending computer. These packages are known as frames. Frames are then transmitted individually. It is convenient to think of a stream of frames on the cable rather like sticks floating on a river. In reality, each frame is a burst of high and low voltages which represents the ones and zeros of binary encoded data. The sending computer's network interface card (NIC) is responsible for generating the rapid pulses of electricity that make up each frame. Whenever a frame is transmitted by a computer, it is actually broadcasting the frame on the network, every other computer can see the frame but only the intended recipient, the one with the correct destination MAC address chooses not to ignore it. At any instant, a cable either has a voltage across it meaning a one, or it doesn't mean a zero. It is in the nature of electricity that they can only be one voltage across the wire at a time and since each frame must be transmitted in its entirety without interruption, only one computer at a time can transmit a frame on the same stretch of cable. If at exactly the same instant, two computers attempt to transmit a frame, there'll be a collision and both frames will fail. Each computer must then wait a random amount of time, possibly only a tiny fraction of a second - the so called back off delay before attempting to transmit the failed frame again.

Frame collisions were common on an old-style LAN. The system for dealing with frame collisions is labeled as the CSMA/ **CD or Carrier Sense Multiple Access with Collision Detection,** fortunately this reaction happens very quickly. A typical Ethernet can carry up to 10 gigabits per second, that's a lot of frames! Modern wireless Ethernet uses a similar system but instead of cables, a wireless network uses high frequency radio waves. A wireless access point does the same job as the backbone cable, all frames are sent to this first and then they're relayed onwards.

Wi-Fi has a range of about a hundred meters, but this also depends on obstacles like walls, or hills, not to mention possible interference from devices like microwave ovens and cordless telephones. The closer you are to a Wi-Fi hotspot, the better.

To transmit Ethernet frames over Wi-Fi, the sender must first make its intention known to the wireless access point. If nothing else is transmitting, the wireless access point will let the sender know that it may continue. Frames are then relayed via the wireless access point to the intended recipient. A wireless network interface card can't transmit and receive at the same time, it is said to be half duplex. Since other computers may be too far away for direct communications, one computer doesn't necessarily know if another is attempting to transmit at the same time.

Therefore, to avoid collisions which would corrupt Ethernet frames, everything must go through the wireless access point. This is called as the **CSMA/CA or Carrier Sense Multiple Access with Collision Avoidance** and it is the essence of how all Wi-Fi works today.

In case you are wondering why your neighbor's Wi-Fi doesn't interfere with yours, well it might. Normally each wireless access point operates within its own radio frequency range. When it sets itself up, it will choose a channel that seems quiet at the time and your wireless computers will tune in to this. Rather like when you tune in to a TV or radio station, a modern wireless access point can select one of twenty-three non-overlapping channels. So hopefully your neighbor's Wi-Fi will be operating in a different frequency range. Nevertheless, it is beneficial sometimes to change your Wi-Fi channel manually, especially in a crowded area. It should be said that wireless ethernet frames are normally encrypted so the data that you broadcast on the airwaves can't read even if it is deliberately intercepted.

LAN Topology

This refers to the placement or layout of the machines in a local area network. Specifically, how the computers are connected together. There are four main ways of connecting the computers in a LAN: the bus, star, ring, and mesh.

· **Bus Topology**

This type of structure involves a main backbone cable and the workstations are attached to this. The backbone cable can be up to a hundred meters long before an amplifier is needed to boost the signals. A typical bus LAN uses Ethernet technology and all of the workstations have an Ethernet network interface card (NIC) inside them. With any LAN, only one computer can transmit a packet of data at a time. Ethernet handles this by allowing any computer to attempt to put a signal on the cable at any time, then if there is a collision it is detected by the network interface card which waits a very brief casual number of time before giving another try to retransmit. The backbone cable has a terminator at either end, there is nothing more than electrical resistors designed to prevent signal echoes on the cable. The bus is the cheapest way to arrange a network because it uses the least amount of cable compared to other arrangements. It is easy to swap workstations or to add new ones without disrupting the rest of the LAN and if one workstation fails, the network will continue as long as there isn't a break in the main backbone cable.

· **Star Topology**

A star-shaped LAN, the computers and devices are all hooked up directly to a main device. Each workstation is independent of the rest so it's easy to add and remove workstations without disruptions. There may be a server at the center of the LAN or there may be a connecting box known as a hub, in which case the server will be connected to it just like the workstations. Although the name may suggest the topology's shape, the cable runs may vary in great length depending on how far away the workstations are from the center. For this reason, the star uses the most amount of cable compared to other arrangements and this makes it potentially the most expensive arrangement. Also, if the server or the central hub fails the whole LAN will go down.

· **Ring Topology**

This is more than just a way of connecting computers together. It's an alternative to Ethernet when it comes to controlling the way computers exchange packets of data. In a ring, an electrical signal called the token is passed from computer to computer at a very high speed and always in the same direction. The so-called token ring network interface card in each machine is responsible for propagating the token. When one computer wants to transmit a packet of data to another it takes control of the token. No other computer can send anything while it has possession of the token. The data is essentially attached to the token and sent on its way. The main benefit of a token ring network is that very fast transmission rates are possible because there are no collisions to be dealt with. However, because the network interface card of each computing devices in the token ring is responsible for maintaining the token if one machine fails, the whole network will fail. Adding new workstations involves shutting the whole network down. The ring is also potentially the most expensive arrangement because special token ring network interface cards cost more than ethernet cards.

· **Hubs**

In its simplest form, a hub is just a connecting box that simplifies the wiring of a local area network. By using a central hub with computers radiating out from the middle, you can create what looks like a star-shaped network. However, inside the hub there might be a ring or a bus. A hub can do more than just tidy up the wiring of a LAN. If it's also repeater, it will amplify signals on long stretches of cable. If a hub is a switch or a router, it can help to reduce the amount of unnecessary traffic on the LAN.

· **Mesh Network**

Wireless mesh networks are becoming more common. In the mesh, every device is connected to every other device. Either directly which is known as a full mesh or indirectly which is called partial mesh. This type of architecture has a lot of advantages, typically the administration tasks are decentralized. There's no controlling server, so there's no single point of failure because there are no cables involved. A wireless mesh is cheaper to set up particularly over a large area such as a whole city. Adding new nodes is easy, the network interface cards usually configure themselves when they detect nearby nodes. As the number of nodes increases, the network becomes even faster and more efficient. In a wireless mesh, data packets hop from node to node and will find the fastest route available.

Quick Notes:
- Topology refers to the layout of computers in a LAN
- Packets transmitted using Token, Ring, or Ethernet
- Layouts include bus, star, and ring
- Mesh is used for Wi-Fi networks
- Hubs can simplify wiring
- A large LAN might have several layouts

Standard Connectors

Connectors are very similar whether it is a loopback cable, whether it is a rollover cable, whether it is an ethernet straight through or crossover; the connectors themselves look exactly the same to our eyes, the only difference is how it is wired inside of that jacket.

- RJ- 11 Connector
  The letters RJ means registered jack; this is a four-wired connector used mainly to connect telephone equipment. As far as computer networking is concerned, it is used to hook up computers to local area network via the computer's modem. The rj-11 locks itself in place by a hinge-locking tab and it resembles the rj-45 but is considerably smaller in size.

- RJ-45 Connector

  By far, the rj-45 is the most common connector. This is an eight-wired connector that is used to connect computers to local area networks. It is used with twisted pair cabling. Like the rj-11, it locks itself in place by a hinge-locking tab.

- RJ-48c Connector

  This connector looks similar to rj-45. The difference between the two, the rj-48c is used with shielded twisted pair instead of unshielded twisted pair. It is primary used with T1 lines and it is also wired differently than the rj-45.

- UTP Coupler

  This is used to connect UTP cables with rj-45 connectors to each other. This is typically used when running a longer cable is either not an option or not available. The user needs to hook the end of the cable into the coupler and then add another cable on the other side. By doing so, it would successfully extend the existing UTP cables.

- BNC Connector

  This belongs to a standard category of RF connector that is utilized in coaxial cables. The letters BNC stands for Bayonet Neill–Concelman. It is used for both analog and digital video transmissions as well as audio.

- BNC Coupler

    This is used to connect two coaxial cables with BNC connectors attached to them. This particular coupler is a BNC female to female coupler.

- Fiber Coupler

    If two fiber connectors are needed to be joined together then a fiber coupler is required to complete the task. This coupler is used to join two of the same fiber optic connectors. The two connectors have to be the same type, this is not to be confused with a fiber adapter which is used for joining two different connectors together such as an SC to an ST and so on.

- F-Type Connector

    This is a threaded connector that is typically used with coaxial cables. These are primarily used by cable providers to attach cable modems. The F-Type tightens by an attached nut.

    USB Connector
- Universal Serial Bus or USB connector is very common in both desktops and laptops. Majority of computer manufacturers make wireless cards that can be plugged to a usb port. The usb has two different connector types: Type A and Type B.

- IEEE 1394

    This connector is also known as the firewire, it can be recognized with its D-shaped connector. This type of connection is also widely common in desktops. Laptops and even tablets and some smartphones. It is widely associated with peripheral devices such as digital cameras, multimedia devices, videos, and printers rather than being used in network connections.

· MT-RJ Connector

This is designated for the fiber optic connection. MT-RJ stands for Mechanical Transfer Registered Jack. It is a fiber optic cable connector and it uses a latched push-pull connector. It has a small-form factor built for high - packed density.

· ST Connector

A straight tip connector uses a half-twist bayonet type of lock. This is commonly used in a single mode fiber optic cable.

· LC (Connector)

The local connector is also used as a fiber optic connector. It uses jack that is similar to rj-45. This is commonly used as a connector for cables between floors in a building.

· SC (Connector)

The standard connector uses a push - pull connector that is similar to audio and video plugs. Like the LC connector, this is also commonly used between floors in a building

- RS-232 Connector

  The term Serial refers to sending data, one bit at a time. Serial cables are the types of cables that carries serial data transmission. The most common form of serial cables is using the standard RS-232 Connector which has the common "D" connector, such as the DB-9 and DB-25.

Network Cable Standards

There are specific cables needed to be used for local area networks (LAN), these are the twisted cables or the ethernet cables that computer users can find as a connection is established from the computer to the router or modem in order to obtain internet access. One end of the cable plugs into the computer's network interface card (NIC) while the other end is connected to the network port of the router switch or modem depending upon what is being used in the network.

Ethernet twisted pair cables come in two different types; the first type is the Unshielded Twisted Pair – is frequently described as the most regular type of cable that is used more recently. This type is consisting of four pairs of wires that are color coded then twisted around within itself, the wires are twisted to prevent electromagnetic interference or crosstalk. This cable can be commonly found in most people's homes or businesses. The second type is the Shielded Twisted Pair (STP). The STP is highly similar to the unshielded twisted-pair except that it has a foil shield that covers the wires. This shielding adds an extra layer of protection against electromagnetic interference leaking into and out of the cable. This type of cable is mainly used for industrial purposes and not so much in homes or businesses.

In some cases where the network administrator or the user prefers to make their own custom cables for the network, typically a bulk roll of twisted pair cable can be purchased from a store. From there, it can be wired correctly by attaching rj45 connectors to each end. To achieve this, the protective shielding at the end of each network cable needs to be removed to expose the wire. This is done by using a cable stripper, the cable is inserted into the cable stripper and then the outer sheathing is removed to expose the wires and then the cable needs to be inserted into a wire crimper to attach a rj45 connector. It is important to note that the wires in the cable have to arranged in a certain order and that order will be different depending upon the purpose of the cable.

Common types of twisted pair cables:
· Straight Patch Cable
· Crossover Cable

When it comes to the wiring order of these twisted pair cables, there are two different standards that are used within the industry: one is the 568A and the other standard is 568B.

The orders are based on the color of the wires.

568A

- White - Green
- Green
- White - Orange
- Blue
- White - Blue
- Orange
- White - Brown
- Brown

568B:

- White - Orange
- Orange
- White - Green
- Blue
- White - Blue
- Green
- White - Brown
- Brown

*The main difference among the A and the B standards is the green wires are swapped with the orange. It doesn't really matter which standard is used, both standards do the same thing. Here in the United States, most people use the B standard.

Whether the A or the B wiring standard is chosen, if both ends of the cable are wired using the same standard, then this is known as a Straight Cable which is also known as a Patch Cable. A straight cable allows signal to pass through from end to end. This is the most common type of cable that is utilized in the local area networks. A straight cable manages to connect computers to hubs, switches, routers or modems. In other words, it is used to connect dissimilar devices together, making it the most common cable that is being used on LANs.

A Crossover Cable is also used on local area networks, but it is not as common as a straight cable. A crossover cable is created when both ends of a cable are wired using the two different standards. For example: one end is wired using the A standard and the other end is wired using the B standard. Crossover cables are used to connect two similar devices together. A common scenario is between two computers, crossover cables are utilized to attach devices directly to each other beyond the use of a hub or a switch. It is capable to be utilized for connection between hubs to hubs, or switches to switches.

There are also the categories of twisted cables. These are Cat 3, Cat 4, Cat 5, Cat 6, and Cat 7. The difference between these categories is the maximum speed they can handle without having crosstalk or interference. The numbers of the category represent the tightness of the twist that are applied to the wires. The speed ranges from the lowest category which is 3 at 10 megabits per second and all the way to Cat 6a and Cat 7 which has speeds of 10 gigabits per second. Most networks of today would use at least Cat 5e on their networks because most networks would be running at least at gigabit speeds. Cat 3 and Cat 5 are slower than gigabit and are pretty much obsolete today. In case the user is at a network speed that is running slower, Cat 7 can still be used because it is backward compatible. The Cat 7 is actually a shielded twisted-pair version of Cat 6a.

CATEGORY	SPEED	
CATEGORY 3	10 Mbps	Currently obsolete
CATEGORY 5	100 Mbps	Currently obsolete
CATEGORY 5e	1 Gbps	Enhanced
CATEGORY 6	1 Gbps	10 Gbps (cable length under 100 meters)
CATEGORY 6a	10 Gbps	Augmented
CATEGORY 7	10 Gbps	Added shielding to the wires
CATEGORY 8	40 Gbps	Distance up to 30 meters

The latest version is Cat 8. It is the ultimate copper cable; it is also a shielded twisted-pair cable which has a delivery speed of up to 40 gigabits per second up to a distance of 30 meters. In comparison, this is 4 times faster than the Cat 6a or Cat 7.

Chapter 4: Firewall

Firewall

A firewall is a procedure in place that has been engineered to restrict unwarranted access from coming into a private network by monitoring the information that arrives from the internet. It stops unwelcomed traffic while it allows valid traffic. A firewall's purpose is to create a safety barrier between a private network and the public internet, because on the internet there's always going to be hackers and malicious traffic that may try to penetrate into a private network to cause harm. A firewall if the primary component on a network to prevent this.

A firewall is especially important to any organization that has a lot of computers and servers in them. It is unideal to have all those devices accessible to everyone on the internet where a hacker can come in and totally disrupt that organization.

Imagine how a firewall works in a building structure, it is very similar to how firewall's used in computer networks work. In fact, this is where the word "firewall" came from. A firewall in a building structure provides a barrier so that in the event of an actual fire, on either side of a building, the firewall is there to keep the fire contained and to keep it from spreading over to the other side. The firewall, in concept, is there to keep the fire from destroying the entire building. If a firewall is not present to contain the flames, it is extremely easy and fast to spread the fire to the entire building structure. A network firewall works in a similar way. It stops harmful activities before it can spread into the other of the firewall and cause harm to a private network.

In today's high-tech world, a firewall is essential to every home and especially in a business or an organization to keep their network safe.

A firewall works by filtering the incoming data and determines by its rules if it is allowed to enter a network. These rules are also known as an Access Control List. These rules are customizable and are determined by the network administrator. The administrator decides not only what can enter a network but also what can leave a network. These rules either allows or denies permission.

Firewall rules can be based on:
- IP Addresses
- Domain names
- Protocols
- Programs
- Ports
- Keywords

Firewalls come in different types. One type is Host-based Firewall - this is a software firewall. This is the kind that is installed on a computer and it protects that computer only and nothing else.

Another type of firewall is called Network-based Firewall. This is a conjunction between a hardware together with software and it operates at the network layer. It is placed between a private network and the public internet. Unlike host-based firewall, where it can only protect the computer where it is installed, a network-based protects the entire network and it does this through management rules that are applied to the entire network. Any harmful activity can be stopped before it reaches the computers. Network-based firewalls can be a standalone product which is mainly used by large organizations, it can also be a built-in as a component of a router which is what a lot of smaller organizations rely on. Another way is to have it deployed in a service provider's cloud infrastructure.

A lot of organizations tend to use both network-based and host-based firewalls, this method provides a multi-layer protection.

DMZ (Demilitarized Zone)

To enhance the security of an organization, another approach is being used - seclusion or separation; this method is called DMZ. Digital devices like servers and computers sit on the contrasting ends of a firewall. The concept is almost like creating two separate networks. The next logical question is, "Why would a user want this? How does the DMZ accomplish this, if it really can?"

For example: In a company's computer network, there could be a web server and an email server. Typically, these kinds of servers sit behind a network's firewall, these servers are inside the company' private network. This would mean that the company is somehow letting in people from untrusted network (the internet), given access behind the company's firewall and into the company's private network where the servers are.

The example set up could cause a security concern because as people are accessing these servers, hackers could use the same opportunity and use as an opening to cause havoc in a computer network. Remember at this point, outsiders have already got past the firewall because servers are behind the firewall. Hackers can try and access other sensitive data from other devices that are also behind the firewall, such as a database server where sensitive data is kept, or hacker may even try to plant a virus in the network.

What if a company or any network administrator put the public access to web and email servers outside the network's internal firewall and put it on the opposite side of the firewall? The servers would still be located within the same building and need not be physically removed, but it would be configured to be on the other side of the firewall.
In this set up, whenever people access the servers from the internet, they are not going to be accessing them behind the network's internal firewall - where most of the sensitive information are kept, the servers are now out in front facing the internet and fully exposed.
This is exactly what DMZ is.

DMZ is sometimes referred to as the Perimeter Network. As a perimeter network, it acts like a screened network to detect any malicious activity before it can get pass the firewall and into the internal network. The DMZ divides the network into two parts: by taking the devices from inside the firewall and then putting it outside the firewall. Some networks that uses DMZ only uses one firewall, however larger companies that have more sensitive data at stake tend to use at least two firewalls to secure its network. Extra firewall will be added and then be put in front of a DMZ, the second firewall adds an extra layer of protection to ensure that only legitimate traffic can access the DMZ. This more secure setup also makes it harder for would - be hackers to penetrate into the network because they have to go through two different firewalls.

There is also a DMZ that can be configured for home - use. This can be done using a standard router. In the advanced settings of the router's configuration page, there is typically a section there that talks about setting up a DMZ. This setup is not entirely a true DMZ but rather it is just setting up a DMZ host. Creating a DMZ in a home-based router appoints a device as a DMZ host and will send and push all the ports to that device.

A common use of a DMZ for a home setup is to put it with gaming consoles such as an Xbox or PlayStation and configuring it as a DMZ host. This is typically done because a lot of these gaming consoles are often used for online gaming. Most gamers do not want any interference that could happen from a firewall, so it is unlikely that gamers would like to change the settings of any kind that would have something to do with port forwarding configuration. Gamers could just go into the DMZ settings in the router and put in the gaming console's IP address as the DMZ.

It is very important to note that the device in the DMZ is set with a static IP address rather than a dynamic IP address.

In summary: In the real world, the DMZ is an area where the military is forbidden. In the computing world, DMZ is where the firewall protection is forbidden.

Chapter 5: Network Components

Hub, Switch, Router and Modems

These apparatuses are similar in concept but there is a contrast in the way they manage data.

Hub

The function of a hub is to hook up all of the network devices together on an internal network, it is a gear that has several ports that can allow ethernet connections from network devices. A hub is not regarded to be intelligent. It does not have the ability to filter any data. The hub also does not have the intelligence to direct where the data should be sent to. The lone element the hub knows is whenever a device is attached to its port, when a data packet reaches one of the ports, it is duplicated to all other ports.

In by doing so, data packets are visible to all the devices on that hub.

A data packet comes in to one port, then the hub will just rebroadcast that data to each of the ports that has a device attached to it.

In a scenario where four computers all belong to the same network, which are also connected to the same hub: if computer A wanted to communicate with computer B, then computers C and D would still receive the data even though the data was not intended for them.

Aside from the security concerns this setup may have constructed, it also generates avoidable traffic on the network which as a result, misuse the bandwidth.

Switch

A switch is immensely comparable to a hub. It is device that has a number of ports that allows ethernet connections from network devices. In comparison with a hub, a switch is intelligent. A switch has the ability to determine the physical addresses of the digital equipment that are attached to it and save these information - the physical addresses called MAC address in its data bank. When a data packet is dispatched to a switch, it is only routed to the planned destination port.

In a scenario where in a private network, there are four computers that are attached to the same hub: if computer D wanted to communicate with computer C, then the switch will seek the information at its data bank of MAC addresses and matching ports and hand over the data to the appropriate port. The data packet would only be passed to the computer C, its intended destination. Computers B and A would not be affected by that instance of communication.

Because of its efficiency, most users and network administrators favor switches than the hubs because of its capacity to reduce unnecessary traffic on the network.

Quick Notes:

- Hubs and switches are utilized to swap data within a LAN
- These devices are not meant to send and receive data outside their own network, for example – the internet
- To exchange or route data outside their own network to another network, i.e., the internet, a device needs to be able to read IP addresses.

- Hubs and switches do not have the ability to scan and interpret IP addresses, only switches can read MAC addresses

Router

A router does correctly what its name suggests, it is a device that directs or forwards data from a network to another network depending on their IP addresses. When a data packet has arrived from the router, the device's job is to inspect the data's IP address and figure out if the packet was intended for its own network or if it is designated to be sent to another network. If the router has concluded that the data packet is originally directed for its own network, it acquires the data. If the packet is determined not to be directed for its own network, the router dispatches it to separate network. A router can be described accurately as a network's gateway.

Quick Notes:
- Hubs and switches are employed to build networks
- Routers are designed to affix networks

What is the difference between a modem and a router?

Others may probably have the impression that modem and a router are equivalent of each other, they are not. These two devices are distinctive with each having independent roles on a network.

If internet is required inside an establishment, a user needs to have a modem. A modem is responsible in delivering the internet into an establishment. A modem establishes and maintains a devoted connection to your internet service provider (ISP) to grant connection to the internet.

The logic why a modem is needed is - as a result of having a couple of types of signals that are utilized on a computer and when the devices are connected to the internet. A computer only has the ability to interpret digital signals, although these signals that are out on the internet are classified to be as analog.

In the process of analog data coming in from the internet, the modem demodulates the arriving analog signals and transcribes it as digital signals so that a computer can read it. A modem also modulates outgoing digital signals from a computer into an analog signal as it goes out on the internet.

The context behind the word modem is a device that is designed as a modulator and demodulator - which precisely how a modem operates. It modulates the data that are on its way out from a computer and demodulates incoming or arriving data from the internet.

There are routers that are being utilized in businesses and larger institutions, and there are smaller routers that are utilized in homes and startup businesses - but essentially these types do the same thing.

In a single computer setup, a user doesn't need a router to access the internet. The user can directly plug the network cable of the computer into the modem and then end user will be able to access the internet. However, in a computer networking set up - like in most homes and businesses, multiple devices need to have access and be connected to the internet and that is where a router is needed.

Types of Modems

Some of the common types are cable and DSL modems. This rests upon what type of internet that is being used, the accurate type of modem is required.

Cable modems are directed and attached to a home or business by means of a coaxial cable. This type of connection - cable internet, is typically provided by the same company that provides you with cable television.

DSL modems are connected using a typical phone line.

For home and small business, ISPs may provide a modem device that acts as combination of router and a modem. It is a modem with an incorporated wireless router in a single physical device.

Mesh Wi-Fi System

The most preferred way of connecting to the internet by many is through wireless connection, it gives the users flexibility to move around and still be connected to the network without the limitations that wired connection might have.

In some instances where a few areas or spots within a structure gets a weaker Wi-Fi signal, it can be described as "spotty". For example, there might be some areas in a house or office where the signal is weak, or it may be totally unavailable. There are several reasons why spotty signal might incur - as we have discussed in the Wi-Fi section of this book, or just the placement of the Wi-Fi router may also affect the way the signal strength in some areas can be.

To remedy this problem, a lot of times people would buy just a Wi-Fi extender to help and extend the Wi-Fi signal. Even though Wi-Fi extenders do work, some issues may occur since Wi-Fi extenders create its own Wi-Fi network that has its own separate SSID. In this case, the user would have to connect to the Wi-Fi where the signal is stronger - whether from the router or to the Wi-Fi extender's network, depending on where the user is at within a structure.

Another option to expand Wi-Fi signal within a structure is by using a Mesh Wi-Fi System. It is the latest technology as an answer to the problems of weak or dead spot issues with Wi-Fi.

A mesh Wi-Fi is a group of routers or Wi-Fi points that are placed in different locations inside an infrastructure. It provides a blanket of Wi-Fi coverage within a closed area like a home or small office. It does the job of eliminating weak Wi-Fi signals.

A good feature of this technology is that the Wi-Fi points communicate with each other wireless to create one large Wi-Fi network. There are no cables involved when Wi-Fi points are communicating with each other which makes the placement of the Wi-Fi points that much easier.

A sample setup using mesh Wi-Fi: A modem - router that brings the internet into the home or office, then attach one of the mesh Wi-Fi points to the modem - router using an ethernet cable and the other Wi-Fi points can be placed around the infrastructure as needed. Once the physical setup is complete, the Wi-Fi points will communicate or talk to each other to create a seamless internet connection that covers the entire house or small office for all of the wireless devices to connect to. This system creates a large Wi-Fi network, each Wi-Fi point is not creating its own Wi-Fi network with SSID like an extender would be like.

A device that is connected to the network will seamlessly disconnect from a Wi-Fi point and then reconnect to another Wi-Fi point.

Quick Notes:

· How hubs and switches relate to modems and modem-routers?

- Most routers will have an in-built switch integrated to it, if this is the case, it is not a requirement to have a switch if you network has a router with a switch built into it.

· A possible reason why you would require to add a switch despite having a router with a built-in switch, is if you needed more wired connections for your devices and all of the ports in your router have been exhausted. A switch can be connected to the router, then additional devices can be connected to the network through the switch.

Chapter 6: Wireless Technology

Wireless network connects computers and other digital devices through the air via radio waves. Wireless networks are commonly called as Wireless Local Area Networks (WLAN), another term that is widely used is "Wi-Fi".

Wireless networks can be structured in various ways; however, the basic components remain the same.

Access Point (AP) - this is the "heart" of the network and the links connect it to the nodes. This is the wireless router; it provides access to the internet and other to the other computers within the network. Typically, a router is hardwired to a modem or in some cases a multipurpose device like the modem - router can be used. Typically, the internet access is going through ethernet wires. From this moment on, the network becomes wireless.

Links

These are radio waves instead of instead of wires, it uses one or two bands of spectrum; 2.4GHz or 5 GHz. The earlier band is shared with microwaves, baby monitors, garage door openers, and many other non Wi-Fi devices - all of which can cause interference to the network. The 2.4 GHz has a longer range compared to 5 GHz spectrum; however, the latter is extremely less crowded but since it does have a shorter range to extend its range capacity, it might require multiple access points as needed

Nodes

These are the computers or workstations and all other digital devices that can be connected to the Wi-Fi. Laptops and desktops have information cards that receive and send data through radio waves, the mobile devices like a smartphone or a tablet are like two-way radios in the sense that they receive and transmit radio waves to link to the access points

How is a device recognized by wireless network?

A custom code is being used by the computer, this the Transmission Control Protocol / Internet Protocol. The TCP follows rules to create and assemble packets of information and the IP sends and receives these data. An IP address is assigned to a computer or every digital device while it in the network.

What is the difference between 2.4 GHz and 5 GHz Wi-Fi Routers?

The technology of today lets us have wider options when it comes to devices. This is also true for Wireless Networks. You might have noticed some Wi-Fi routers that have both 2.4GHz and 5 GHz frequency bands.

A frequency band is how wireless data is transmitted between devices. These bands are radio waves that carry the data and these bands are either 2.4GHz and 5 GHz. Previously, most Wi-Fi routers will only transmit one of these bands which is the 2.4 band since it is the most common frequency, and these are called Single Band

Routers. Newer routers that can transmit both bands are referred to as Dual Band Wi-Fi routers.

At this point we have learned how the 2.4 GHz is the standard band, however it is not just a standard band that is being used in Wi-Fi routers. It is also the standard band that is utilized in a lot of other devices like microwave ovens and cordless phones, Bluetooth devices, wireless cameras, just to name a few. This became a problem because the fact that so many other devices use the 2.4 band the signal tend to become overcrowded and was causing a lot of interference with Wi-Fi signals. Whenever this happens, it slows down the Wi-Fi network speed and sometimes can cause to disrupt or lose connection to the Wi-Fi router.

The 5 GHz band was added to try to resolve the overcrowding issue of the previous band. The newer band is not as commonly used as the 2.4 so it is used by fewer devices, as a result there is minimal to no interference in the signal. Using the 5 GHz would relieve the problem related to slow network speeds and connection drops that is typically caused by interference from other devices.

Another reason why the 2.4 band is more vulnerable to interference is because of the difference in wireless channels. A wireless channel is a way to fine-tune and alter a frequency. Sometimes it is needed to change the channel in the router whenever high-interference is being experienced within a channel. The 2.4 GHz band has 11 channels to choose from (1,2,3,4,5,6,7,8,9,10,11); but of these 11 channels only three are non-overlapping (channels 1, 3, and 11). Basically, in this band there are only 3 solid channels to choose from. The 5Ghz band has more channels, it has 25 non-overlapping channels.

Another difference between the two are the speed and range that it can cover. The 2.4 GHz band transmits data at a slower speed than the 5 GHz, but it does have a broader dimension covered. The 5GHz band has the ability to broadcast data at a faster speed but it has a shorter range because it has higher frequency, and as the frequency gets higher it gets difficult for it to pass through or penetrate solid objects such as floors and walls in a building.

Overview:
2.4 GHz
- · Advantages:
- - Farther range
- - Can penetrate solid objects
- · Disadvantages
- - Vulnerable to interference
- - Slower speed

5GHz
- · Advantages:
- - Higher transfer speed
- - Less vulnerable to interference

- · Disadvantages
- - Shorter range

-   Harder time penetrating solid objects

802.11 Channel Access

RF is an open shared medium, since we operate in a license-free space with 802.11 such as 2.4 GHz, portions of the 5 GHz all the way down to 50 GHz for some of the television whitespace and all the way up to 60 GHz with 802.11a/d or Multi-Gigabit (DMG) devices physical layers. There is more frequency space that we use today than ever with 802.11, however the one thing they all share in common is that they are open shared medium. Meaning, multiple devices on the same channel must share access and the device cannot detect what is happening somewhere else. There is no way for a transmitting station to know as it is sending information that the receiving station does not have interference or some other factor that might be impacting it there. We utilize a special type of communication in 802.11 networks like Acknowledgement Frames to acknowledge the receipt of information. An algorithm is needed to assist in the prevention of collisions.

Devices should be able to detect signal at the lowest modulation rate used within the channel. This is a requirement of 802.11 channel access; it needs to be able to see that signal at the lowest possible data rate. The lowest data rate is the one that you can demodulate at the greatest distance. If something is sent at a low data rate even at a distance, you should be able to decode or demodulate that data. This is the primary key to proper wireless LAN shared access, the need to be able to detect signal at the lowest modulation rate.

Quick Notes:
· RF is an open medium
· Multiple devices in the same channel must share access
· Devices cannot detect what is happening in other locations
· An algorithm is needed to assist in the prevention of collisions (Collision Avoidance)
· Devices should be able to detect signals at the lowest modulation rate within the channel
· This is the primary key to proper WLAN shared access

The wireless technology has helped us to transfer data from one device to another without using wires or cables. Using this technology, we can now establish a network is more flexible, intangible and has ease of access.

The use of smartphones or tablets or any other wireless devices that support Wi-Fi, wireless networking has allowed us to move around an area without hesitation since the device is still connected to the network.

In wires connection, data passes through cables whereas in wireless connection the data is passing through radio frequency (RF) signal.

The frequency of the Radio Frequency or RF signals ranges from 30kHz to 300 GHz, it falls under the category of EM waves or electromagnetic waves. A light is a good example of an electromagnetic wave; however, we can see a light as it passes through, RF signal on the other hand is completely not visible to us.

In radios, FM radio stations uses RF signal to broadcast signals. The frequency signal being used is frequently the same as the station name, for example KIIS-FM 102.7 (the 102.7 in the station name is the frequency it uses).
RF Signal range: 30kHz to 300 GHz

Types of Wireless Network
· Wireless LAN
· Wireless MAN
· Wireless WAN
· Wireless PAN

Wireless LAN (Local Area Network)
This is a network where there are two or more computers or devices connected to the network and it only covers a limited area, for example a home or small business. The NIC is sed in this type of network, we often call this the Peer-to-Peer Network (P2P). Another form of this is an ad-hoc network which is used in temporary manner.

Unlike using switch in a wired network, in the WLAN setup we use a device called an access point. This is a central device from which the RF signal is being generated. WLAN which uses access point are called Basic Service Set (BSS), it acts as the coordinator between different devices within the network.

Wi-Fi
RF signal Frequency: 2.4 GHz or 5 GHz
Range: 100 meters

Wi-Fi products are certified and tested by the Wi-Fi Alliance

Wireless MAN (Wireless Metropolitan Area Network)
Collected unit of many WLANs located at various places
Uses WIMAX technology (Worldwide Interoperability for Microwave Access) which is controlled by WiMAX Forum
Maximum Speed: 1 Gbits/ sec
IEEE 802.16 Standard

WWAN (Wireless Wide Area Network)
This is an extensive network that has been distributed across an immense amount of space. It connects cities together. Mobile phones use WWAN to make communication possible.

The technology in WWAN are subdivided in generations: 2G, 3G, and 4G
Most analog devices are utilizing this technology
· Examples of 2g
- General Packet Radio Service (GPRS)
- Enhanced Data rates for GSM Evolution (EDGE)

· Examples of 3G (third generation technologies)
- Code Division Multiple Access (CDMA)
- Universal Mobile Telecommunication System (UMTS)
- High Speed Packet Access (HSPA)
- Evolved High Speed Packet Access (HSPA+)

- 4G (High Speed Network accessibility can be achieved with this technology)
- Long Term Evolution (LTE)
- Voice Over Long-Term Evolution (VoLTE)

Time Evolution

In 1G in the 2980s, the only single voice was going from one device to another device. The analog protocol was being utilized during this period. In mid 1980s 2G network has introduced, with it came voice and text capabilities. Both voice and text messages are going from one device to another device with the use of digital standards. The speed from 1G (2.4 kbps) has increased when 2G was invented (16 kbps). In 2003, 3G has evolved from voice and text, with now including data. It uses the multimedia technologies and has a speed of up to 2 Mb per second. In 2009 4G was introduced to the market, this technology allows voice to go through data. IP protocol is utilized, and the speed can reach up to 100 Mb per second. 5G technology is the next one to hit the market soon, it will have more bandwidth mobility which a key factor for it would be to succeed.

WPAN (Wireless Personal Area Network)

This kind of network is used smaller distance
Technologies that are mostly used for WPAN are Bluetooth and Infrared Data Association

Bluetooth
· Uses ISM band of 2.4 GHz
· Speed of up to 721Kbps

- Range goes anywhere between 10 to 100 meters

If you are using Bluetooth technology, let's say in your headset or keyboard or speakers and it is connected to your smartphone or tablet, this is an example of a personal wireless area network

VLAN (Virtual Local Area Network)

A VLAN is a local area network where the computers, servers, and other network devices are logically connected regardless of their physical location. This means, even if the devices connected to the network are scattered in different places, it would not matter because a VLAN can logically group these devices into separate virtual networks.

The purposes of a VLAN

- Improved security
- Traffic management
- Make a network simpler

A VLAN capable switch can logically create several virtual networks to separate network broadcast traffic. This can be done by designating specific ports on the switch and assigning those ports to a specific VLAN.

VLAN helps with traffic management because as a local area network grows and more network devices are added, the frequency of the broadcast will also increase, and the network will get heavily congested with data. By creating VLANs, it will divide up the network into smaller broadcast domains, it will help alleviate the broadcast traffic

Security Options

Data can be easily hacked in Wireless Network without using proper security protocols. RF signals can be intercepted by other antennas.

IEEE Standards

The acronym stands for Institute of Electrical and Electronics Engineers.

Since there are various types of technology available for wireless networks, IEEE was established to determine standards for functioning of wireless networks.

Most networking standards are designed by 802 LAN/MAN Standards Committee.

IEEE Wireless Standards

- The first Wireless LAN was successfully made in 1997
- IEEE 802.11 Standard was designed because of WLAN
- Frequency used: 2.4 GHz
- Maximum Speed: 2Mbps
- This is now referred to as 802.11 Legacy

802.11a

Frequency: 5 GHz

Maximum Speed: 54 Mbps

802.11b

Frequency: 2.4 GHz

Maximum Speed: 11 Mbps

These standards were introduced in the same year in the late 1990s

802.11g

Frequency: 2.4 GHz

Maximum Speed: 54 Mbps

Introduced in 2003

802.11n

Frequency: 2.4 GHz and 5 GHz

Maximum Speed: 300 Mbps

Usual drawbacks of Wireless Networking

· RF signal strength gets weaker as the distance increases

· The signal may be affected by structures like concrete walls, big objects, and other similar items

· Unsecured signal can be easily targeted for hacking and can be intercepted

Chapter 7: OSI Reference Model

OSI Model or Open System Interconnection Model

OSI model defines and is used to understand how data is transferred from one computer to another in a computer network in the most basic form two computers connected to each other with a LAN cable and connectors sharing data with the help of network interface card forms a network but if one computer is based using Microsoft Windows and the other computer has Mac OS installed, then how are these two computers are going to communicate with each other in order to successful communication between computers or networks or different architectures seven layers OSI models or Open System Interconnection Model was introduced by the International Organization for Standardization or ISO in 1984 containing:

- Application Layer
- Presentation Layer
- Session Layer
- Transport Layer
- Network Layer
- Data Link Layer
- Physical Layer

Each layer is a package of protocols, independent of each other.

For example, in Application Layer, it does not mean it includes computer applications like Chrome, Firefox, or similar web browsers, but it includes application layer protocols that are needed to make these applications work correctly in the network or on the Internet.

Application Layer:

Used by network applications. Network Application means, computer applications that utilize the internet, like web browsers, Microsoft Outlook, Skype just to name a few.

The web browser is a network application running in your computer, but it uses application layer protocols like HTTP or HTTPS to do web surfing. Not only web browsing but all network applications are dependent on application layer protocols to function. There are dozens of application layer protocols aside from HTTP and HTTPS (FTP, NFS, FMTP, DHCP, SNMP, TELNET, POP3, IRC, NNTP) that enable various functions at this layer all these protocols collectively are the basis for various network services like file transfer, web surfing, emails, virtual terminal, etc.

· File transfer is done with the help of FTP protocol
· Web surfing is done with HTTP or HTTPS
· Emails utilizes SMTP
· For virtual terminal, telnet is used

Application layer provides services for network applications with the help of protocols to perform user activities

Presentation Layer

The presentation layer receives data coming from the application layer. This data is in the form of characters and numbers. Presentation layer converts these characters to machine-understandable binary format

For example: Conversion of ASCII ---> EBCDIC this function of the presentation layer is called translation. Before data is transmitted, the presentation layer reduces the number of bits that are used to represent the original data. this bit reduction process is called data compression and the results can be "lossy" or "lossless". Data compression reduces the amount of space used to store the original file as the size of the file is reduced it can be received at the destination in very little time, data transmission can be done faster thus data compression is helpful in real-time video and audio streaming. To maintain the integrity of the data before transmission, data is encrypted. Encryption enhances the security of sensitive data. At the sender side, data is encrypted and at the receiver side, the data is decrypted. SSL or Secure Sockets Layer protocol is used in the presentation layer for encryption and decryption. The presentation layer performs three basic functions: translation, compression, and encryption/decryption.

Session Layer

Suppose, you have planned for a party, you have hired a few helpers ensuring that each activity runs smoothly. Helpers will help you in setting up, assist in cleaning, and then closing the party. It is similar to the session layer. In this part of the process, this layer helps in setting up and managing connections, enabling sending and receiving of data followed by termination of connections or sessions. Like when you hired some helpers for a party, session layer too has its own helpers called APIs or Application Programming Interfaces, NETBIOS (network basic input/output system) is an example of APIs which allows applications on separate computers to talk with each other just before a session or a connection is established with the server. The server performs a function called authentication. Authentication is the process of verifying who you are. For this process, the server uses a username and a password, once this information is entered, it is masked a session, or a connection is established between your computer and the server. After authenticating the user authorization is checked. Authorization is the process used by a server to determine if you have permission to access a file, if not you will typically get a message saying, "you are not authorized to access this page". Both of these functions for authentication and authorization are performed by the session layer.

The session layer keeps track of the files that are being downloaded. For example, a web page contains text and images, this information is stored as separate files on the webserver. When you request a website in your web browser, your web browser offers a separate session to the webserver to download each of these text and image files separately these files are received in the form of data packets. The session layer keeps a track of which data packet belongs to which file either text file or image file and tracks where the received data packet goes, for this example it goes to the browser that is session layer helps in session management so.

The session layer helps in session management, authentication, and authorization. Your web browser performs all functions of the session, presentation, and application layer.

Transport Layer

The transport layer controls the reliability of communication through segmentation, flow control, and error control. In segmentation, data received that came from the session layer is divided into small data units called segments. Each segment contains a source, a destination a port number and a sequence number. A port number helps to direct each segment to the correct application. The sequence number helps to reassemble segments in the correct order to form the correct message at the receiver. Inflow control, the transport layer controls the amount of data being transmitted. For example, our smartphone is connected to a server, supposed a server can broadcast data maximum at 100 Mbps and our smartphone can process data at a maximum of 10 Mbps. Now, if we download a file from the server, but the server starts sending data at 50 Mbps, which is a lot higher than the rate of our smartphone can process. With the help of the transport layer, a smartphone can tell the server to slow down the data transmission rate up to 10 Mbps so no data gets lost. Similarly, is a server is sending data at 5 Mbps, a smartphone can request the server to increase the data transmission rate to 10 Mbps to maintain system performance.

The transport layer also helps in error control. If some data does not arrive at the destination, the transport layer uses automatic repeat request schemes to rebroadcast the missing or damaged data. A group of bits called checksum is added to each segment by the transport layer to find out the received can update segment. Protocols of the transport layer are the TCP and UDP (transmission control protocol and user datagram protocol). Transport layer performs two types of services: connection-oriented transmission and connectionless transmission. Connection-oriented transmission is done via TCP while Connectionless Transmission is done via UDP. UDP is faster than TCP because it does not provide any feedback whether data was really delivered. Whereas TCP provides feedback. Therefore, lost data can be retransmitted in TCP. UDP is used where it does not matter whether we have received all data. For example, online streaming movies, songs, games, voice over IP (VOIP), TFTP, DNS, etc. On the other hand, TCP is used were full data delivery is a must. For example, world wide web, email, FTP, etc. Transport layer is involved in segmentation, flow control, error control, connection oriented, and connectionless transmission. Transport layer passes data segments through the network layer.

Network Layer

Network layer works for the transmission of the received data segments from one computer to another located in different networks. Data units in the network layer are called packets. It is the layer where routers reside.

The function of network layer are logical addressing routing and path determination. IP addressing done in network layer is called logical addressing. Each computer in a network needs to have a distinct IP address. Network layer assigns sender and receiver's IP address to each segment to form an IP packet. IP addresses are assigned to ensure that each data packet can reach the correct destination. The routing is a method of moving data packet from source to destination and it is based on the logical address format of IPV4 or IPV6. Suppose computer A is connected to network one and computer B is connected to network two. From computer B we have requested to access Facebook or communication and now there is a reply from Facebook server for them to be in the form of packets. This packet needs to be delivered to computer B only. Since in a network, each device has a unique IP address, so these both computers will be having a unique IP address as well. Network layer of the Facebook server has already added sender and receiver's IP address in the packet. Suppose mask used is 225.225.225.0, this mask tells that the first 3 combination represents network while the last combination represents host or computer B so based on IP address format received data packet will move first to network 2 and then to computer B. So, based on IP address and mask routing decisions are made in a computer network. Now path determination. A computer can be connected to internet server for a computer in a number of ways. Choosing the best possible path for data delivery from source to destination is called Path Determination. Layer C devices uses protocols such as Open Shortest Path First (OSPF), Border Gateway Protocol (BGP), Intermediate System to Intermediate System (IS-IS) to determine the best possible path for data delivery.

Data Link Layer

Data link layer receives and accepts data packet that were being sent by the network layer. Data packets contain IP addresses of sender and receiver. There are two kinds of addressing; logical addressing and physical addressing. Logical addressing is done at network layer where sender and receivers IP addresses are assigned to each segment to form a data packet. Physical addressing is done at data link layer where MAC addresses of sender and receiver are assigned to each data packet to form a frame. MAC addresses are a 12-digit alphanumeric code embedded in network interface card of your computer by your computer manufacturer. The data unit located inside the data link layer is labeled as the "frame". Data link layer is embedded as software in network interface card of the computer and provide means to transfer data from one computer to another via local media. Local media includes copper wire, optical fiber or air for radio signals. Please note, air media does not correspond to audio, video, or animation. It refers to the physical links between two or more computers or networks.

Data Link Layer executes dual basic functions, it permits upper layers of OSI model to retrieve and gain access to the media by means of techniques parallel to framing. It manages and restricts how data is planted and received from media using various modes like the media access control and error detection. Consider two distant hosts; a laptop and a desktop communication with each other. As laptop and desktop are connected to different networks, so they will be using network layer protocols - IP for example, to communicate with each other. In this example, desktop is connected to router r1 through an ethernet cable. Router r1 and r2 are connected via satellite link, and laptop is connected to router r2 via wireless link. Now person1 wants to send some data to laptop, based on the medium used to connect desktop and router r1 data link layer adds some data in the head and tail of IP packet and converts it to a frame. Ethernet frame in this case, router r1 receives this ethernet frame pick up and split into an IP packet and then encapsulate it again to a frame so that it can cross satellite link to reach the router r2. Router r2 will again be encapsulate the frame and encapsulate it again to form a wireless data link frame. Laptop receives this wireless data link frame de-encapsulate it and then forwards the IP packet to network layer.

Finally, data arrives at the application layer.
Application layer protocols then make the received data visible on computer screen. So, network layer or higher-level layers are able to transfer data over media with the help of data link layer. Data link layer lends admittance to the media for higher layers of OSI model. Data link layer also set the oversight on how data is arranged and received from the media. The technique used to get the frame move the switch between on and then off, the media is named Media Access Control, there may be a number of devices connected to a common media. If there is more than one device that is connected to the same media that sends data at the same time, then there may be a possibility of collision of the two messages resulting in a useless message that neither

recipient can understand. To avoid these situations, data link layer keeps an eye on when the shared media is free so that device can transmit data for the receiver. This is called carrier sense multiple access, so data link layer with this media access control methods controls data transmission. Tail of each frame contains bits which are used to detect errors in the received frame. Errors occur due to certain limitations of the media used for transmitting data.

Physical Layer

Till now, data from the application layer has in segmented and compartmented by the transport layer which plays toward the packets by network layer and framed by datalink layer which is a sequence of binary zeroes and ones. Physical layer converts these binary sequences into signal and transmitted over local media. It can be an electrical signal in the case of copper cable or LAN cable, light signal in case of optical fiber and radio signal in case of air. Signal generated by a physical layer depends on the type of media used to connect two devices. At the receiver physical layer receives, converts it to bits and pass it to data link layer as a frame. Frame is further de-encapsulated as data moves through higher layers. Finally, data is moved to application layer. Application layer protocols makes the sender's message visible in the application in the receiver's computer screen. In this way, OSI model is helping to transfer data between distant hosts. These multi-level layers of the OSI model are lying behind the smooth functioning of internet.

Chapter 8: Transmission Control Protocol and Internet Protocol (TCP /IP)

Internet protocols are needed for proper functioning of internet and it includes TCP, HTTP, UDP, FTP, protocols that interact with web browsers while, ARP, ICMP interact with network adapters (IC). Network Protocols are required for Wi-Fi, Bluetooth and LTE to fully function. Network routing protocols are needed for the best download path for a device to download a file or data from the internet. These includes EIGRP, OSPF, and BGP.

TCP/IP

It is a collection of several protocols, but the core functionality of TCP / IP comes from two separate protocols working together, the so-called Transmission Control Protocol (TCP) and Internet Protocol (IP). The job of the TCP is to break up the data from the sending computer into small packets and get these packets ready for transmission. Each packet is given a sequence number at this stage. The content of each packet is used to calculate extra information which is then added to the packet as it's been created the calculation is done again at the receiving end to check for corruption during transmission.

Transmission Control Protocol (TCP)

TCP on the receiving computer reassembles the packets in the correct order according to their sequence numbers and if there are any packets that have been damaged on the way or haven't been received at all, TCP will request that those packets be sent again. You can see them that transmission control protocol is all about ensuring the integrity of the data.

· Breaks data into packets before sending
· Adds error checking information to packets
· Reassembles packets when received
· Requests retransmission of failed packets

Internet Protocol (IP)

The Internet Protocol on the other hand will add addressing information to each packet information to each packet information to identify the intended recipient of the packets. This is the recipient's so-called IP address. The sender's IP address is also added to the packet. The IP addresses also indicate where the recipient and the sender are located. This information is used by the network routers to guarantees that the packets are being dispatched to the right direction.

· Identifies devices on the network
· Routes packets from source to destination via routers

Notes on IP Address:
· Each computer running TCP/IP must have a unique IP address
· 32-bit number expressed as 4 denary octets for convenient notation
· Computers can be statically or dynamically configured (DHCP)

- Subnet mask identifies computer's location on a segmented network
- Default gateway's IP address provides access to the wider network

TCP/ IP Suite of Network Protocols

Other protocols that collectively provide the data transport services utilized by just about everything on the internet

- HyperText Transfer Protocol (HTTP) - This is used over the world wide web, to deliver multimedia rich webpages to your browser.
- File Transfer Protocol (FTP) - Can be used when you want to relocate files quickly between computers
- Simple Mail Transfer Protocol (SMTP) - Used when email messages are sent between mail servers
- Post Office Protocol (POP) - This comes into play when you retrieve email messages from a mail server so you can work with it locally on a PC-based application such as Outlook
- Internet Message Access Protocol (IMAP) - Allows you to work with mail live on the server using webmail system such as Hotmail or Gmail
- Voice Over Internet Protocol (VOIP) - This is specifically for transferring voice and video data over the internet allowing for telephone-style conversations. VOIP is itself a suite of programs.
- User Datagram Protocol (UDP) - A lightweight substitute to TCP. It is much less reliable than TCP because it does not perform any of the error checking, but it is much faster. UDP is suitable for applications where the quality

of transmission is not a big issue such as live video stream and online games

- Internet Control Message Protocol (ICMP) – Utilized by routers to exchange status information and error messages. For example, to report that a particular route that cannot be reached
- Address Resolution Protocol (ARP) - allows one device to discover another's MAC address if its IP address is known. Once the target network segment has been reached, the MAC address comes into play

Most TCP/IP packets begin and end their journey on a LAN using ethernet, but IP addresses can only get packets so far, the last leg of the journey depends on each packet bearing the destination MAC address.

How do these protocols work together to get data ready for network transmission?

For our example, let's start with a data we want to transmit, it might be a web page being delivered by a web server to a user's browser. A file being copied from one machine to another.

To begin with, the data must be collected from the application software and formatted for further processing the protocols that performs this task includes - HTTP, FTP, SMTP, and POP3, dependent upon the quality of the data.

Then the data is fragmented down onto packets a sequence number and error-checking data is added to each packet. In addition, something called a "port number" is added to indicate the nature of the data and therefore the application it is heading for. This port number, in concept is different from a physical port on a device that you plug a cable into. Port 80 means that it is HTTP data which is a web page, port 20 is delegated for FTP, while port 25 is SMTP data, and the list goes on. Port numbers are not only used by the receiving application but also by routers to control the movement of certain types of data in a process known as Port Forwarding. Packetizing the data is the job of the TCP.

The source and destination IP addresses are added to each packet, this is essential information for the routers. IP addressing information is added by the Internet Protocol (IP) or ICMP if it is control information.

Finally, the source and destination MAC addresses are added to each packet. MAC addresses are essential for ethernet communication on a LAN segment. Each IP packet is now enclosed within an ethernet frame. Imagine, as if it is a package inside a package. ARP is an example of a protocol that's important when performing this task.

The four distinct layers of software, each layer with a name according to the job of the software operating at that layer. The Application Layer sits at the top, underneath is the Transport Layer, then the Network Layer, and finally the Link Layer at the bottom. This is the so-called four-layer model. The software at each layer can only communicate with what is directly above directly below. The interfaces between these layers now are the rules for passing data from one program to another are standardized and well-known. This means that software from manufacturers like

Sun, Microsoft, Cisco, and the open-source community can write new programs to slot in at any position, confident about the compatibility of the programs.

TCP / IP

Transmission Control Protocol and Internet Protocol. It is a series of multi-step protocols that are meant and utilized for connection and communication across the internet. The standard of communication of this suite can be asserted as a client-server model. TCP/IP model is a layered implementation of that OSI, in this case TCP / IP has 4 layers.

Layers of TCP/IP

- Application Layer
- Transport Layer
- Network Layer
- Data Link Layer

All the activities that were being done in the OSI physical model is being covered by these four layers itself.

TCP/IP is a client-server suite, that means the client is sending a request and a server machine is fulfilling that request. In the TCP/IP model, since it is an implementation of the OSI model, there will be different protocols at each level.

Application Layer

HTTP protocol or FTP protocols are used. HTTP Hypertext Transfer Protocol it is the most commonly used protocol for transferring of text, whereas FTP or File Transfer Protocol is used for transferring files.

Transport Layer

This layer uses TCP or Transmission Control Protocol to establish the session between the client machine and the server machine

Network Layer

This stage utilizes Internet Protocol. At this point, all the machines, all the workstations are the nodes even the servers are attached to the TCP/IP network is assigned an IP address. Whatever is the source desk or the destination address that is to be reflected in the form of the IP address. When the client is sending a request, it will give its own address and it will give the IP address of the server machine.

Data Link Layer

The last layer in this structure is where it actually transmits the data physically and it goes to the server machine at server end again at the network layer that data is assembled, until it passes through the entire TCP layers at the server end and the data is assembled completely.

Chapter 9: IP Address

Computers on the Internet communicate with each other with underground or underwater cables or wirelessly. If someone wants to download a file from the internet, then that person's computer should have an address so that other computers in the internet can find and locate my computer. In internet terms, that address of computer is called IP address.

Let us understand it with other examples: If someone wants to send you a mail then that person should know and have your home address, similarly, your computer also needs an address in order for the computers in the internet can send you a file that you want to download.

IP address can be described as a string of numbers written in a certain format. IP address is the shortened term for Internet Protocol Address. An array of guidelines and rules that is responsible to make the internet to function in order, this is what the Internet Protocol is about.

There are two types of IP address; IPv4 and Ipv6

IPv4

This type of IP address consists of 4 numbers separated with a dot in between range. Each number can range from 0 to 255 in decimal numbers, but computers do not understand the decimal numbers so these numbers are converted to binary form which is understandable to computer language. In binary, this range can be written a (00000) Since each number N is represented by a group of a binary digit so the whole IPv4 address is represented by a sequence of 32 ones and zeros or simply by a sequence of 32 bit.

IPv4 is a 32-bit address.

In IPv4 a unique sequence of ones and zeros is assigned to each computer therefore a total of 2 raised to the power of 32 devices, that is approximately 4 billion devices (4,294,967,296 devices) can be addressed and connected to the internet with IPv4.

IPv6

To address the ever-growing number of devices that need to connect to the internet and requires its own IP address, we are slowly moving towards IPv6 which is a 128-bit IP address.

IPv6 is written as a group of 8 hexadecimal numbers separated by colons.

A total of 2 to the power of 128 devices can be connected to the internet or **340282366920938463463374607431768211456 devices** which is far more than enough for many future generations to come.

How to find my IP address?

· To find your computer's public IP address, write "what is my IP" in Google search bar and Google will provide you the information.

- For your smartphone, you can type "what is my IP" in Google search bar or say the command for voice activated search. Again, Google will provide you with the information about your device's public IP address.

Without this protocol, we would not be able to connect to the internet, connect our apps, send messages or calls via the internet and other simple tasks that we tend to overlook, not knowing we need internet for.

Classifications of IP addresses
Dynamic IP Address
When a device like a smartphone or computer is connected to the internet, the Internet Service Provider (ISP) lends the user an IP address from the range of available IP addresses. Once connected, the device now has an IP address in order to browse the internet and to send and receive data to and from the computers in the internet. The next session you connect to the internet, the ISP then provides you with a different IP address within the same available range in their system. Since IP address keeps on changing every time a device connects to the internet, such IP addresses are called Dynamic IP addresses.

Static IP Address
These are IP addresses that never change. They serve as permanent internet address. It is mostly used by DNS servers (these are servers that help us to open a website on our end). Static IP addresses provides information such as which device is located in which continent, which country,

which city and which ISP is providing the internet connection to the device. Once the ISP is known, trace location of the device can be done in no time. Static IP address are considered somewhat less secure than Dynamic IP address because they are easier to track. However, following safe internet practices can help you to keep your computer secure.

Dynamic Host Configuration Protocol (DHCP)

Each digital device that resides within a network is required to have an IP
address for communication purposes. An IP address is an identifier for a computer or device on a network. There are two ways that a computer can be assigned an IP address, it could be done by using a Static IP or Dynamic IP.

Static IP is where a user assigns a computer or device with an IP address manually. This was the original method that was done in the beginning of networking. Each digital device that resides within a network, the user would want to obtain computer's network configuration page and manually type in an IP address. In addition to an IP address, it was also required to type in other information such as the Subnet Mask, then the Default Gateway, and lastly a DNS Server. In cases when there is another computer or device needed to be added to the network, the process needs to be repeated again. This process was tedious and requires a lot of work especially if the user is dealing with a large network that has a lot of computers. It was also important to remember that each computer has a unique IP addresses assigned, because if the same IP address is used twice in the same network it would cause an IP conflict. Those computers with conflicting IP addresses will not have the ability to gain access to the network.

A better and easier way of assigning computers an IP address was made - the Dynamic IP.

The set up where a DHCP server voluntary provides an IP address to a computer is called Dynamic IP. A DHCP server automatically assigns a computer an IP address, it can also assign a subnet mask, a default gateway, and a DNS server.

As an example, at the Network Connection Properties window for the Network Interface Card (NIC) on a Microsoft Windows computer. In there, an option to set 'Obtain an IP address automatically' is available. When this option is selected, the computer would broadcast a request for an IP address on the network then the DHCP server will assign an IP address from its pool and deliver it to the computer. Once it is done, the user can verify all the different settings that the DHCP server has given the computer and the user can do this by opening up a Command Prompt and then type in the keyword "ipconfig" space forward slash all [ipconfig /al] then press enter. It should show that DHCP is enabled on the computer, which means it is getting its IP address from a DHCP server. Other information that will be displayed: the DNS server, default gateway, subnet mask and most importantly the IP address - all configurations were provided by DHCP server. The Dynamic IP Addressing is the preferred choice by many because it is automatic, and it makes managing a network a lot easier.

The DHCP server assigns IP addresses to computers on a network from its scope. A scope is a spectrum of IP addresses that are being handed out by the DHCP server. These values can be customized to either increasing or decreasing the range, it all depends on what the network administrator prefers.

The servers assign the IP addresses as a lease, so the computer does not actually own the IP address. A lease is the amount of time an IP address is designated to a digital device within the network. For example, a lease of IP could be for one day. The reason behind the concept of lease is to help make sure that the DHCP does not run out of IP addresses in its scope. After a certain period of time during the lease, the computers will transmit a signal to the DHCP server asking the

server to renew its lease of the IP address. In some ways, the computers in the network are informing the DHCP server that it is still present on the system and its IP address is still being used. If a computer is removed from the network, that device is not going to be able to ask the DHCP server for a renewal, and if it does not ask a renewal then the lease will expire. The IP address from the computer with expired lease, will go back to the IP address pool, it is now renewed and can now be used for another computer.

If a network administrator prefers for a computer within a network to have a specific IP address all the time meaning the IP address would not change, one option is to create a reservation on the DHCP server. A reservation ensures that a specific computer that has been recognized by its MAC address will always be given the same IP address when that computer or device seeks the DHCP server for an IP address. Reservations are not typically given to regular computers, it is typically allocated to special devices or computers such as network printers, servers, routers, or something similar; because devices like these should be given the same IP address constantly.

Notes:

· DHCP is a service that runs on a server such as Microsoft server or a Linux server.

· It is also a service that runs on routers, whether it is a business router or a small office/ home office router, these routers will have a DHCP service built into them.

Chapter 10: Domain Name System (DNS)

DNS

Across the internet, computers can distinguish a device's identity with a distinctive and one of a kind identifier called the IP address. Computers cannot comprehend nor understand human vocabulary. If computers cannot comprehend and understand the human vocabulary, then if you are wondering how can a computer pull up a webpage whenever we put in a site's URL on the address bar? The simplest answer to that inquiry: DNS

For example, a person who only knows how to speak English would want to communicate with another person, but that person only knows Mandarin. To have a successful communication, a translator would be vital. The concept is similar when it comes to the internet. The digital side of the conversation, the computers, can discern IP addresses. Its counterpart in this conversation, humans, can only comprehend our own language. The DNS operates as a decoder that is placed in the middle of the two participants of the conversation.

The DNS controls and manages a table where names or identifiers have been charted into numbers, especially the domain names of websites that are charted to its corresponding IP addresses. When a user keys in google.com in the address bar, the DNS converts it to the language that the web browser can comprehend which in this case would be the IP address and hands it off to the web browser. The web browser recognized the command that the user needs to reach Google's website, it makes an attempt to reach the Google server and loads its website on the computer. The DNS functions like a phone book of the internet whenever computer seeks with identifiers to obtain numbers.

How DNS works internally?

To understand this, we should know what our DNS servers. Servers are computers storing HTML files, images, sounds, videos, or any other file types. Servers that work together to provide IP address of the requested website to the web browser are called DNS Servers.

Types of DNS Servers:

- DNS recursive resolver / DNS resolver
- Root name server
- Top Level Domain / TLD name server
- Authoritative name server

DNS resolver is furnished by the ISP. It conjoins the web browser of our digital devices, like the computer, to the DNS name servers. The series of root name servers are currently counted to be at thirteen at the moment. It is rationally called letter.root-servers.net ; it is regulated and managed by twelve various organizations. The spectrum of letters, with the only exception of the letter g, are from letters a up to m. For every particular series, a number of servers are situated throughout the globe. The informational page is present for all root name servers at letter.root-servers.org ;

the information is organized alphabetically with an exception of the letter g. The letter g is the home page. For the domains that are using a common domain extension, the TLD name server keeps all of its information. To illustrate this, .com TLD name server manages and preserves the data and materials of all websites with the .com extension; .net TLD name server manages and preserves the data and materials of all websites with the .net extension. In the domain name system, the authoritative name server is conclusive stop in the chain. It safe keep the IP address of the website that is being asked for. By using certain CMD commands, the authoritative name server for a website can be detected.

(nslookup, set query=ns, etc)

What is master and the slave DNS?

The slave is the absolute likeness of master DNS and is utilized to distribute the DNS server load

How a computer loads a website?

If a user types in facebook.com in the address bar of a web browser, since the internet needs an IP address, so it transmits the inquiry to the operating system of the computer. The OS is engineered to transmit the inquiry to the DNS resolver. The OS then establishes a communication with the DNS resolver. The DNS resolver monitors its cache if the IP address of the website that is being requested is present. If not, the root name server receives the inquiry from the DNS. The root name server examines the website's extension to find out if it is a .com or .org or .net . Knowing what the extension is at this point, the IP address of the TLD name server can now be provided by the root name server to the DNS resolver.

For this sample context, the DNS resolver provides the IP address of the .com TLD name server, the DNS resolver contacts the .com TLD name server, it lends the IP address of the authoritative name server that shall automatically save the information which is the IP address of the sought website. Lastly, the authoritative name server allocates the correct IP address of facebook.com to the DNS resolver. This information is kept and saved by the DNS resolver in its cache, this information is ready to be used whenever it is needed again. The operating system of the computer also receives a copy of the IP address so it can store its information. The web browser then receives the information that was forwarded to it by the operating system. The web browser then reaches out to the Facebook server and displays facebook.com - the website that was originally requested by the user.

How TLD name server knows which authoritative name server stores the IP address of the requested website?

It starts when a domain name is bought and acquired from a registrar. There are several providers in the market today, for this scenario let us use WordPress. The domain that shall utilize as the authoritative name server can be designated on the registrar's website. From the time that a web hosting plan is acquired, for example - Amazon Web Hosting, the specifics of the authoritative name server can be obtained. As soon as the registrar's website receives the specifics of the authoritative nameserver, the TLD name servers managing the authority registry get a directive from the registrar to amend TLD name server with the particulars of the authoritative name server that the user has supplied. The precise IP address of the requester website can be generated since the TLD name server has identified which authoritative nameserver can accomplish it.

Is DNS important?

As a part of product research conducted by a Europe-based internet provider in 2016, they methodically surveyed 2,000 people and were surprised to learn that only 1 in 5 people can easily recall their home phone number or have memorized in some way. In a study done in 2019 by a medical diagnostic company based in the United States, only 57% of 1004 adult respondents know confidently what their blood type is.

Phone numbers and blood type are important information that we cannot easily remember, and that's ok. But imagine for every website you need to visit, whether it is Google, Facebook, Twitter or Netflix, you have to remember a set of numbers just to get on their webpage. It could be so daunting for a lot of us!

Domain Name System or more commonly referred to as DNS Servers is a computer server that houses the data on public IP addresses and its corresponding hostname.

Chapter 11: Remote Access Protocols, Network Storage Systems & File Transfer Protocols

Remote Access Protocols

· Remote Access Service (RAS)

This is a technology that enables the user to connect to a computer from a remote location. For example; accessing an office computer while the user is miles away at home. It allows the services on a remote network to be accessed over a dial-up connection. This service was originally engineered by Microsoft and built into the older Windows operating system (NT line of server software). It works with most of the major set of protocols suchlike as NetBeui, IPX / SPX, and TCP / IP

· Serial Line Internet Protocol (SLIP)

This is a protocol that is designed for communication between two computers using serial connection, such as a typical phone line. SLIP is rarely used anymore because it is not a secure protocol. During a dial - up connection, it sends all the data including sensitive data like passwords in clear text. This protocol falls short in today's need for security when it comes to data - handling. SLIP does not provide any error - checking and is limited to only utilizing the TCP / IP protocol - a better protocol was needed to address these issues.

- **Point - To - Point Protocol (PPP)**

This was the answer to the SLIP's pressing issues. This is a standard remote access protocol that is being used even to this day. It was developed to replace SLIP's limitation in security, error - checking and protocol support. Like SLIP that is used for communication between two computers using a serial connection such a typical phone line. Unlike SLIP, PPP is a secure protocol, it supports encryption and authentication. Most internet service providers (ISP) utilize this protocol for their customers who may opt to access the internet through a dial up connection.

- **Point - To - Point Protocol Over Ethernet (PPPoE)**

The moniker is exactly what it implies. This protocol uses PPP over Ethernet (Note: refer to the text for PPP for its details). The PPPoE works by encapsulating PPP in ethernet frames. The users of this protocol are typically connected to the internet via DSL broadband, cable modem, or wireless connection. It was also developed for connecting multiple users within a local area network towards a remote site sharing a common device.

- **Point - To - Point Tunneling Protocol (PPTP)**

This technology is utilized for establishing Virtual Private Networks (VPN). In fact, this is the default protocol associated with VPNs. PPTP ensures that the data transfer from one device to another is secure by creating a secure tunnel between the two points.

- **Generic Route Encapsulation (GRE)**

This is a protocol that is used along with Point - To - Point Tunneling Protocol (PPTP) as part of creating a VPN network. GRE is what actually creates the tunnel in PPTP. It is used to encapsulate the data in a highly secure method.

- **Virtual Private Network (VPN)**

This is a secluded or a private network that utilizes a public network, such as the internet, in order to establish or create a remote connection. The data is encrypted as it sends and decrypted as received. It provides a dedicated link between two points over the internet.

Network Storage Systems

Network Attached Storage (NAS)

This storage system is ideal if the user / network administrator wanted to set up a network storage in a way that stored data goes to a centralized location where it can be accessed from all of the devices that are connected on the network. This can be done by using a network attached device. A NAS is designed for storing data and it does not do anything else besides storing data. Typically, a NAS is a box that will have multiple hard drives in a RAID configuration for redundancy. It will also have a network interface card (NIC) that will directly attach to a switch or router in order for the data to be accessed over a network. Once it is on and active within the network, it can be accessed from other devices such as desktops, laptops, servers, and it can be accessed as a shared drive.

NAS can be ideally used in homes and are more typically present in home office or small to medium-sized businesses. A main disadvantage of utilizing the NAS is how it has a sole point of failure, to put in more context – if a component fails power supply on the NAS then all of the other devices will not have the ability to access its data.

Storage Area Network (SAN)

This storage system is engineered as a special high-speed network device that stores and provides access to large amounts of data. Ideally, it is a dedicated network that is used for data storage. This network consists of multiple disk arrays, switches, and servers. Since it is composed of multiple components, a SAN is fault tolerant while still having the data being shared among several disk arrays. In the event that a switch, or a disk array, or if a server goes down or have a malfunction, the data can still be accessed. Whenever a server accesses the data on a SAN, it accesses the data as if it was a local hard drive because that is how operating systems (OS) recognize a SAN. It is recognized as a local attached hard drive rather than a shared network drive like in a NAS. Another advantage of using NAS is how highly scalable it can be, adding more storage space can easily be done without interruption on the network.

SAN is a high-speed network and that is because in a SAN, all the devices are interconnected - all of the devices are connected to each other and it uses fiber channel to link with each other. Fiber channel is a standard for SAN, because it is fiber optics it has the speed capability of between gigabits per second all the way up to 128 gigabits per second making it extremely fast hence, making it expensive. As an alternative to fiber channel, some SANs have also been using iSCSI (Internet Small Computer System Interface) instead which is a more affordable alternative but not as fast as the fiber channel.

Another important factor about SAN is how it is not affected by network traffic such as bottleneck that can occur in a local area network (LAN), this is because SANs are configured not to be part of a local area network. SANs are partitioned off; it is basically a network all by itself.

Due to the design and trade off price of SANs, it is mainly used by large companies and large organizations.

Standard Protocols

Hypertext Transfer Protocol (HTTP)

Hypertext Transfer Protocol or HTTP; this is possibly the most widely used protocol in the world today. HTTP is the protocol that is used for viewing web pages on the internet. So, when you type in a web address like google.com, you'll notice that HTTP is automatically at the beginning of the web address after you hit enter, this indicates that you are now using HTTP to retrieve this web page. Now in standard HTTP, all the information is sent in clear text, so all the information that is exchanged between your computer and that web server which includes any text that you type on that website that information is transferred over the public internet and because it is transferred in clear text, it is vulnerable to anybody who wants it such as hackers. Now normally this would not be a big deal if you were just browsing regular websites and no sensitive data such as passwords or credit card information are being used but if you were to type in personal sensitive data like your name, address, phone number, date of birth, password or SSN, that sensitive data goes from your computer and then it has to travel across the public internet to get to that web server and this makes your data vulnerable because a hacker that somewhere on the internet listen in as the data is being transferred and steal your information. "So, a hacker can steal personal information as it is traveling over the internet, he has a name, phone number, address, credit card number and other information. "This is a problem as far as security and this why HTTP was developed.

Hypertext Transfer Protocol Secure (HTTPS)

Stands for Secure Hypertext Transfer Protocol. This is HTTP with a security feature. Secure HTTP encrypts that is being retrieved by HTTP, it ensures that all the data that is being moved and relocated across the internet among computers and servers is secure by making the data impossible to read and it does this by using encryption algorithms to scramble the data that is being transferred. For example, if you were to go to a website that requires you to enter personal information such as passwords or credit card information, you will notice that an S will be added to the HTTP in the web address and this S indicates that you are now using secure HTTP and have entered a secure where sensitive data is going to be passed and that data is going to be protected. In addition to the S being added, a lot of web browsers will also show a padlock symbol in the address bar to indicate that secure HTTP is being used. So, by using secure HTTP, all the data which includes anything that you type is no longer sent in clear text, it is scrambled in an unreadable form as it travels across the internet. So, if a hacker tries to steal your information, he would get a bunch of meaningless data because the data is encrypted, and the hacker would not be able to crack the encryption to unscramble the data.

SSL

Secure Socket Layer

Secure HTTP protects the data by using one of two protocols. One of these protocols is the Secure Socket Layer or SSL. It is a set of rules that is used to ensure security on the internet. It uses public key encryption to secure data. This is how SSL works: when a computer connects to a website that is using SSL, the computer's web browser will ask the website to identify itself then the web server will send the computer a copy of its SSL certificate.

An SSL certificate is a small digital certificate that is used to authenticate the identity of a website. Basically, it is used to let your computer know that the website you're visiting is trustworthy. Your computer's browser will check to make sure that it trusts the certificate and if it does it will send a communication to the web server then after the web server will respond back with an acknowledgement so when SSL session can proceed, then after all these steps are complete, encrypted data can now be exchanged between your computer and the web server.

TLS

Transport Layer Protocol is the other protocol being used by secure HTTP. TLS is the latest industry standard cryptographic protocol. It is the successor to SSL, and it is based on the same specifications and like SSL, it also authenticates the server, client, and encrypts the data. It is also important to point out that a lot of websites are now using secure HTTP by default regardless is sensitive data is going to be exchanged or not. A lot of this has to do with Google, because they are now flagging websites as not secure if they are not protected with SSL and if a website is not SSL-protected, Google will penalize that website in their search rankings. This is one of the major reasons, you'll notice that secure HTTP is being used rather than standard HTTP.

File Transfer Protocols

Protocols that are used to transfer files over network.

File Transfer Protocol (FTP)

FTP is a standard set of rules that is used to move or relocate files among computers and servers above a network, the internet is a good example of it. In a nutshell, FTP is the language that computers use to transfer files over a TCP / IP network.

A sample scenario of using the FTP: When a computer user somewhere in the world wanted to make their files available for other people to download, all that user needs to do is to simply have the file that is meant to be shared, uploaded to the FTP and then other people from anywhere in the world can simply connect to that FTP server and download the files using the FTP protocol. A dedicated FTP server can be used but is not always necessary to do this type of file transfer, a simple workstation or computer can be configured to act as an FTP server. In Microsoft Windows, this can be done using the Internet Information Services Manager.

There are a couple of ways to transfer files using the FTP
· Internet Browser
· FTP Client
· Command Prompt

For example, a user wants to download a few mp3 files that someone else has put on the FTP server. One way of retrieving the files is by using an internet browser. On the browser's address bar, type in the address of the FTP server that is intended to be reached, as if just going to a regular website. In other words, type in the FTP address as the URL.
The only difference between going to a regular website and accessing an FTP server via web browser is the prefix that needs to be used. In web browsing "HTTP" or "HTTPS" are the prefix that can be used, in FTP it is simply "FTP" as the prefix to be used.
Once the user has reached the FTP server site, folders and files can easily be browsed depending on what the owner has made available. The user can simply view and download the file.
In most cases, FTP servers will require an account with a username and password. Though there are some FTP

servers that lets users to login anonymously. It just depends on the type of authentication the owner of the FTP server has set up.

Another way to connect to an FTP server is by using an FTP client. There are a number of FTP clients available for use, an example of a commonly - used and free FTP client is Filezilla. Using an FTP client provides a graphical user interface which can attribute to a better overall experience than using a web browser. Once connected to an FTP server using an FTP client, users can drag and drop the files that it wants to be downloaded. For some users who have permission access, it is easier to upload files to the FTP server using the FTP client.

Today, accessing FTP server via the Windows command prompt is mostly used whenever there is a software repair needs to be done in the system. This happens mostly whenever the web browser and FTP client are either not available or not working. This can be caused by malware, virus or corrupted files.

Transferring files is a common use of FTP especially for transferring files in bulk. Another common use of FTP is to give the ability web designers to upload files to their web servers.

A drawback of using the FTP is how it is not a secure protocol. The data that is being transferred is not encrypted. All the data that is being moved is sent in clear text which can cause security concerns. Ideally, FTP should only be used on a limited basis or on trust - worthy networks or better yet when the data that is being transferred is not sensitive because of its minimal level of security protocol.

Secure File Transfer Protocol (SFTP)

If a user needs to transfer data that needs to be protected, then a more secure transfer protocol should be used. Here is where SFTP becomes practical. Secure FTP is just like its predecessor, the FTP, except it adds a layer of security. The data using Secure FTP is fully encrypted by utilizing secure shell during data transfer. In this way, no data is being sent in clear text, it is all encrypted. Secure FTP authenticates both the user and the server, and it uses port 22.

It is also important to note that both FTP and SFTP are connection - oriented protocols that use Transmission Control Protocol (TCP) for file transfer, so it guarantees file delivery.

Trivial File Transfer Protocol (TFTP)

This is an absolute straightforward protocol for file transferring; however, it is not meant to send files over the internet unlike with FTP and SFTP does. It is used mainly for transferring files within a local area network (LAN). It is often used to transfer configuration files and firmware images to network devices such as firewalls and routers. TFTP is more often used by network admins rather than for home users. Unlike FTP and SFTP that uses TCP protocol to transfer files, TFTP is a connectionless protocol that uses the User Datagram Protocol (UDP) instead. Since the TFTP is utilizing UDP instead of TCP, it is unreliable protocol. Lastly,

TFTP does not provide any security and not does it need to since it is used for local area network and not over the internet.

Chapter 12: SECURITY PROTOCOLS

Defense in Depth Principle

There are threats to every system and several ways an attacker may try to exploit them. When we consider how to secure a system, we need to consider Defense in Depth.

The *Defense in Depth Principle* states that there is no one thing or even two that can completely secure a system. This contention is that if one part of the security solution would have failed then another part should be able to resist or prevent the attack from succeeding.

In practice, this means applying security in layers. For example: we could have a firewall and an IPS (Intrusion Prevention System) on the edge of the network, behind the firewall there may be an email scanning service, and on the workstations, there would be antivirus software.

An attacker may try to send some malicious code through email, the firewall and IPS may not be able to pick this up as email is a valid application. In this scenario, we would rely on the email scanner.

But what if the email scanner service is down for whatever reason? Maybe it crashed or maybe it just did not pick up that this email is a threat. In that case, we still have the antivirus software on the workstation to fall back on.

This example is a simplified look at the Defense in Depth. This strategy reduces the risk of a successful and possibly very expensive security breach.

A common misconception in network security for beginners is to rely too heavily on the firewall. All too often people think that the firewall should suffice. Unfortunately, that is just not true. Firewalls are only just a piece of a much larger puzzle. A simple firewall uses IP address and ports to allow or deny traffic. An IPS can look into this information further and deeply into the traffic to see if it matches known patterns of attacks. These two are just part of the edge of the network.

What about encrypting traffic with HTTPS, requiring authentication and authorization before accessing secure resources. New security flaws are found regularly, patching these flaws regularly would definitely help with the security of the network systems. Also, we need to consider our endpoints - workstations, laptops, smartphones, and any other device that connects to the network. This is where we think about antivirus, host-based firewalls, and VPN (Virtual Private Network) connections.

We cannot consider something to be reasonably secured without considering all aspects of the systems. Aside from the technical controls like firewalls and antivirus, but there are also other things to consider like the physical and administrative controls. We need to consider things like the security of the building where the servers or workstations are based, locking the door to the server room, or putting equipment in locked racks or cabinets. When it comes to administrative controls, these relate to policies and procedures. It can start with identifying the proper way to handle data, a big part of this is simply educating the users. Having controlled set of who can access the data. Reminding the users to use strong passwords, how to avoid social engineering, and how to recognize threats in general.

Security should be applied in layers and these layers are more than just technical controls. Having a contingency plan in the event one of the security layers failed, what actions can be taken to put everything back together and minimize the threat or damage.

Intrusion Prevention Service (IPS)

Intrusion Prevention Service is designed to prevent malicious actions from occurring within the network. For modern implementations, we always deal with IPS than IDS (Intrusion Detection System) since aside from preventing malicious actions, it also logs each incident where malicious actions have been prevented.

IPS can be either network based (NIPS) or host based (HIPS). The network-based monitors the entire network for malicious traffic by analyzing all tcp/ip traffic entering the network. The host based on the other hand, monitors a single host for malicious activity, usually for unauthorized changes.

NIPS requires that IPS be installed on a device at the network perimeter. The HIPS require that IPS be installed on every host that requires protections - usually it is only installed on specific servers.

IPS detection can be signature-based or anomaly-based. There is always one signature for every exploit that is capable of preventing, the signature works by zeroing in on some unique aspect of the particular exploit that is always present. One of the advantages of this method is the low rate of false-positives. On the other hand, signature based can only detect exploits for which a signature exists, so signatures must always be updated.

In anomaly-based, the system looks for abnormal traffic and assumes that the abnormal traffic is malicious. The advantage of this method - it requires less maintenance; it does not need to be updated constantly. The only downside with the anomaly-based is the higher rate of false-positives.

Newer IPS systems are primarily signature-based employed in a physical security device. This is highly recommended for the needs of the majority of networks. Signature-based IPS can be put on a physical security client such as a firewall that sits on the perimeter of the network. A subscription is typically needed to be obtained from the vendor to keep the signatures up to date. Generally, the signatures updates automatically, on a daily basis similar to how antivirus does its updates.

Types of threat:
- DoS (denial of service)
- Ransomware
- Phishing
- Data theft

- Tracking
- Botnet

Sources of Threats

Threat actors: Individuals with malicious intent, nation state sponsored groups

Sources of Vulnerabilities
Design problems

When somebody has designed an application or a system and there's just a fundamental problem with that design

Implementation flaws

The design is fine but actually when that design has been translated into the appropriate code, will probably be at hardware, there's problem at that stage and there's resulting in weaknesses

Configuration issues

This is quite common. Systems are insecure when it shouldn't be, because somebody either misunderstood how to configure the item

Changes over time

Too many changes have been done to the point that the system is no longer secure because the original intent has been lost

Failure to provide security updates

Most of the recent security attacks have been successful purely because people have not applied security updates.

Assumption of trust

Devices that do not belong to the network are plugged to the computer, making it the network system highly vulnerable for phishing scams. Email attachments that we easily open without examining a few details.

Vulnerabilities: Wi-Fi

· Do you control the hardware?
· Do you control the software / firmware?
· Are the protocols broken?
· Who have you given access to? Are their systems secure?
· Whose network have you connected to?
· Non-physical connection increases attack surface

Risk Management

· Apply security in layers
· Know your gear
· Port scanning - a sample program is Nmap
· Firewall logging
· Intrusion Detection and Intrusion Prevention Service

Risk Management: Wi-Fi

· SSID hiding doesn't work
· WEP is broken
· Don't use SSIDs that can make you a target

Wireless Security

Most of us had connected to a Wi-Fi network with our laptop, tablet, or our smartphones. To join a network connection with a device, a network name needs to be selected and a password needs to be supplied.

Wi-Fi network can be just open with no password required; in that scenario it means anybody can join it. However, in the majority of cases, Wi-Fi networks will be secure and will require a password. There are several different protocols for securing a Wi-Fi network.

Wired Equivalent Privacy (WEP)

This protocol was developed in 1999 making it the earliest security protocol that was used for wireless networks. As the term suggests, it is meant to supply an equal level of security to wireless networks as it did for wired networks. However, this turned out not to be 100 percent the case, it was learned that the 40-bit encryption that WEP used was vulnerable and not secure making it easily hackable. This is the main reason why WEP is no longer used today and modern Wi-Fi routers won't even have it as an option anymore.

Wi-Fi Protected Access (WPA)

After WEP, better security protocol was needed for wireless networks. WPA is a wireless security protocol that was developed to solve the problems of WEP. WPA uses a stronger encryption method called Temporary Key Integrity Protocol (TKIP). The new encryption method dynamically changes its keys as it is being used that way it ensures the data integrity. Even though WPA is a lot more secure than WEP, even today the WPA is outdated. TKIP did eventually have some vulnerabilities.

WPA2

WPA2 was developed to provide even stronger security than WPA, it does this by requiring the use of a stronger encryption method. While WPA uses TKIP for encryption, WPA2 uses AES which stands for Advanced Encryption Standard. The newer encryption uses a symmetric encryption algorithm which makes it strong enough to resist a brute-force attack. In fact, AES is classified to be secure that the U.S. federal government has adopted to use it, it is being utilized to encrypt sensitive government data.

Now when you log in to the Wi-Fi router's configuration page and proceed to the Wi-Fi security section, this is where you would find the different security protocols that you can choose from to protect your Wi-Fi network. In most routers, there is an option that has both WPA and WPA2 - this is a mixed security option. This option enables WPA and WPA2 at the same time, it will use both TKIP and AES security. The reason for this option is for compatibility purposes because some older devices (dated prior to 2006) may not be compatible with using AES encryption that is being used with WPA2. In this option, older devices will connect to the older WPA protocol, but at the same time modern devices will connect to WPA2.

Using the mixed option all the time, though it is the most compatible with all devices, with this option while it uses

AES it also is utilizing TKIP which is the lesser secure encryption. This leaves your network more vulnerable to a breach.

WPA3

This is the next generation of wireless security; it was introduced in 2018. According to the Wi-Fi Alliance, WPA3 contributes top of the line security protocols available for commerce. To facilitate further vigorous authentication, additional features were placed to streamline Wi-Fi security. It will also receive increased protection from password guessing attempts. The WPA3 option is available to newer routers.

Wi-Fi Protected Setup (WPS)

This is another type of wireless security method that does not require the user to type in a password. The WPS was designed for people who know a little or novice about wireless networks, to make it easy as possible for their devices to join a wireless network.

There are a couple of different methods that are used with WPS, but by far the most common method is the Push Button method. In this method the user would just need to press a couple of buttons to be connected to the network.

Most routers today will have a physical WPS button that you can press, and a lot of Wi-Fi printers will also have a software or physical WPS button.

For example, you want to connect a printer via WPS, you would need to push and hold the WPS button that is located on the Wi-Fi router and in the span of 120 seconds you would press the WPS button on your printer. After a few seconds, the printer should be connected to the Wi-Fi router.

Another method for WPS is if the client you are using has a WPS pin number. If this is the set-up, the user just needs to enter a pin number to the field provided and within a few seconds it will connect to the network.

WPS is the easiest way to join a wireless network, a lot of manufacturers have built wireless products with WPS. This is just to make it as simple as possible for the users to join a device to a wireless network.

ACCESS CONTROL

Access Control is called MAC filter in some routers, with this option the network administrator can either allow or block devices from joining a network. Every network adapter has a MAC address (MAC address can be described as the hexadecimal number - numeral system made up of 16 symbols, that exclusively pinpoint the identity of each device that resides on a network) and with Access Control the network administrator can manage the devices that can and cannot connect to the network using the MAC address of the specific device. When a device is blocked, it would exclusively be able to obtain an IP address from the router, but it would not be able to communicate with any other device and it would not be able to connect to the internet.

The Access Control can be used as an extra layer of security that is in addition to the network's Wi-Fi password. Access Control also works for wired devices.

Chapter 13: BASIC NETWORK UTILITIES

PING Utility

The ping command is the most widely used of all network utilities. It is a tool that is used to test issues such as network connectivity and name resolution

In a sample scenario given, if a user would ping a host IP address: At a command prompt, then the user needs to type "ping" space, then the IP address of the host then hit enter. The command will send out four data packets to the destination IP address we chose, then the destination will send back those packets to you as a reply. These replies are called Echo Reply Requests. These replies will tell you what is happening to the destination host you tried to ping. For instance, 4 packets sent, and 4 packets received, and 0 loss means there is a general connectivity between you and the destination. If you did not get a reply, that means there is no reply from the host, and it could mean there is no network connectivity between you and the destination.

In some cases, you might get a result from a ping that says, "request timed out", this could mean that the host network is down, or it is blocking all the ping requests.

Another message that you might get is "destination host unreachable", that message is coming from the router, that means that the route to the destination cannot be found.

The ping command can also be used to test DNS name resolution issues. Instead of using the IP address in the ping command, try using the domain name of the website you are trying to reach. For example, type "ping" space, the domain name, then hit enter. If by pinging the domain name, if you get the same successful result as typing the IP address when you ping the same destination, then this would indicate that the name resolution by the DNS is working fine.

If you ping the domain name and it failed, then the next step is typing the ip address instead. If by typing the IP address and the ping is successful this time, then you can isolate the issue to DNS

Trace Route Utility

Tracert is used to find the exact path the data packet is taking on its way to the destination.

For example: to trace a route from one computer to another, key in "tracert" space, then the destination computer's IP address at the command prompt,

then press enter. By doing this, the data packet will find its way to the destination. Each time the data reaches a router on its path, it will report back information about that router such as its IP address and the time it took between each hop.

TraceRT utility is a great tool that can be used to pinpoint where the problem lies within a network if the data cannot reach its destination.

IPCONFIG

This is a useful tool to display network configurations for your computer and this information can be used as part of the problem-solving process.

- Ipconfig – shows the default gateway, the IP address, and the subnet mask
- Ipconfig /all – shows the full TCP/IP configuration
- Ipconfig /renew - releases and renew the IP address lease
- Ipconfig /release - releases the IP address lease

Chapter 14: NETWORKING ISSUES

Most network designs can be classified as either wired or wireless. Networks do not have to use either types of networks solely, but it can certainly be combined. If you have a wireless network, there is a possibility that at one point a wired connection existed within your network.

Most businesses today adopt the usage of incorporating both wired and wireless networks due to ease of access and business needs. It is important to know how to diagnose problems related to wired and wireless issues.

Wired Factors

A common fault point is the media. In a wired network, this involves copper cables. Overtime, cables can become worn out or damaged which makes it prone to short circuits. It is also important to remember to use the right type of cable depending on what kind of network you are using.

If you are going to use copper cabling, it is important to recognize the environment around the cable because certain electronic equipment that might seem harmless (like fluorescent lights, microwave ovens, fans, etc.) can interfere with the copper media therefore altering or reducing the strength of the signal which is known as attenuation.

Another factor to consider is the length of the cable. If the cable exceeds the maximum recommended length, then this could also cause problems within the network. Using the wrong type of cable could be another cause of network issue, for example you are using a crossover cable, but your network requires straight cable.

Wireless Factors

Antennas are another factor that affects wireless service. Since wireless devices operate using radio waves, the antenna is a big factor that can determine the range and speed of a signal.

- Omni-directional antenna - one of the most common types of antenna. This type of antenna transmits signal in all directions. Every wireless device within its direction can pick up its signal as long as the device is in range

- Directional antenna - this type directs the signal to one direction. That direction is to wherever the antenna is pointed to.

Problems that can arise in a wireless environment one of these is an interference. Microwave ovens can cause interference and certain wireless devices can interfere with the network's wireless signal (like mobile phones, Bluetooth devices such as a wireless keyboard and mouse). The waves that are being produced by other wireless devices can alter the signal of a wireless network.

A cordless phone is another device that is known to cause issues to wireless networks, that is because a lot of this type of phone operates on the same frequency as wireless routers do. An example of this issue is when the wireless phone rings and it affects the network connectivity of a laptop. This happens if both the wireless network and wireless phone are using the same wireless channel. To quickly resolve this, you can log on to the router's configuration page and change the channel in the wireless signal - this should take care of it most of the time.

The structure of a building is another factor that can affect a wireless signal. Depending on the materials used and structured in the building like concrete walls, window film, and metal studs - these can all have an effect on the strength and stability of the wireless signal. If this scenario occurs, the placing of the router needs to be in a strategic location within the building.

Wrong Encryption

Using the wrong type of encryption could prevent other devices from joining a network. This might happen if a router is using a newer encryption method like WPA2 in its wireless network but a device like a laptop is using an older encryption like WEP or WPA, the laptop would not be able to join the wireless network because the newer encryption may not be recognized by older devices.

Link LED (Light Emitting Diode)

Simple indicators that are used to tell us basic information about a network device. On a network interface card (NIC), if network cable is plugged in to the NIC port then a green led light indicates a successful network connection has been established, this is called the link light. If after connecting the cable and the indicator does not light up, this might indicate an issue such as a bad cable or simply the computer is turned off. A yellow blinking light indicates there is network activity whether the speed of the light's blinking is fast or not, this indicates normal operation.

One of the most obvious things to check when it comes to network connectivity issue is the physical connectivity. Check to see if your computer is connected to the network. Thoroughly examine the led indicators. See if the switch is turned on. Check for loose cables either from the NIC or switch connection.

Troubleshooting Strategy
1. Determine the manifestations of the issues and its likely cause
- Gather information about the problem
- What is the problem?
- When did the problem occur?
- Specific error messages
- Does the problem happen all the time or intermittently?

2. Identify the affected area
- Is the problem isolated or spread across several locations
- If the problem affects everyone, check the switch
- If the problem is isolated, check individual cable

3. Establish what has changed: problem do not occur at random; it happens for a reason.
- Did anything change just prior to the problem happening?
- Was there any hardware removed or added?
- Was there any software installed or uninstalled?
- Was anything downloaded from the internet?

4. Select the most probable cause

· Look for the simplest solutions first
· Does the device have power?
· Are the cables plugged in?
· Check the LEDs

5. Carry out a game plan and resolution as well as its probable effects

· This is the cautious phase
· Must know what effect the action will have on the network
· Will it affect the entire network or be isolated at one area?

6. Test the result

· Where you drive the operation to resolve the obstacle
· Where you will know if the resolution strategy will iron out the obstacle at hand or not

7. Pinpoint the conclusion and the aftermath of the resolution

· Has the solution strategy fix the dilemma or not?
· What effect did it have on everyone else?
· Do the results show a temporary fix or a permanent one?

8. Document the solution and the process

· Document the problem
· Document what caused the problem
· Document how the problem was fixed

- This is an important step. If the problem has been resolved it is important to document what transpired within the issue and how was it resolved. In the event that the same issue occurs again, you or anyone who has access to that documentation would know the resolution in the fastest possible time and may take preventive measures so the problem will not occur again.

Conclusion

Thank you for making it through to the end of *Computer Networking Beginners Guide: What is the computer network and how to learn it in a simple way. The Easy step by step Guide for beginners*, let's hope it was informative and able to provide you with all of the tools you need to achieve your goals whatever they may be.

Computer Networking enables us to share resources and use data no matter what scale of architecture you might have. It helps us to exchange information between different people and computers. This has been faster and more reliable than the method of manually handing files or mailing it or retrieving a reel of magnetic tape on the other side of a building.

This technology has also let us to share physical resources; computers within a network can now share a printer or storage drives – ones too expensive to have attached to every machine.

In order for you to be online, your computer or smartphone is connected to a large, distributed network, called the internet. The internet is arranged as an ever-enlarging web of interconnected devices.

The World Wide Web is not the same thing as the internet, even though people often use the two terms interchangeably. The World Wide Web runs on top of the internet, in the same way as Skype or Instagram do. The internet is the underlying plumbing that conveys all the data for all these applications.

These are some of the technologies that keeps us connected online.

Finally, if you found this book useful in any way, a review on Amazon is always appreciated!

www.ingramcontent.com/pod-product-compliance
Lightning Source LLC
Chambersburg PA
CBHW071059050326
40690CB00008B/1067